Seventh Edition

Workplace Communications
The Basics

George J. Searles
Mohawk Valley Community College

D0573834

New! 2016 MLA Updates

PEARSON

Boston   Columbus   Indianapolis   New York   San Francisco
Amsterdam   Cape Town   Dubai   London   Madrid   Milan
Munich   Paris   Montreal   Toronto   Delhi   Mexico City   São Paulo   Sydney
Hong Kong   Seoul   Singapore   Taipei   Tokyo

To Ellis

Senior Acquisitions Editor: Brad Potthoff
Product Marketing Manager: Jennifer Edwards
Project Manager: Shannon Kobran
Program Manager: Katharine Glynn
Project Coordination, Text Design, and
    Electronic Page Makeup: SPi-Global
Media Editor: Kelsey Loveday

Design Lead: Beth Paquin
Cover Designer: Studio Montage
Cover Art: Kzenon/Fotolia, Mark Adams/123RF,
    Wavebreak Media Ltd./123RF
Senior Manufacturing Buyer: Roy L. Pickering, Jr.
Printer/Binder: LSC Communications
Cover Printer: Lehigh-Phoenix Color/Hagerstown

Acknowledgments of third-party content appear below or on the appropriate page within the text.

Photo credits. Pg. 46: Arcady/Fotolia, Chrisdorney/Fotolia, Elenarts/Fotolia. Pg. 58: Peter Bull/Dorling Kindersley, Ltd. Pg. 107: 123RF, Monkey Business/Fotolia

Text credits. Pg. 36: US Postal Service. Pgs. 49, 51: US Bureau of Labor Statistics. Pg. 56: WPClipart.com. Pg. 59: Reprinted with permission from NFPA 54-2012. Copyright 2011 National Fire Protection Association. This reprinted material is not the complete and official position of the NFPA on the referenced subject, which is represented only by the standard in its entirety. Pg. 91: NASA. Pg. 109: Couresty of Mohawk Valley Community College. www.mvcc.edu. Pg. 200: Modern Language Association. Pgs. 212, 215: United States Office of Drug Control Policy. Pg. 216: New Solutions for Ensuring a Drug-Free Workplace. *Occupational Health & Safety 71*.4 (2002): 34–35. Print. p. 34. Pg. 217: Drug Testing in the Workplace: The Challenge to Employment Relations and Employment Law, *Chicago-Kent Law Review 63*:3 (1987).

Library of Congress Cataloging-in-Publication Data
Searles, George J. (George John), 1944- author.
  Workplace communications : the basics / George J. Searles, Mohawk Valley Community College.—
Seventh Edition.
    pages cm
  Includes bibliographical references and index.
  ISBN 978-0-13-412069-0
1. English language—Business English. 2. English language—Technical English. 3. Business writing—Problems, exercises, etc. 4. Technical writing—Problems, exercises, etc. 5. Business communication—Problems, exercises, etc. 6. Commercial correspondence—Problems, exercises, etc.   I. Title.
  PE1479.B87S43 2016
  808.06'665—dc23

                                                                                        2015032116

2   17

Student ISBN-10:   0-13-470130-5
Student ISBN-13: 978-0-13-470130-1

A la Carte ISBN-10:   0-13-470316-2
A la Carte ISBN-13: 978-0-13-470316-9

www.pearsonhighered.com

Contents

Short Reports: Page Design, Formats, and Types   64

Summaries   86

Preface

What's New in the Seventh Edition?

The seventh edition retains all the essential features of the earlier versions while incorporating much new material:

- Ongoing focus on international communications
- New exercises that address cross-cultural dynamics
- Collaborative exercises in all chapters
- Coverage of work-related text messaging
- Advice on writing for Web sites and other on-line media
- Enhanced guidance about on-line job searching
- Updated model documents throughout

Hallmark Approach of *Workplace Communications*

Workplace Communications: The Basics originated as the solution to a problem. Semester after semester, I had searched unsuccessfully for a suitable text to use in my English 110 course, Oral and Written Communication, at Mohawk Valley Community College. Designed as an alternative to traditional first-year composition, the course satisfies curricular English requirements for students anticipating careers in such fields as welding, heating and air conditioning, and electrical maintenance. As might be expected, English 110 is a highly practical, hands-on course that meets the specialized needs of its target audience by focusing exclusively on job-related communications.

Although some excellent texts had been written in the fields of business and technical communication, nearly all were aimed at the university level and were therefore quite beyond the scope of a course like English 110. Finally, I decided to fill the gap and meet my students' needs by creating a textbook of my own. My students at Mohawk Valley responded enthusiastically, citing the book's accessibility, clarity, and pragmatic, down-to-earth emphasis as particularly appealing qualities. To my great satisfaction, it has met with similar success at many other colleges both here and abroad, with new editions appearing in 2003, 2006, 2009, 2011, and 2014.

Short on theory, long on practical applications, and written in a simple, conversational style, it's exceptionally user-friendly. The book is appropriate not only for recent high school graduates but also for returning adult students and other non-traditional learners. It's comprehensive and challenging enough for trade school and community college courses such as English 110 and for similar introductory-level classes at most four-year institutions.

Like the earlier editions, this seventh edition includes many helpful features:

- Learning objectives and outlines for each chapter
- Numerous examples and sample documents based on actual workplace situations
- Useful checklists at the ends of most sections
- Realistic exercises that reflect each chapter's focus

Supplements

Instructor's Manual. The updated Instructor's Manual offers teaching guidelines for each chapter, sample course outlines, keys to the exercises, and additional material. All the visuals are available at high-quality resolution to facilitate the creation of PowerPoint slides. Please send me your comments and suggestions by e-mail to gsearles@mvcc.edu or by conventional mail to the Center for Arts & Humanities, Mohawk Valley Community College, 1101 Sherman Drive, Utica, NY 13501.

MyTechCommLab. This supplement saves time and improves results by offering you the best available online resources for technical communication. This dynamic, comprehensive site offers engaging and interactive content that will help you improve the technical communication skills you will need most—writing, research, and document design. A built-in grade book allows you to track progress with a click of the button.

PowerPoints. PowerPoints that cover key concepts discussed in the text are available for you to download and use in your classes.

Test Bank. Each chapter of *Workplace Communications* has a corresponding chapter in the Test Bank with thirty-five multiple-choice questions and six short essay questions.

Acknowledgments

Permit me some acknowledgments. First, I thank my reviewers: Rima S. Gulshan, George Mason University; Katherine McEwen, Cape Fear Community College; Melissa McFarland, Central Carolina Technical College; Debbie Montgomery, Athens Technological College; Diane Paul, Central New Mexico Community College; and Genny Yarne, Kirkwood Community College.

I also thank my publishing team: Katharine Glynn, Shannon Kobran, and Teresa Ward at Pearson and Michelle Gardner at SPi Global.

On a more personal note, I wish also to thank my students and colleagues, who have taught me so much over the years. And I would be remiss indeed if I failed to acknowledge the assistance of Mohawk Valley Community College librarians Colleen Kehoe-Robinson and Barb Evans. In addition, I salute my lifelong friend Frank Tedeschi and my "basketball buddy," John Lapinski; both continue to provide much-appreciated diversion, encouragement, and companionship.

Most importantly, of course, I thank my wife, Ellis; and my sons, Jonathan and Colin.

GEORGE J. SEARLES, Ph.D.
Mohawk Valley Community College

The Keys to Successful Communication: Purpose, Audience, and Tone

1

LEARNING OBJECTIVES

When you complete this chapter you'll be able to:

- determine your purpose for writing.
- identify your intended audience.
- perform productive prewriting activities.
- complete revision-ready first drafts.
- rewrite effectively to achieve appropriate tone.

Every instance of workplace writing occurs for a specific reason and is intended for a particular individual or group. Much the same is true of spoken messages, whether delivered in person or by phone. Therefore, both the purpose and the audience must be carefully considered to ensure that the tone of the exchange is appropriate to the situation. Although this may seem obvious, awareness of purpose, audience, and tone is crucial to ensuring that your communication succeeds. Equally important is the need to understand that writing is actually a three-step process involving not only the writing itself but also prewriting and rewriting. This opening chapter concentrates on these fundamental concerns, presents a brief overview of the basic principles involved, and provides exercises in their application.

Purpose

Nearly all workplace writing is done for at least one of three purposes: to create a record, to request or provide information, or to persuade. For example, a caseworker in a social services agency might interview an applicant for public assistance to gather information that will then be reviewed in determining the applicant's eligibility. Clearly, such writing is intended both to provide information and to create a record. On the other hand, the purchasing director of a manufacturing company might write a letter or e-mail inquiring whether a particular supplier can provide materials more cheaply than the current vendor. The supplier will likely reply promptly. Obviously, the primary purpose here is to exchange information. In yet another setting, a probation officer composes a presentencing report intended to influence the court to grant probation to the offender or impose a jail sentence. The officer may recommend either, and the report will become part of the offender's record, but the primary purpose of this example of workplace writing is to persuade.

At the prewriting stage of the writing process—before you attempt to actually compose—you must first do some *thinking* to identify which of the three categories of purpose applies. Ask yourself, "Am I writing primarily to create a record, to request or provide information, or to persuade?" Once you make this determination, the question becomes, "Summarized in one sentence, what am I trying to say?" To answer, you must zoom in on your subject matter, focusing on the most important elements. A helpful strategy is to use the "Five W's" that journalists use to structure the opening sentences of newspaper stories: Who, What, Where, When, Why. Just as they do for reporters, the Five W's will enable you to get off to a running start.

Audience

Next, ask yourself, "Who will read what I have written?" This is a crucial part of the prewriting stage of the communication process.

An e-mail, letter, report, or oral presentation must be tailored to its intended audience; otherwise, it probably won't achieve the desired results. Therefore, ask yourself the following questions before attempting to prepare any sort of formal communication:

- Am I writing to one person or more than one?
- What are their job titles and/or areas of responsibility?
- What do they already know about the specific situation?
- Why do they need this information?
- What do I want them to do as a result of receiving it?
- What factors might influence their response?

Because these questions are closely related, the answers sometimes overlap. A good starting point for sorting them out is to classify your audience by level: layperson, expert, or executive. The layperson doesn't possess significant prior knowledge of the field, whereas an expert obviously does. An executive reader has decision-making power and, one hopes, considerable expertise. By profiling your readers or listeners this way, you'll come to see the subject of your planned communication from your audience's viewpoint as well as your own. You'll be better able to state the purpose of your communication, provide necessary details, cite meaningful examples, achieve the correct level of formality, and avoid possible misunderstandings, thereby achieving your desired outcome.

In identifying your audience, remember that workplace communications fall into four broad categories:

- **Upward communication:** Intended for those above you in the hierarchy. (Example: An e-mail reply to a question from your supervisor.)
- **Lateral communication:** Intended for those at your own level in the hierarchy. (Example: A voice mail to a coworker with whom you're collaborating.)
- **Downward communication:** Intended for those below you in the hierarchy. (Example: An oral reminder to an intern you've been assigned to train.)
- **Outward communication:** Intended for those outside your workplace. (Example: A letter to someone at a company with which you do business.)

These differences will influence your communications in many ways, particularly in determining format. For in-house communications (the first three categories), the memo was traditionally the preferred written medium. The memo has now been almost totally replaced by e-mail. And text messaging, of course, has became another major form of in-house communication. For outward communications, such as correspondence with clients, customers, or the general public, the standard business letter has been the norm. Business letters are either mailed or transmitted by fax machine. Even for outward communications, though, e-mail is often the best choice because of its speed and efficiency. If a more formal document is required, a confirmation letter can always be sent later.

Global Audience

Increasingly, outward communication involves transcultural interactions. In the global marketplace, you face particular challenges when composing documents intended for readers in other countries. Although it's always foolish to embrace cultural and ethnic stereotypes, cultural differences do indeed exist. In fact, specialized terminology has been developed to address this issue. For example, experts in the field of communications differentiate between *high-context* and *low-context* cultural mind-sets. Business and technical communications in high-context cultures such as many in Asia, the Middle East, and South America typically exhibit an emphasis on background information and often contain an interpersonal component. Those in low-context cultures such as Australia, much of western Europe, and certainly the United States do not. Such differences can result in very dissimilar handlings of essentially identical situations, as Figures 1.1 and 1.2 illustrate.

3-Dynamics

221 River Street
Hoboken, New Jersey 07030

February 2, 2015

Mr. Yukio Tanaka
Shinchoku International
7-3-1 Hongo
Bunkyo, Tokyo 113-8654
Japan

Dear Mr. Yukio Tanaka:

Everyone at 3-Dynamics enjoyed your recent visit to our corporate offices, but we must apologize for the frigid New Jersey weather. We are sure that your wife and family are glad that you have returned safely and are delighted with the lovely gifts you bought for them at Bloomingdale's, one of our most highly regarded department stores.

As you know, 3-Dynamics was founded in 2010 and was an early leader in three-dimensional printing. Since then we have expanded and become the most well-known American company in this field. Much of our success is the result of our decision to develop both hardware and software, rather than focusing exclusively on one area of this exciting technology.

Certainly we are enthusiastic about the prospect of cooperating with Shinchoku International in a joint venture. Such an undertaking would be very rewarding for both companies, allowing us to capture a much greater segment of the world-wide market than either can claim at present.

With your permission, we will contact you in the very near future to arrange for the next step in establishing our partnership.

Respectfully,

Edward Ahern

Edward Ahern
Assistant Director of Marketing

FIGURE 1.1 • Letter to an overseas reader

3-Dynamics

**221 River Street
Hoboken, New Jersey 07030**

February 10, 2015

Mr. Richard Gray
SxSW Technologies
50 Sixth Street, Suite 56
Austin, TX 78700

Dear Richie,

Thanks for making the trip east last week to discuss our possible merger.

Everybody here agrees it's something we should explore further, with an eye toward capturing a much greater share of the rapidly expanding 3-D market. Could be a major win-win for both SxSWT and 3-Dynamics.

Someone here will contact you very soon to start putting the wheels into motion. Stay tuned!

Best,

Ed

Edward Ahern

Assistant Director of Marketing

FIGURE 1.2 • Letter to American Reader

The letter to the Japanese company "shoots the breeze" through its more formal tone and conclusion of personal detail before getting down to the "take-away." The letter to the American company "cuts to the chase." Idioms such as these, while well-known by American English speakers, might be quite confusing—in fact meaningless—to readers elsewhere. Indeed, that's the definition of an idiom: an expression that defies direct translation. This is another key feature of global communication. Colloquialisms vary greatly around the world, even among native speakers of English in England, Ireland, Scotland, Wales, Canada, and elsewhere. Therefore, they should definitely be avoided when writing to readers outside the United States. Even contractions—which can be seen as too informal—should not appear. The same is true of slang, abbreviations, acronyms, and other varieties of nonstandard phrasing. Of course, it's *always* better to avoid such expressions in workplace writing, but especially so in transcultural situations. These usages not only increase the likelihood of miscommunication but are difficult or impossible to translate meaningfully if your writing must be recast in your reader's language.

Also important when writing in an international setting is to use familiar, commonplace vocabulary and strive for direct, straightforward sentence structure that follows the basic subject/verb/object pattern. This is always preferable to a complex, roundabout style, but never more so than in the global context.

In addition, it's necessary to avoid cultural references, which may not be understood by readers in other countries. Many American idioms presuppose a familiarity with our popular culture, particularly sports. If we refer to a "hail Mary," for example, or a "slam dunk," we'll be understood "in a New York minute," but only if our reader is also from this country. Such expressions are useful only in rather informal exchanges and are never appropriate when addressing readers in other parts of the world.

This is equally true of attempts at humor, which may not only puzzle but perhaps unintentionally insult the reader. While we must always consider questions of audience when composing workplace documents, attention to this fundamental issue is absolutely paramount in the international context.

Tone

As Table 1.1 reflects, the drafting stage of the three-part writing process is the least complicated. If you've devoted enough time and attention to prewriting, you'll know what you intend to say, you'll have *enough* to say, and you'll know what goes where, so you'll be able to compose fairly quickly. Indeed, at the drafting stage, you should simply push ahead rather than stopping to fine-tune because it's best not to disrupt the flow of your ideas. Of course, if you notice an obvious miscue (a typo, for example), it's OK to correct it, but keep the emphasis on completing the draft before you run out of time and energy. Any additional polishing that may be needed can be done during the final, most challenging stage of the process, rewriting.

Prewriting	Drafting	Rewriting
• Identify your purpose and your intended audience.	• Create a first draft, concentrating on content rather than fine points of mechanics, style, and tone.	• Consider the organization of the content.
• Decide what needs to be said.		• Check for accuracy, completeness, and ethical validity.
• Choose the most appropriate format (e-mail, letter, report).		• Revise for style, striving for concision and simplicity.
		• Adjust the tone to suit the audience.
		• Edit for mechanical errors (typos, spelling, grammar, punctuation).

TABLE 1.1 • Writing: A Three-Step Process

Nobody produces good writing on the first try. You *must* rewrite. But rewriting involves far more than simply correcting mechanical errors. For example, what may have seemed sufficient and logical at the drafting stage might now strike you as much less so. Therefore, you might want to add something here and there or take something out. How about organization?

- Are the individual words in each sentence precisely the right ones, and is each exactly where it belongs?
- Are the sentences in each paragraph presented in the best possible order?
- Are the paragraphs in the best sequence, or should they be rearranged?

In addition, you should look for ways to tighten your style by avoiding wordiness and expressing yourself as simply and directly as possible. Very important, is your tone appropriate to your purpose and your intended reader?

Your hierarchical relationship to your reader plays a major role in determining your tone, especially when you're attempting to convey "bad news" (the denial of a request from an employee you supervise, for example) or to suggest that staff members adopt some new or different procedure. Although such messages can be phrased in a firm, straightforward manner, a harsh voice or belligerent attitude is seldom productive.

Any workforce is essentially a team of individuals cooperating to achieve a common goal: the mission of the business, organization, or agency. A high level of collective commitment is needed for this to happen. Ideally, each person exerts a genuine effort to foster a climate of shared enthusiasm. But if coworkers become defensive or resentful, morale problems inevitably develop, undermining productivity. In such a situation, everyone loses.

Therefore, don't try to sound tough or demanding when writing about potentially sensitive issues. Instead, appeal to the reader's sense of fairness and cooperation. Phrase your sentences in a nonthreatening way, emphasizing the reader's viewpoint by using a reader-centered (rather than a writer-centered) perspective. For obvious reasons, this approach should also govern your correspondence intended for readers outside the workplace, especially those in other countries.

Here are some examples of how to creatively change a writer-centered perspective into a reader-centered perspective:

Writer-Centered Perspective	**Reader-Centered Perspective**
If I can answer any questions, I'll be happy to do so.	If you have any questions, please ask.
We shipped the order this morning.	Your order is on its way.
I'm happy to report that . . .	You'll be glad to know that . . .

Notice that changing *I* and *we* to *you* and *your* personalizes the communication. Focusing on the reader is also known as the "you" approach. Another important element of the you approach is the use of *please, thank you,* and other polite terms.

Now consider Figures 1.3 and 1.4. Both e-mails have the same purpose—to change a specific behavior—and both address the same audience. But the first version adopts a writer-centered approach and is harshly combative. The reader-centered revision, on the other hand, is diplomatic and therefore much more persuasive. The first is almost certain to create resentment and hard feelings, whereas the second is far more likely to gain the desired results.

In most settings, you can adopt a somewhat more casual manner with your equals and with those below you than with those above you in the chain of command or with persons outside the organization. But in any case, avoid an excessively conversational style. Even when the situation isn't particularly troublesome and even when your reader is well-known to you, remember that "business is business." Although you need not sound stuffy, it's important to maintain a certain level of formality. Accordingly, you should never allow personal matters to appear in workplace correspondence. Consider, for example, Figure 1.5, an e-mail in which the writer has obviously violated this rule. Although the tone is appropriately respectful, the content should be far less detailed, as in the revised version shown in Figure 1.6.

A sensitive situation awaits you when you must convey unpleasant information or request assistance or cooperation from superiors. Although you may sometimes yearn for a more democratic arrangement, every workplace has a pecking order that you must consider as you choose your words. Hierarchy exists because some individuals—by virtue of more experience, education, or access to information—are in fact better positioned to lead. Although this system sometimes functions imperfectly, the supervisor, department head, or other person in charge responds better to subordinates whose communications reflect an understanding of this basic reality. Essentially, the rules for writing to a person higher on the ladder are the same as for writing to someone on a lower rung. Be focused and self-assured, but use the "you"

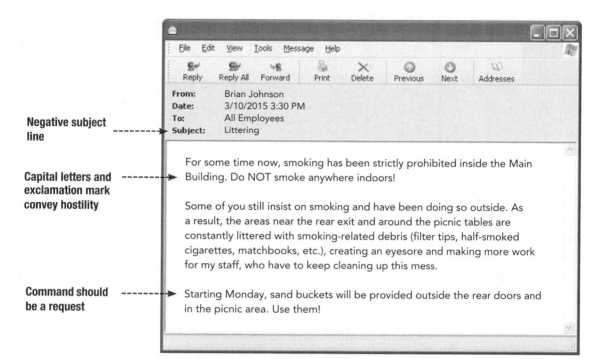

FIGURE 1.3 • Original E-mail

Negative subject line ----→ Subject: Littering

Capital letters and exclamation mark convey hostility ----→ For some time now, smoking has been strictly prohibited inside the Main Building. Do NOT smoke anywhere indoors!

Some of you still insist on smoking and have been doing so outside. As a result, the areas near the rear exit and around the picnic tables are constantly littered with smoking-related debris (filter tips, half-smoked cigarettes, matchbooks, etc.), creating an eyesore and making more work for my staff, who have to keep cleaning up this mess.

Command should be a request ----→ Starting Monday, sand buckets will be provided outside the rear doors and in the picnic area. Use them!

FIGURE 1.4 • Revised E-mail

Positive subject line ----→ Subject: Outdoor Ashtrays

Because the Main Building is a No Smoking zone, some of you have been taking your breaks outdoors.

Upbeat tone encourages compliance ----→ We appreciate your compliance with company regulations and wish to minimize your inconvenience. As of Monday, sand bucket "ashtrays" will be provided for your use outside the rear doors and near the picnic tables. This will help maintain a more pleasant atmosphere for us all by minimizing litter behind the building.

Polite closing ----→ Again, thanks very much for your cooperation!

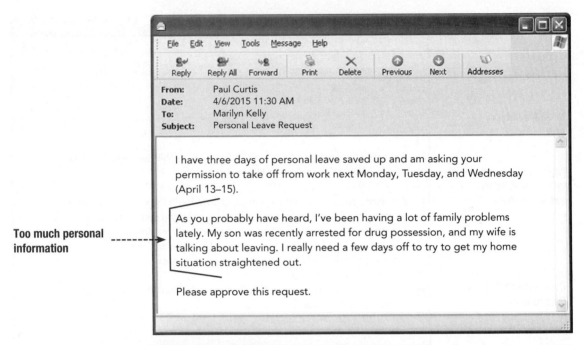

Too much personal information

FIGURE 1.5 • Original E-mail

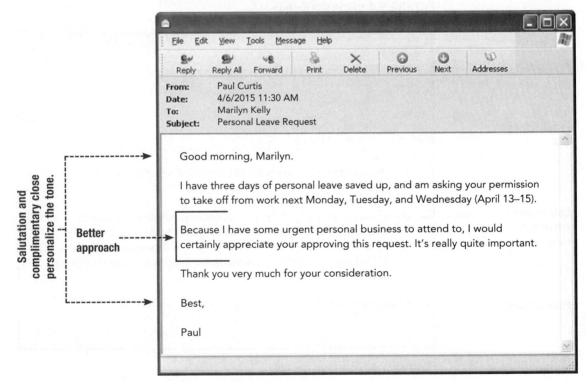

Salutation and complimentary close personalize the tone.

Better approach

FIGURE1.6 • Revised E-mail

Tech**Tips**

A slangy, vernacular style is out of place in workplace writing, as are expletives and any other coarse or vulgar language. Something that may seem clever or humorous to you may not amuse your reader and will probably appear foolish to anyone reviewing the correspondence later. Keep this in mind when sending e-mail, a medium that seems to encourage looser, more playful phrasing.

Avoid abbreviations and acronyms hatched in Internet chat rooms and other informal contexts such as text messaging. Although inventive, most are inappropriate for the workplace because they may not be readily understood—especially by older workers and those for whom English is not their native language. Here are ten examples.

BTW: by the way	IRL: in real life
FWIW: for what it's worth	OTOH: on the other hand
HAND: have a nice day	TMOT: trust me on this
IMHO: in my humble opinion	TTYTT: to tell you the truth
IOW: in other words	WADR: with all due respect

At the same time, *technical* acronyms specific to particular businesses and occupations facilitate dialogue among employees familiar with those terms. As with so many aspects of workplace communications, the use of acronyms is largely governed by considerations of audience, purpose, and tone.

approach, encouraging the reader to see the advantage in accepting your recommendation or granting your request.

Nowhere is this more crucial than in the global context. Obviously, it would be impossible to familiarize oneself with all the many cultural differences that exist around the world. Nevertheless, it's important to recognize that in the realm of workplace communications, most cultures place a very high value on tact and courtesy. Informality can easily be viewed as disrespect, and indirection is often preferable to outright refusal or disagreement. In many Asian countries, for example, "maybe" is often understood to mean "no," as is the phrase "we'll think about it." This is in direct contrast to the American tendency toward bluntness, which can be interpreted as overly aggressive or even combative.

An especially polite tone is advisable when addressing those who outrank you. Acknowledge that the final decision is theirs and that you are fully willing to abide by that determination. This can be achieved either through "softening" words and phrases (*perhaps, with your permission, if you wish*) or simply by stating outright that you'll accept whatever outcome may develop. For example, consider the e-mails in Figures 1.7 and 1.8. Although both say essentially the same thing, the first is completely inappropriate in tone, so much so that it would likely result in negative

Hostile tone creates negative climate

> Just wanted to let you know that you'd better forget about the random drug-testing policy you announced in your memo yesterday. It's a dumb idea that will never work. All the drivers are angry about it, and there are a lot of questions that your memo left completely unanswered! From what I hear, people in other departments have a lot of questions too. Better clear some of this stuff up or nobody's ever going to hold still for it.

FIGURE 1.7 • Original E-mail

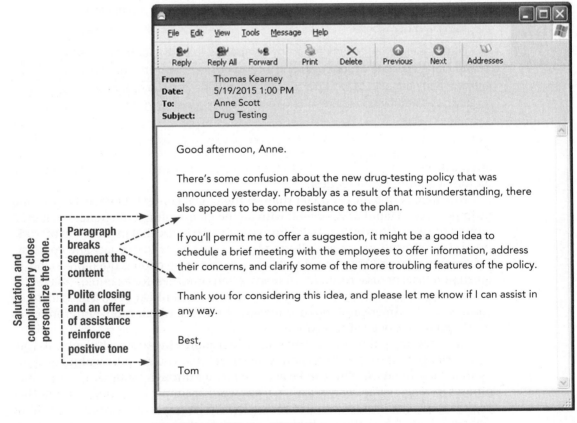

Salutation and complimentary close personalize the tone.

Paragraph breaks segment the content

Polite closing and an offer of assistance reinforce positive tone

> Good afternoon, Anne.
>
> There's some confusion about the new drug-testing policy that was announced yesterday. Probably as a result of that misunderstanding, there also appears to be some resistance to the plan.
>
> If you'll permit me to offer a suggestion, it might be a good idea to schedule a brief meeting with the employees to offer information, address their concerns, and clarify some of the more troubling features of the policy.
>
> Thank you for considering this idea, and please let me know if I can assist in any way.
>
> Best,
>
> Tom

FIGURE 1.8 • Revised E-mail

consequences for the writer. The second would be much better received because it properly reflects the nature of the professional relationship.

Communicating with customers or clients also requires a great deal of sensitivity and tact. This is especially important when communicating with readers abroad, many of whom are accustomed to a more formal and polite tone than is common here. When justifying a price increase, denying a claim, or apologizing for a delay, you'll probably create an unpleasant climate unless you present the facts in a gentle manner. Always strive for the most upbeat, reader-centered wording you can devise. Here are some examples of how to rephrase negative content in more positive, reader-centered terms:

Negative Wording	Positive Wording
We cannot process your claim because the necessary forms have not been completed.	Your claim can be processed as soon as you complete the necessary forms.
We do not take phone call after 3:00 p.m. on Fridays.	You may reach us by telephone on Fridays until 3:00 p.m.
We closed your case because we never received the information requested in our letter of April 2.	Your case will be reactivated as soon as you provide the information requested in our April 2 letter.

When the problem has been caused by an error or oversight on your part, be sure to apologize. However, do not state specifically what the mistake was or your letter may be used as evidence against you should a lawsuit ensue. Simply acknowledge that a mistake has occurred, express regret, explain how the situation will be corrected, and close on a conciliatory note. For example, consider the letter in Figure 1.9. The body and conclusion are fine, but the introduction practically invites legal action. Here's a suggested revision of the letter's opening paragraph, phrased in less incriminating terms:

> Thank you for purchasing our product and for taking the time to contact us about it. We apologize for the unsatisfactory condition of your Superior microwave dinner.

Moreover, given the serious nature of the complaint, the customer services representative should certainly have made a stronger effort to establish a tone of sincerely apologetic concern. As it stands, this letter seems abrupt and rather impersonal—certainly not what the context requires. (For a much better handling of this kind of situation, see the adjustment letter in Figure 2.6.)

This is not to suggest, however, that workplace communications should attempt to falsify reality or dodge responsibility. On the contrary, there's a moral imperative to uphold strict ethical standards. Recent corporate misdeeds have put ethical questions under the spotlight and greatly increased the public's appetite for investigative reporting by the media. The online *Encyclopedia Brittanica* defines *ethics* as "the discipline concerned with what is morally good and bad, right and wrong." Essentially, ethics involves choosing honesty over dishonesty, requiring us to act with integrity

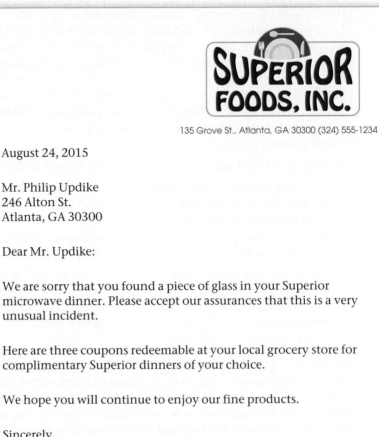

SUPERIOR FOODS, INC.

135 Grove St., Atlanta, GA 30300 (324) 555-1234

August 24, 2015

Mr. Philip Updike
246 Alton St.
Atlanta, GA 30300

Dear Mr. Updike:

Wording is too explicit ⤑ We are sorry that you found a piece of glass in your Superior microwave dinner. Please accept our assurances that this is a very unusual incident.

Here are three coupons redeemable at your local grocery store for complimentary Superior dinners of your choice.

Positive tone despite negative situation ⤑ We hope you will continue to enjoy our fine products.

Sincerely,

John Roth

John Roth
Customer Services Dept.

Enclosures (3)

FIGURE 1.9 • Letter to Customer

even when there would be short-term gains for behaving otherwise. Ethical communication must therefore be honest and fair to everyone involved.

By their nature, workplace communications can greatly affect people's lives. Accordingly, customers and clients, investors, taxpayers, and workers themselves should be able to treat such materials as accurate, reliable, and trustworthy—in short, ethical. Documents fail the ethics test if corrupted by any of the following tactics:

- **Suppression of information:** The outright burying of data to hide inconvenient truths. (Example: A company fails to reveal product-testing results that indicate potential danger to consumers.)

- **Falsification or fabrication:** Changing or simply inventing data to support a desired outcome. (Example: A company boasts of a fictitious enterprise to lure investors into supporting a new venture.)

- **Overstatement or understatement:** Exaggerating the positive aspects of a situation or downplaying negative aspects to create the desired impression. (Example: A public-opinion survey describes 55 percent of the respondents as a "substantial majority" or 45 percent as "a small percentage.")

- **Selective misquoting:** Deleting words from quoted material to distort the meaning. (Example: A supervisor changes a report's conclusion that "this proposal will seem feasible only to workers unfamiliar with the situation" to "this proposal will seem feasible . . . to workers.")

- **Subjective wording:** Using terms deliberately chosen for their ambiguity. (Example: A company advertises "customary service charges," knowing that "customary" is open to broad interpretation.)

- **Conflict of interest:** Exploiting behind-the-scenes connections to influence decision making. (Example: A board member of a community agency encourages the agency to hire her company for paid services rather than soliciting bids.)

- **Withholding information:** Refusing to share relevant data with coworkers. (Example: A computer-savvy employee provides misleading answers about new software to make a recently hired coworker appear incompetent.)

- **Plagiarism:** Taking credit for someone else's ideas, findings, or written material. (Example: An employee assigned to prepare a report submits a similar report written by someone at another company and downloaded from the Internet.)

Workers must weigh the consequences of their actions, considering their moral obligations. If this is done in good faith, practices such as those outlined in the preceding list can surely be avoided. Decisions can become complicated, however, when obligations to self and others come into conflict. Workers often feel pressure to compromise personal ethical beliefs to achieve company goals. All things being equal, a worker's primary obligation is to self—to remain employed. But if the employer permits or requires actions that the employee considers immoral, an ethical dilemma is created, forcing the worker to choose among two or more unsatisfactory alternatives.

For example, what if an employee discovers that the company habitually ignores Occupational Safety and Health Administration (OSHA) or Environmental Protection Agency (EPA) standards? As everyone knows, whistle-blowing can incur heavy penalties: ostracism, undesirable work assignments, poor performance reviews—or even termination. Although the Sarbanes-Oxley Act of 2002 prohibits such retribution, it's quite difficult to actually prove retaliation unless the worker is prepared for potentially lengthy and expensive legal combat with no guarantee of success and the added threat of countersuit. And even if the attempt does succeed, the worker must then return to an even more hostile climate. Should the person seek employment elsewhere, blacklisting may have already sabotaged the job search.

There are no easy resolutions to ethical dilemmas, but we all must be guided by conscience. Obviously, this can involve some difficult decisions. By determining your purpose, analyzing your audience, and considering the moral dimensions of the situation, you'll achieve the correct tone for any communication. As we have seen, this is crucial for dealing with potentially resistive readers (especially those above you in the workplace hierarchy) and when rectifying errors for which you're accountable. In all instances, however, a courteous, positive, reader-centered, and ethical approach leads to the best results.

EXERCISES

EXERCISE 1.1

Revise each of the following three communications to achieve a tone more appropriate to the purpose and audience.

SOUTHEAST INSURANCE COMPANY

Southeast Industrial Park   Tallahassee, FL 32301
Telephone: (850) 555-0123   FAX: (850) 555-3210

November 9, 2015

Mr. Francis Tedeschi
214 Summit Avenue
Tallahassee, FL 32301

Dear Mr. Tedeschi:

This is to acknowledge receipt of your 11/2/15 claim.

Insured persons entitled to benefits under the Tallahassee Manufacturing Co. plan effective December 1, 2005, are required to execute statements of claims for medical-surgical expense benefits only in the manner specifically mandated in your certificate holder's handbook.

Your claim has been quite improperly executed, as you have neglected to procure the Physician's Statement of Services Rendered. The information contained therein is prerequisite to any consideration of your claim.

Enclosed is the necessary form. See that it's filled out and returned to us without delay or your claim cannot be processed.

Yours truly,

Ann Jurkiewicz

Ann Jurkiewicz
Claims Adjustor

Enclosure

File Edit View Tools Message Help

Reply | Reply All | Forward | Print | Delete | Previous | Next | Addresses

From: CALSTON
Date: 3/17/2015 2:00 PM
To: All Caseworkers
Subject: Goofing Off

A lot of you seem to think that this is a country club and are spending entirely too much time in the break room! As you well know, you're entitled to one <u>15-minute</u> break in the morning and another in the afternoon. The rest of the time, you're supposed to be AT YOUR DESK unless signed out for fieldwork.

Cheryl Alston

Case Supervisor

File Edit View Tools Message Help

Reply | Reply All | Forward | Print | Delete | Previous | Next | Addresses

From: CRIGNEY
Date: 5/4/2015 10:00 AM
To: All Faculty, Staff, Students
Subject: Burglarized Vehicles

Recently, there's been a rash of burglaries in the faculty/staff parking lot. Items such as CD players, cellular phones, and even a personal computer have been reported missing from vehicles.

After investigating, however, we've learned that several of these vehicles had been left unlocked. Don't be stupid! Always lock your car or else be prepared to get ripped off. My staff can't be everywhere at once, and if you set yourself up to be victimized, it's not our fault.

Charles Rigney

Chief of Campus Security

EXERCISE 1.2

Revise each of the following three communications to eliminate inappropriate tone and/or content.

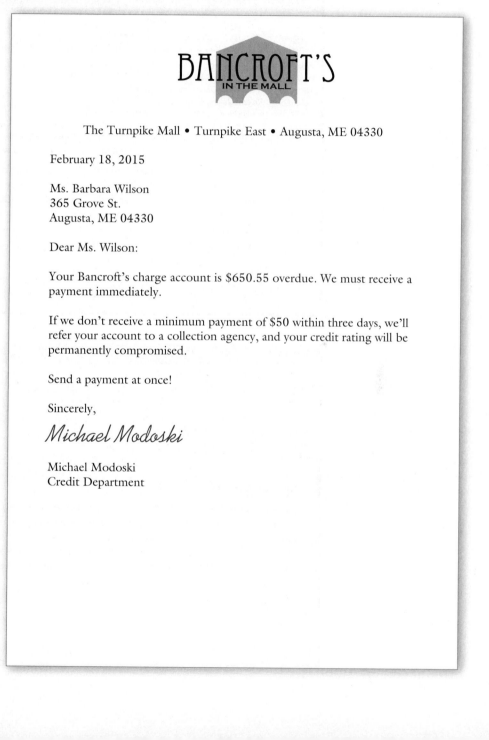

BANCROFT'S
IN THE MALL

The Turnpike Mall • Turnpike East • Augusta, ME 04330

February 18, 2015

Ms. Barbara Wilson
365 Grove St.
Augusta, ME 04330

Dear Ms. Wilson:

Your Bancroft's charge account is $650.55 overdue. We must receive a payment immediately.

If we don't receive a minimum payment of $50 within three days, we'll refer your account to a collection agency, and your credit rating will be permanently compromised.

Send a payment at once!

Sincerely,

Michael Modoski

Michael Modoski
Credit Department

EXERCISE 1.2   *Continued*

File   Edit   View   Tools   Message   Help

Reply   Reply All   Forward   Print   Delete   Previous   Next   Addresses

From: Carl Roberts
Date: 11/10/2015 2.30 PM
To: Marketing Department Employees
Subject: Rescheduling of Meeting

The Friday afternoon department meeting has been rescheduled for Monday at 9 a.m. because I have to leave work early on Friday.

My son's high school football team (the mighty 7 & 0 Centerton Lions—rah! rah!) has an out-of-state game Friday night against another undefeated team in Illinois. From what I understand, they're a real powerhouse, but I'm sure Centerton will beat them, especially since Carl Junior's averaging nearly 14 yards per carry!

:-):-):-):-):-):-):-)

GO, LIONS!!!

File   Edit   View   Tools   Message   Help

Reply   Reply All   Forward   Print   Delete   Previous   Next   Addresses

From: Ellen Miller
Date: 7/14/2015 11:00 AM
To: Richard Rhodes
Subject: Excuse for Absence

Dear Mr. Rhodes:

Sorry I missed work on Monday. What happened was that my husband's company picnic was on Sunday. As you may have heard, he has a really bad drinking problem. Needless to say, he tied one on big time and insisted on staying out half the night, so I didn't get any sleep. But I gave him a good talking-to, and I can promise you that nothing like this will ever happen again.

Sincerely,

Ellen

EXERCISE 1.3

Revise each of the following two letters to eliminate wording that might create legal liability.

133 Court St.   Olympia, WA 98501

January 13, 2015

Mr. Robert Ryan
352 Stegman St.
Olympia, WA 98501

Dear Mr. Ryan:

We have received your letter of January 6, and we regret that the heating unit we sold you malfunctioned, killing your tropical fish worth $1,500.

Because the unit was purchased more than three years ago, however, our storewide warranty is no longer in effect, and we are therefore unable to accept any responsibility for your loss. Nevertheless, we are enclosing a Fin & Feather discount coupon good for $20 toward the purchase of a replacement unit or another product of your choice.

We look forward to serving you in the future!

Sincerely,

Sandra Kouvel

Sandra Kouvel
Store Manager

Enclosure

EXERCISE 1.4

The following idioms are well-known in the United States but might not be understood by readers elsewhere. Replace them with straightforward, literal expressions of the meanings.

after the dust settles   _____

all in the same boat   _____

back to square one   _____

bend over backward   _____

bite the bullet   _____

count on me   _____

dead on arrival   _____

foot the bill   _____

hands down   _____

hit the ground running   _____

on thin ice   _____

running on fumes   _____

slip through the cracks   _____

tough act to follow   _____

turn up the heat   _____

Workplace Correspondence: Memos, E-mail, Text Messages, and Business Letters

LEARNING OBJECTIVES

When you complete this chapter you'll be able to:

- follow established guidelines specific to various genres of workplace writing.
- compose clear, focused memos.
- use e-mail protocols efficiently.
- craft clear, concise text messages that convey information with maximum economy.
- write effective business letters in a variety of situations.

Until fairly recently, the memo was perhaps the most common form of workplace correspondence. Along with the business letter, the memo was fundamental to office procedure. Any large company, agency, or other organization would generate thousands of such documents daily. Now, however, the memo—and, to a lesser extent, the business letter as well—has been largely replaced by e-mail. And e-mail itself is now in competition with text messaging, at least in relatively informal contexts. This chapter explores the connections among the memo, e-mail, texts, and the business letter, and explains how to handle each.

Memos

Traditionally, the memo was a vehicle for internal or "intramural" communication—a message from someone at Company X to someone else at Company X. The memo may have been written to one person or to a group, but it was almost always a form of in-house correspondence.

Although the usual purpose of a memo was to inform, often its function was to create a written record of a request or other message previously communicated in person, over the phone, or through the grapevine.

Accordingly, a memo was usually quite direct in approach. It would come to the point quickly and not ramble on. A good memo would focus sharply, zooming in on what the reader needed to know. Depending on the subject, a memo would make its point in three or four short paragraphs: a concise introduction, a middle paragraph or two conveying the details, and perhaps a brief conclusion. But some memos were as short as one paragraph or even one sentence. Like so many other features of workplace communications, memo length was determined by purpose and audience.

Although minor variations did exist, practically all memos shared certain standard format features:

- The word *Memo, Memorandum,* or some equivalent term at or near the top of the page.
- The DATE line.
- The TO line, enabling the memo to be "addressed," and the FROM line, enabling it to be "signed."
- The SUBJECT line, identifying the topic. Like a newspaper headline but even more concise, the SUBJECT line would orient and prepare the reader for what was to follow. A good subject line answers this question: "In no more than three words, what is this memo really about?"
- Of course, the message or content of the memo. As explained earlier, three or four paragraphs were usually sufficient.

The memo in Figure 2.1 embodies all these features and provides an opportunity to further explore the principle of *tone* introduced in Chapter 1.

The personnel manager picked her words carefully to avoid sounding bossy. She says "You *may want* to send him a . . . card," not "You *should* send him a . . . card," even though that's what she really means. As discussed in Chapter 1, a tactful writer can soften a recommendation, a request, or even a command simply by phrasing it in a diplomatic way. In this situation, an employee's decision whether to send a card would be a matter of personal choice, so the memo's gentle tone is particularly appropriate. But the same strategy can also be used when conveying important directives you definitely expect the reader to follow.

For the sake of convenience in situations where a paper memo may still be preferable to e-mail, most word-processing programs include at least one preformatted memo form, called a *template.* The template automatically generates formatted headings and inserts the date. The writer simply fills in the blanks.

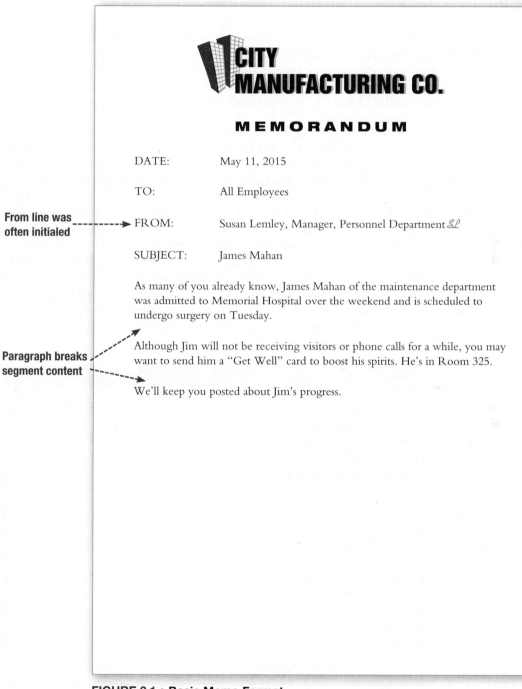

**From line was
often initialed**

**Paragraph breaks
segment content**

**CITY
MANUFACTURING CO.**

M E M O R A N D U M

DATE: May 11, 2015

TO: All Employees

FROM: Susan Lemley, Manager, Personnel Department *SL*

SUBJECT: James Mahan

As many of you already know, James Mahan of the maintenance department
was admitted to Memorial Hospital over the weekend and is scheduled to
undergo surgery on Tuesday.

Although Jim will not be receiving visitors or phone calls for a while, you may
want to send him a "Get Well" card to boost his spirits. He's in Room 325.

We'll keep you posted about Jim's progress.

FIGURE 2.1 • Basic Memo Format

E-mail

Because an e-mail is essentially just an electronic memo, practically everything that's already been said here about traditional memos also applies to e-mail.

Figure 2.2 is a typical e-mail memo, similar to those you saw in Chapter 1.

There are good reasons e-mail has been so widely adopted since becoming generally available in the 1990s. On the most obvious level, it's incomparably faster than traditional correspondence.

It allows for rapid-fire exchanges, and the most recent transmittal can reproduce a complete record of all that has gone before. When you're engaged in a lengthy back-and-forth e-mail "conversation," however, the focus of the discussion most likely evolves. So it's smart to continuously revise the subject line to reflect that fact.

Despite its many obvious advantages, e-mail can also create some problems. One major drawback is that the very ease with which e-mail can be generated encourages overuse. Sometimes a text or simple phone call is more efficient, even if voice mail is involved. In the past, a writer would not bother to send a memo without good reason; too much time and effort were involved to do otherwise. Now, though, much needless correspondence is produced. Many of yesterday's writers would wait until complete information on a given topic had been received, organized, and considered before acting on it or passing it along. But today, it's not uncommon for many e-mails to be written on the same subject, doling out the information piecemeal, sometimes

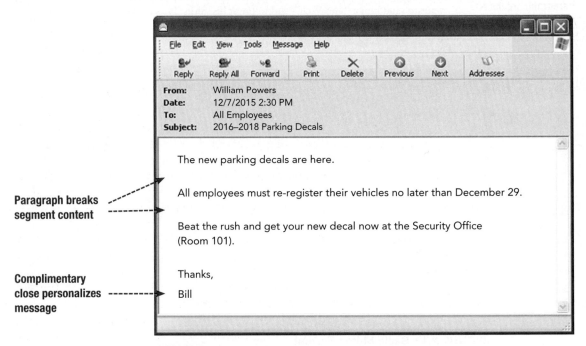

Paragraph breaks segment content

Complimentary close personalizes message

FIGURE 2.2 • E-mail

within a very short time span. The resulting fragmentation wastes the energies of writer and reader alike and increases the possibility of confusion, often because of premature response. One way to minimize this danger is to scan your entire menu of incoming messages, taking special note of multiple mailings from the same source before responding to any.

Similarly, e-mails about sensitive issues are often dashed off "in the heat of battle," without sufficient reflection. In the past, most writers had some time to reconsider a situation before reacting. There was usually the option of revising or simply discarding a memo if, upon proofreading, it came to seem a bit too harsh or otherwise inappropriate. The inherent rapidity of e-mail, however, all but eliminates any such opportunity for second thoughts. In addition, hasty composition causes a great many keyboarding miscues, omissions, and other fundamental blunders. These must then be corrected in subsequent messages, creating an inefficient proliferation of "e-mail about e-mail." Indeed, hurried writing combined with the absence of a secretarial "filter" has given rise to a great deal of embarrassingly bad prose in the workplace. You risk ridicule and loss of credibility unless you closely proofread every e-mail before sending it. Make sure that the information is necessary and correct and that all pertinent details have been included. Be particularly careful to avoid typos, misspellings, faulty capitalization, sloppy punctuation, and basic grammatical errors. Virtually all e-mail systems include spell-checkers; although not foolproof, they help minimize typos and misspellings. Similarly, grammar checkers can detect basic sentence problems.

Be aware that although the To and From lines of an e-mail eliminate the need for a letter-style salutation ("Dear Ms. Bernstein") or complimentary close ("Yours truly"), most writers employ these features when using e-mail to make their messages seem less abrupt and impersonal. The relative formality or informality of these greetings and sign-offs depends on the relationship between writer and reader. In any case, if your own e-mail name and address don't fully reveal your identity, you *must* include a complimentary close to inform your readers who you are. Most e-mail systems enable you to create a "signature file" for this purpose. (See Figure 2.3.)

Understand that e-mail is not private. Recent court decisions—some involving high-profile government scandals—have confirmed the employer's right to monitor or inspect workers' e-mail (and Internet activity). Indeed, it's not uncommon for workers to be fired for impropriety in this regard. A good rule of thumb is, "Don't say it in an e-mail unless you'd have no problem with it appearing on the front page of your company newsletter." In some situations, a given message may be entirely appropriate but may contain highly sensitive information. In such cases, the best choice may be a paper memo personally delivered in a sealed envelope.

As mentioned in Chapter 1, the company e-mail network is no place for personal messages or an excessively conversational style. Many employers provide a separate e-mail "bulletin board" on which workers can post and access announcements about garage or vehicle sales, carpooling, unwanted theater and sports tickets, and the like. Such matters are appropriate only as bulletin board content.

Now that nearly all organizations are online, e-mail is no longer just an intramural communications medium; indeed, it's beginning to rival the business letter as the major form of correspondence across company boundaries. When you're sending e-mail to

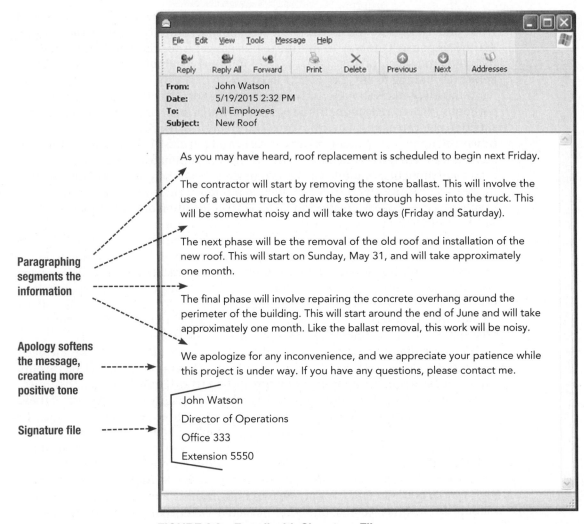

FIGURE 2.3 • E-mail with Signature File

readers at other locations, tone takes on even greater importance than usual. Because the writer and the reader probably do not know each other personally, a higher level of courteous formality is in order. Additionally, the subject matter is often more involved than that of in-house correspondence, so e-mail sent outside the workplace is commonly longer and more fully developed than messages intended for coworkers. And outside e-mail nearly always includes a letter-style salutation and complimentary close unless the writer and the reader have established an ongoing professional relationship.

To sum up, e-mail is no different from any other form of workplace communication in requiring close attention to audience, purpose, and tone—not to mention ethical considerations. Just as you would after composing a conventional memo on paper, assess your e-mail by consulting the checklist on page 30.

Tech**Tips**

Despite its seemingly informal, spontaneous nature, e-mail is no less "official" and permanent than a memo printed on paper. Therefore, it's important to use this medium thoughtfully, efficiently, and responsibly. These guidelines will help.

- Resist the temptation to forward chain letters, silly jokes, political rants, pornographic images, and the like. This not only wastes people's time but, in certain circumstances, can also be hazardous to your professional health.

- Never forward legitimate e-mail to other readers without the original writer's knowledge and permission. The message may have been intended for you alone.

- When composing an e-mail of your own, however, remember that your reader may indeed forward it to others.

- When responding to a mass mailing, do not click Reply All unless there's a valid reason to do so; reply only to the sender.

- Some readers routinely ignore attachments, so don't create one if you can build the information into the body of the e-mail, where it's more likely to be read. If that's not practical, provide a one- or two-sentence summary in the body of the e-mail to prompt the reader to open the attachment. Because very large attachments can clog readers' accounts, it's better to send a hard copy of such material.

- Remember that e-mail is only partially able to convey "tone of voice." For this reason, voice mail or actual conversation is often preferable, allowing your reasoning and feelings to be understood more accurately. This is especially true in complicated or delicate situations, particularly those involving negative messages—the denial of a request, for example.

- Never attempt to communicate when angry. Observe the standard rules of e-mail etiquette. Avoid "flaming" (openly hostile or abusive comments, whether directed at the reader or at a third party). The fact that you're communicating electronically doesn't exempt you from accepted norms of workplace courtesy.

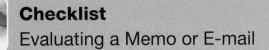

Checklist
Evaluating a Memo or E-mail

A good memo or e-mail

___ follows a standard format;

___ includes certain features:

☐ Date line (appears automatically in e-mail)

☐ To line, which includes the name and often the title and/or department of the receiver

☐ From line, which includes the name (appears automatically in e-mail) and often the title and/or department of the sender; on a paper memo, the From line must be initialed by the writer before the memo is sent

☐ Subject line, which is a clear, accurate, but brief statement of what the message is about

___ is organized into paragraphs (one is often enough) covering the subject fully in an orderly way;

___ includes no inappropriate content;

___ uses clear, simple language;

___ maintains an appropriate tone—neither too formal nor too conversational;

___ contains no typos or mechanical errors in spelling, capitalization, punctuation, or grammar.

Text Messages

According to the old saying, "time is money." In the world of work, therefore, information must be conveyed rapidly, in a punctual manner. Of course, e-mails and phone calls can accomplish this reasonably well. But not everyone constantly monitors e-mail, and phone calls can waste a lot of time because of the necessary "small talk" involved. Moreover, the caller is often detoured to the other person's voice mail, resulting in further delay. But *texts*—very short messages typed on the writer's cell phone keypad and sent to the reader's cell phone—are more efficient. When a text message is sent, the receiver of the text knows immediately and can reply (then or later), either by return text or phone call. Depending on the circumstances, a rapid-fire series of text message exchanges may be the fastest and most practical way to address a given situation.

One major advantage of text messaging is that it's well-suited to today's multi-tasking environment. Virtually everyone carries a cell phone at all times, and most of us have become fairly adept at one-handed "thumb typing." This enables messages to be sent, received, and answered on the fly, even while the persons involved are engaged in other activities. Needless to say, however, no one should ever attempt to text while driving a motor vehicle or operating potentially dangerous equipment of any kind. Although surveys reveal that texting while driving is quite common, this is an extremely hazardous practice, directly responsible for thousands of highway fatalities every year.

Texting can be tricky in less dangerous ways as well. Because every message is limited to only 160 characters (including spaces and punctuation marks), there's a widespread tendency to rely on abbreviation, phonetic spelling, substitution of numerals or single letters for words, and so forth. This is very typical of texts between friends and in other social contexts. The following example illustrates this:

ru goin 2 party 2nite? starts @9. cul8r
(Translation: Are you going to the party tonight? It starts at 9:00. See you later.)

In the workplace, however, these shortcuts can create misunderstanding and confusion, partly because of generational and cultural differences among coworkers, and should therefore be minimized. Since most workplace texts are only a brief sentence or two, there's no real need for extreme concision because there's seldom much danger of exceeding the 160-character limit. As in all writing, the use of conventional spelling, punctuation, and grammar is certainly the best way to ensure clarity in text messages.

As speedy as texting is, there are situations in which it may not be the best choice. If the subject matter is fairly important or sensitive, for example, an e-mail or phone call is preferable. One reason is that cell phones are sometimes lost or temporarily misplaced, thereby creating the possibility of a security breach. Another is that text message accounts reach capacity even faster than e-mail accounts. As the oldest messages must be deleted to create room for new ones, the "paper trail" becomes shortened. This makes it somewhat difficult (though not impossible) to completely reconstruct a scenario if there's any future need to do so.

Of course, employer-provided cell phones should be used only for business purposes, not for social conversation or non-work-related texting. When texting co-workers, it's necessary to observe all the same norms of courtesy that govern e-mail and other workplace interactions. Specifically, there should be absolutely no flirting, rumor-spreading, or exchanging of tasteless jokes and/or politically enflamed rants. Even though texts are by nature very brief, they should still be phrased politely and respectfully. On a related note, it's very rude to text while in face-to-face conversation or while attending a meeting—unless, of course, the texting directly pertains to the business at hand. People you're conversing with, including your fellow participants in meetings, expect (and are entitled to) your undivided attention.

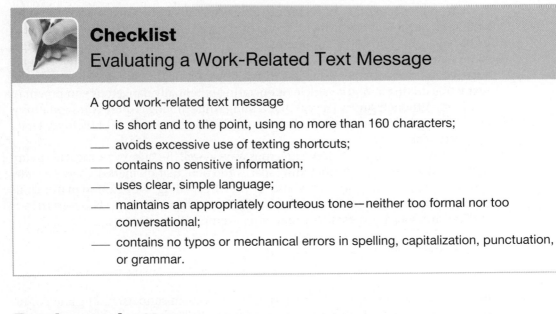

Checklist
Evaluating a Work-Related Text Message

A good work-related text message

____ is short and to the point, using no more than 160 characters;

____ avoids excessive use of texting shortcuts;

____ contains no sensitive information;

____ uses clear, simple language;

____ maintains an appropriately courteous tone—neither too formal nor too conversational;

____ contains no typos or mechanical errors in spelling, capitalization, punctuation, or grammar.

Business Letters

Business letters are typically used for *external* communication: a message from someone at Company X to someone elsewhere—a customer or client, perhaps, or a counterpart at Company Y. As mentioned earlier, however, e-mail is now often used in situations that in the past would have required letters, and this trend is increasing. Nevertheless, countless letters are still written every day for an enormous variety of reasons. Some of the more typical purposes of a letter are to do the following:

- Ask for information (inquiry)
- Sell a product or service (sales)
- Purchase a product or service (order)
- Request payment (collection)
- Voice a complaint (claim)
- Respond to a complaint (adjustment)
- Thank someone (acknowledgment)

Figures 2.4 through 2.6 provide some examples.

Regardless of its purpose, however, every letter includes certain essential components that appear on the page in the following sequence:

1. Writer's address (often preprinted on letterhead) at the top of the page. (Figure 2.7 lists standard abbreviations used in letter writing.)
2. Date (like e-mail, letters sent by fax are also automatically imprinted with the exact *time* of transmission)

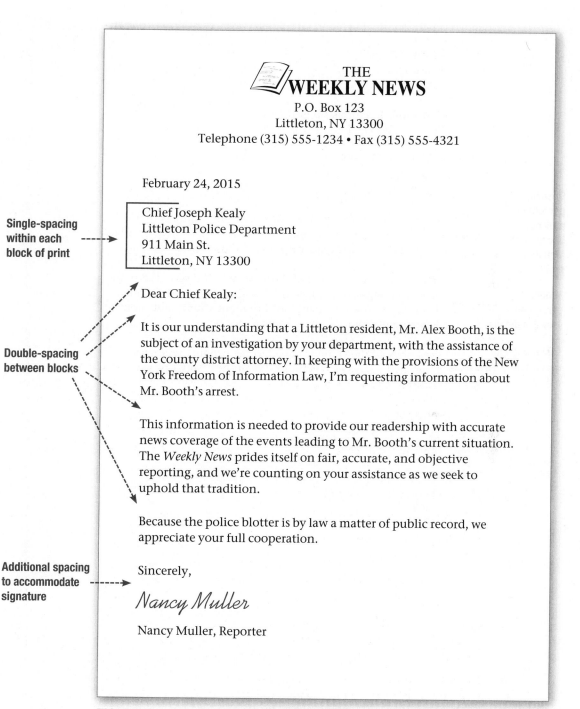

Single-spacing within each block of print

Double-spacing between blocks

Additional spacing to accommodate signature

THE WEEKLY NEWS
P.O. Box 123
Littleton, NY 13300
Telephone (315) 555-1234 • Fax (315) 555-4321

February 24, 2015

Chief Joseph Kealy
Littleton Police Department
911 Main St.
Littleton, NY 13300

Dear Chief Kealy:

It is our understanding that a Littleton resident, Mr. Alex Booth, is the subject of an investigation by your department, with the assistance of the county district attorney. In keeping with the provisions of the New York Freedom of Information Law, I'm requesting information about Mr. Booth's arrest.

This information is needed to provide our readership with accurate news coverage of the events leading to Mr. Booth's current situation. The *Weekly News* prides itself on fair, accurate, and objective reporting, and we're counting on your assistance as we seek to uphold that tradition.

Because the police blotter is by law a matter of public record, we appreciate your full cooperation.

Sincerely,

Nancy Muller

Nancy Muller, Reporter

FIGURE 2.4 • Inquiry Letter in Full Block Style

41 Allan Court
Tucson, AZ 86700
June 30, 2015

Consumer Relations Department
Superior Foods, Inc.
135 Grove St.
Atlanta, GA 30300

Dear Superior Foods:

Opening paragraph provides background, identifies problem.

Superior microwave dinners are excellent products that I've purchased regularly for many years. Recently, however, I had an unsettling experience with one of these meals.

Middle paragraph provides details.

While enjoying a serving of Pasta Alfredo, I discovered in the food what appeared to be a thick splinter of wood. I'm sure this is an isolated incident, but I thought your quality control department would want to know about it.

Last paragraph concludes politely.

I've enclosed the splinter, taped to the product wrapper, along with the sales receipt for the dinner. May I please be reimbursed $4.98 for the cost?

Sincerely,

George Eaglefeather

George Eaglefeather

Enclosures

FIGURE 2.5 • Consumer Claim Letter in Full Block Style

135 Grove St. Atlanta, GA 30300 • (324) 555-1234

July 7, 2015

Mr. George Eaglefeather
41 Allan Court
Tucson, AZ 86700

Dear Mr. Eaglefeather:

Opening paragraph thanks reader, apologizes for problem -------> Thank you for purchasing our product and for taking the time to contact us about it. We apologize for the unsatisfactory condition of your Pasta Alfredo dinner.

Middle paragraph provides solution to problem. -------> Quality is of paramount importance to all of us at Superior Foods, and great care is taken in the preparation and packaging of all our products. Our quality assurance staff has been notified of the problem you reported. Although Superior Foods doesn't issue cash refunds, we have enclosed three coupons redeemable at your grocery for complimentary Superior dinners of your choice.

Last paragraph concludes politely. -------> We appreciate this opportunity to be of service, and we hope you'll continue to enjoy our products.

Sincerely,

John Roth

John Roth
Customer Services Department

Enclosure line. -------> Enclosures (3)

FIGURE 2.6 • Adjustment Letter in Full Block Style

Alabama	AL	Kentucky	KY	Ohio	OH
Alaska	AK	Louisiana	LA	Oklahoma	OK
Arizona	AZ	Maine	ME	Oregon	OR
Arkansas	AR	Maryland	MD	Pennsylvania	PA
California	CA	Massachusetts	MA	Puerto Rico	PR
Colorado	CO	Michigan	MI	Rhode Island	RI
Connecticut	CT	Minnesota	MN	South Carolina	SC
Delaware	DE	Mississippi	MS	South Dakota	SD
District of	DC	Missouri	MO	Tennessee	TN
Columbia		Montana	MT	Texas	TX
Florida	FL	Nebraska	NE	Utah	UT
Georgia	GA	Nevada	NV	Vermont	VT
Hawaii	HI	New Hampshire	NH	Virginia	VA
Idaho	ID	New Jersey	NJ	Washington	WA
Illinois	IL	New Mexico	NM	West Virginia	WV
Indiana	IN	New York	NY	Wisconsin	WI
Iowa	IA	North Carolina	NC	Wyoming	WY
Kansas	KS	North Dakota	ND		
Avenue	AVE	Expressway	EXPY	Parkway	PKWY
Boulevard	BLVD	Freeway	FWY	Road	RD
Circle	CIR	Highway	HWY	Square	SQ
Court	CT	Lane	LN	Street	ST
Turnpike	TPKE				
North	N	West	W	Southwest	SW
East	E	Northeast	NE	Northwest	NW
South	S	Southeast	SE		
Room	RM	Suite	STE	Apartment	APT

FIGURE 2.7 • Standard Abbreviations

Source: U.S. Postal Service.

3. Inside address (the full name, title, and address of the receiver)
4. Salutation, followed by a colon (avoid gender-biased salutations such as "Dear Sir" or "Gentlemen")
5. Body of the letter, using the three-part approach outlined below
6. Complimentary close ("Sincerely" is best), followed by a comma
7. Writer's signature
8. Writer's name and title beneath the signature
9. Enclosure line, if necessary, to indicate item(s) accompanying the letter

Along with these standard components, all business letters also embrace the same three-part organization:

1. A brief introductory paragraph establishing context (by referring to previous correspondence, perhaps, or by orienting the reader in some other way) and stating the letter's purpose concisely. In international correspondence, the introduction is often more lengthy, comprising as many as two or even three paragraphs of polite "ice-breaking" and background before the specific purpose is identified.
2. A middle section (as many paragraphs as needed) conveying the content of the message by providing all necessary details presented in the most logical sequence
3. A brief concluding paragraph politely requesting action, thanking the reader, or providing any additional information pertinent to the situation

Table 2.1 provides guidance in applying this three-part approach in each of the basic letter-writing situations.

Format

Over the years, letters have been formatted in various ways. Today, however, "full block" style is the norm. As shown in Figures 2.4 through 2.6, full block style requires that every line (including the date, the receiver's address, the salutation, the complimentary close, and the sender's name) begin at the left margin. If, as in Figure 2.5, the sender's address isn't preprinted on letterhead, it should also begin at the left margin.

Note also that in full block style, even the first line of each paragraph begins at the left margin rather than being indented.

As shown, a full block letter is single-spaced throughout, with double spacing between the blocks of print. A common practice is to triple- or even quadruple-space between the complimentary close and the sender's name to provide ample room for the sender's signature.

A growing trend in letter writing is the fully abbreviated, "no punctuation, all capitals" approach to the inside address. This derives from the U.S. Postal Service recommendation that envelopes be so addressed to facilitate automated scanning and sorting. Because the inside address has traditionally matched the address on the envelope, such a feature may well become standard, at least for letters sent by conventional mail rather than by electronic means. Indeed, many companies using

Letter Type	Introduction	Middle Paragraphs	Conclusion
Inquiry	Briefly explain the reason for your inquiry, and clearly identify what you're inquiring about.	Provide all relevant details about your inquiry. Concretely specify what you want to know, why the reader should provide this information, and what you'll use it for. If you have more than one question, create a bulleted or numbered list.	Thank the reader in advance for complying with your request. If you must have a reply by a certain date, specify it. Make sure you've provided all the information the reader will need to reply (address, phone number, e-mail address). It's a good idea to provide a stamped, self-addressed envelope.
Sales	Get the reader's attention, perhaps by asking a question, describing a situation, presenting an interesting fact, or using a quotation (the same strategies are explained in Chapter 9 for opening a speech), and state what you're selling.	Provide all relevant details about the product or service you're selling and create an incentive by explaining to the reader the advantages of purchasing.	Thank the reader in advance for becoming a customer and make sure you've provided all the information the reader will need to place an order (price list or catalog, order form, address, Web site, phone number, e-mail address).
Order	Establish that this is indeed an order letter, and state what you want to purchase.	Provide all relevant details about your order (product numbers, prices, quantities, method of payment, etc.). A table is often the best format for presenting this information.	Thank the reader in advance for filling the order. If you must have the product or service by a certain date, specify it. Make sure you've provided all the information the reader will need to ship the order (address, billing address, method of delivery).

Collection	Open with a polite but firm reminder that the reader's payment is overdue. (In a second or third collection letter, the tone of the introduction can be more urgent.)	If you have not already done so in the introduction, provide all the relevant details about how much is owed, when it was due, and when it must be paid to avoid penalty, but acknowledge the possibility of error at your end.	Repeat the payment request and encourage the reader to contact you with any concerns or to discuss payment options. Make sure you've provided all the information the reader will need to respond (address, phone number, e-mail address). It's a good idea to include a stamped, self-addressed envelope.
Claim	Provide some background information, but come quickly to the point, identifying the problem.	Politely provide all relevant details about what has gone wrong and what you want the reader to do about it. If appropriate, provide copies of bills, receipts, contracts, etc.	Thank the reader in advance for correcting the problem and make sure you've provided all the information the reader will need to contact you (address, phone number, e-mail address).
Adjustment	Thank the reader for bringing the problem to your attention, and if the complaint is justified, apologize.	If the complaint is justified, explain what you'll do to fix the problem. If not, tactfully explain why you must deny the claim.	Thank the reader again for writing to you and provide reassurances that everything will be satisfactory in the future.
Acknowledgment	Briefly explain why you are writing the acknowledgment and identify the person, group, or situation you're commending.	Provide all relevant details about why the person, group, or situation deserves commendation.	Conclusions vary greatly depending on the nature of the situation. Commonly, you'll thank the reader for considering the remarks and invite a reply. In such cases, make sure you've provided all the information the reader will need to contact you (address, phone number, e-mail address).

TABLE 2.1 • Letter Content Guidelines

TechTips

Letters and other documents are often sent by a facsimile (fax) machine. Like e-mail, this technology has the obvious advantage of speed; a letter that might take two or three days to arrive by conventional mail can be received instantaneously by fax.

But whenever you fax anything, you must fax a cover memo along with it. In this memo, you should include any additional information that might be necessary to orient the reader and indicate how many pages (including the cover memo itself) you have included in the transmission so the reader will know whether there's anything that was sent but not received. You should also include your fax number, telephone number, and e-mail address so the reader has the option of replying. Here's an example:

DONROC, INC.
36 Clinton St., Collegeville, NY 13323
FAX

DATE: November 9, 2015 (3:15 p.m.)

TO: John Lapinski, Main Office Comptroller (fax #212-123-4567)

FROM: Mark Smith, Branch Office Manager (fax #212-891-0111) Telephone 212-555-2595, e-mail msmth@sarge.com

SUBJECT: Cosgrove Letter

PAGES: 2

Here's Michael Cosgrove's letter of November 3. Let's discuss this at Thursday's meeting.

"window" envelopes have already adopted this style. Again, see Figure 2.7 for the Postal Service's guidelines for abbreviations in addresses.

As mentioned earlier, more and more companies are communicating with each other by e-mail and other forms of electronic messaging rather than by business letter. The letter is still preferred, however, for more formal exchanges, especially those in which speed of delivery isn't a major factor. In situations involving individual customers and clients (some of whom may still rely on conventional mail), the business letter is also the best choice. At least for the immediate future, therefore, the letter will continue to be a major form of workplace correspondence, although its role will almost certainly undergo further redefinition as various forms of electronic communication become increasingly widespread.

Like all successful communication, a good letter must use an appropriate tone. Obviously, a letter is a more formal kind of communication than in-house correspondence because it's more public. Accordingly, a letter should uphold the image of the sender's company or organization by reflecting a high degree of professionalism. However, although a letter's style should be polished, the language should be natural and easy to understand. The key to achieving a readable style—in a letter or in anything else you write—is to understand that writing shouldn't sound pompous or "official." Rather, it should sound much like ordinary speech—shined up just a bit. Whatever you do, avoid stilted, old-fashioned business clichés. Strive instead for direct, conversational phrasing. Here's a list of overly bureaucratic constructions, paired with "plain English" alternatives:

Cliché	Alternative
As per your request	As you requested
Attached please find	Here is
In lieu of	Instead of
Please be advised that X	X
Pursuant to our agreement	As we agreed
Until such time as	Until
We are in receipt of	We have received
We regret to advise you that X	Regrettably, X

If you have a clear understanding of your letter's purpose and have analyzed your audience, you should experience little difficulty achieving the appropriate tone for the situation. In addition, if you have written your letter following full-block format and if you have used clear, accessible, and mechanically correct language, your correspondence will likely accomplish its objectives. As noted earlier, you must scrupulously avoid typos and mechanical errors in memos and e-mails. This is equally important when you compose letters intended for outside readers, who will take their business elsewhere if they perceive you as careless or incompetent. Always proofread carefully, making every effort to ensure that your work is error-free, and consult the following checklist.

Checklist
Evaluating a Business Letter

A good letter

___ follows full block format;

___ includes certain features;

- ☐ Sender's complete address
- ☐ Date
- ☐ Receiver's full name and complete address
- ☐ Salutation, followed by a colon
- ☐ Complimentary close ("Sincerely" is best), followed by a comma
- ☐ Sender's signature and full name
- ☐ Enclosure notation, if necessary

___ is organized into paragraphs, covering the subject fully in an orderly way:

- ☐ First paragraph establishes context and states the purpose
- ☐ Middle paragraphs provide all necessary details
- ☐ Last paragraph politely achieves closure

___ includes no inappropriate content;

___ uses clear, simple language;

___ maintains an appropriate tone, neither too formal nor too conversational;

___ contains no typos or mechanical errors in spelling, capitalization, punctuation, or grammar.

EXERCISES

EXERCISE 2.1

You're the assistant to the personnel manager of a metals fabrication plant. Monday is Labor Day, and most of the 300 employees will be given a paid holiday. The company is under pressure, however, to meet a deadline. Therefore, a skeleton force of forty—all in the production department—will be needed to work on the holiday. Those who volunteer will have the option of being paid overtime at the standard time-and-a-half rate or receiving two vacation days. If fewer than forty employees volunteer, others will be assigned to work on the basis of seniority, with the most recently hired employees chosen first. The personnel manager has asked you to alert affected employees. Write an e-mail to the staff in the production department.

EXERCISE 2.2

You're a secretary at a regional office of a state agency. Normal working hours for civil service employees in your state are 8:30 a.m. to 4:30 p.m., with a lunch break from 12:00 to 12:30 p.m. During the summer, however, the hours are 8:30 a.m. to 4:00 p.m., with lunch unchanged. Summer hours are in effect from July 1 to September 2. It's now mid-June, and the busy office supervisor has asked you to remind employees of the summer schedule. Write a memo to be posted on the main bulletin board and sent via e-mail.

EXERCISE 2.3

You work in the lumberyard of a building supplies company. Every year during the July 4 weekend, the town sponsors the Liberty Run, a 10K (6.2-mile) road race. This year, for the first time, local businesses have been invited to enter five-member teams to compete for the Corporate Cup. The team with the best combined time takes the trophy. There will be no prize money involved but much good publicity for the winners. Because you recently ran the Boston Marathon, the company president wants you to recruit and organize a team. It's now April 21. Better get started. Write an e-mail to your coworkers.

EXERCISE 2.4

You're an office worker at a large paper products company that has just installed an upgraded computer system. Many employees are having difficulty with the new software. The manufacturer's representatives will be onsite all next week to provide training. Because you're studying computer technology, you've been asked to serve as liaison. You must inform your coworkers about the training, which will be delivered in Conference Room 3 from Monday through Thursday in eight half-day sessions (9:00 a.m. to 12:00 p.m. and 1:00 to 4:00 p.m.), organized alphabetically by workers' last names as follows: A–B, C–E, F–I, J–M, N–P, Q–SL, SM–T, and U–Z. Workers unable to attend must sign up for one of two makeup sessions that will be held on Friday. You must ensure that everyone understands all these requirements. Write a memo to be posted on all bulletin boards and sent via e-mail.

EXERCISE 2.5

You're the manager of the employee cafeteria at a printing company. For many years, the cafeteria has provided excellent service, offering breakfast from 7:00 to 8:30 a.m. and lunch from 11:00 a.m. to 2:00 p.m. It also serves as a breakroom, selling coffee, soft drinks, and snacks all day. But the cafeteria is badly in need of modernization. Work is scheduled to begin next Wednesday. Naturally, the cafeteria will have to be closed while renovations are in progress. Employees will still be able to have lunch and breaks, however, because temporary facilities are being set up in Room 101 of Building B, a now-vacant area formerly used for storage. The temporary cafeteria will provide all the usual services except for breakfast. Obviously, employees need to know about the situation. Write an e-mail to the employees.

EXERCISE 2.6

Proofread and rewrite the following memo, correcting all errors.

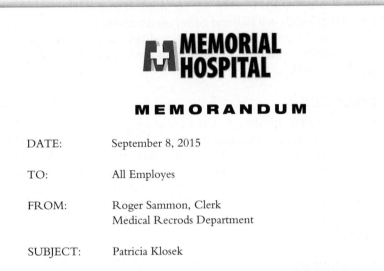

MEMORANDUM

DATE: September 8, 2015

TO: All Employes

FROM: Roger Sammon, Clerk
Medical Recrods Department

SUBJECT: Patricia Klosek

As many of you allready know. Patricia Klosik from the Medical records Depratment is retiring next month. After more then thirty years of faithfull service to Memorial hospital.

A party is being planed in her honor. It will be at seven oclock on friday October 23 at big Joes Resturant tickets are $50 per person whitch includes a buffay diner and a donation toward a gift.

If you plan to atend please let me no by the end of next week try to get you're check to me by Oct 9

EXERCISE 2.7

A consumer product that you especially like is suddenly no longer available in retail stores in your area. Write the manufacturer a letter ordering the product.

EXERCISE 2.8

Imagine you've received the product ordered in Exercise 2.7, but it's somehow unsatisfactory. Write the manufacturer a claim letter expressing dissatisfaction and requesting an exchange or a refund.

EXERCISE 2.9

Team up with a classmate, exchange the claim letters you each wrote in response to Exercise 2.8, and then write adjustment letters to each other.

EXERCISE 2.10

Many businesses, nonprofit agencies, and other organizations routinely send "snail mail" letters in an effort to advertise products and services, solicit monetary contributions, or achieve some other objective. Select one such letter you've recently received and write a brief evaluation of its effectiveness. Comment on the letter's purpose, format, clarity, and tone. If the letter could be better, provide specific suggestions for improvement.

3

Effective Visuals: Tables, Graphs, Charts, and Illustrations

LEARNING OBJECTIVES

When you complete this chapter, you'll be able to:

- understand the principles governing effective visual representation.
- produce user-friendly tables.
- design informative line graphs and bar graphs.
- create clear flow charts, organizational charts, Gantt charts, and circle charts.
- use illustrations (photos, drawings, and diagrams) effectively.

People often communicate without written or spoken language—through gestures and facial expressions, for example, and of course by means of diagrams, pictures, and signs. Consider the familiar displays shown here:

Workplace communications make extensive use of visual aids along with text. Proposals, manuals, instructions, Web pages and reports of all kinds contain numerous illustrations to capture and hold people's attention and help convey information. To function successfully in today's increasingly sophisticated workplace, an employee must be well-acquainted with these visual elements. This chapter begins with a brief overview of basic principles governing the use of visuals. It then explores the four main categories of visuals—tables, graphs, charts, and illustrations—and explains the principal features and applications of each.

Principles of Effective Visuals

With today's software packages, you can assemble data on a spreadsheet and then display it in whatever format is most suitable. For drawings and photographs, you can choose from a vast array of readily available electronic clip art and stock images. Computer technology produces highly polished results while encouraging a great deal of experimentation with various design features. Like computerized text, graphics stored electronically have the added advantage of easy revision if your data changes.

Ironically, the one potential drawback of computer-generated graphics derives from the same versatility that makes these programs so exciting to work with. Inexperienced users can become carried away with the many options at their disposal, creating cluttered, overly elaborate visuals that confuse rather than illustrate. As with writing and page design, simpler is better. Always bear in mind that visuals should never be introduced simply for their own sake to "decorate" a document. Theoretically, every visual should be able to stand alone, but its true purpose is to clarify the text it accompanies.

Like good writing, effective visuals are simple, clear, and easy to understand. It's also very important to choose the most appropriate *type* of visual for the task at hand. When using any kind of visual aid, however, you must observe the following fundamental rules:

- Number sequentially and title every visual in your document, with outside sources clearly identified. If the document contains only one visual, you can omit the number. Titling a visual is much like writing a subject line for a memo or e-mail. The title should be brief, accurate, and informative. To write a good title, answer this question: In just a few words, what does this visual depict? The number, title, and source usually appear *beneath* the visual rather than above. (Tables are the exception to this rule; they're often numbered and labeled *above*.)

- Any information you provide in a visual you must first discuss in the text. The text should refer the reader to the visual (for example, "See Figure 5"), and the visual should be positioned logically, as soon as possible *after* the reference.

- Present all visuals in an appealing manner. Each visual should be surrounded by ample white space, not crowded by the text or squeezed between other visuals.

- Clearly label all elements of the visual and provide a "key" whenever necessary to show scale, direction, and the like. Labels must be easy to read, with their terms matching those used in the text; you can't call something "x" in the text and label it "y" in the visual if you expect the reader to find it easily.

- When visuals accompany instructions, the point of view in the visuals must be the same as that of the reader performing the illustrated procedure. For example, an overhead view might be confusing if the reader will be approaching the task head-on.

- A visual should never omit, distort, or otherwise manipulate information to deceive or mislead the reader. Because the purpose of a visual is to reinforce the meaning of your text, any visual you include is subject to the same ethical standards of honesty and accuracy that your text must meet.

- Avoid spelling mistakes, poor grammar, inconsistent formatting, or other blunders in the labels, key, title, or other text accompanying a visual. Nothing undermines the credibility of a visual faster than a careless error.

Tables

The purpose of tables is to portray statistical and other information for easy comparison. Tables consist of horizontal rows and vertical columns in which the data are presented. The top row, which holds the column headings, is called the *boxhead;* the leftmost column, which holds the row headings, is called the *stub.* This arrangement permits ready access to information that would be exceptionally difficult to sort out if it were presented only as text. A convenient example is the league standings that appear on the sports pages of most newspapers, enabling fans to determine at a glance the ranking, won/lost records, and other information pertaining to team performance.

For example, consider the following paragraph, which is so full of statistical detail that it's impossible to retain it all.

St. Louis finished the 2014 season in first place in the National League Central Division, with a record of 90 wins and 72 losses, for a .556 percentage. Pittsburgh was in second place, 2 games behind, with 88 wins and 74 losses, for a .543 percentage. Milwaukee was third, 8 games behind, with 82 wins and 80 losses, for a .506 percentage. Next was Cincinnati, 14 games behind, with 76 wins and 86 losses, for a .469 percentage. Chicago was last, 26 games behind, with 73 wins and 89 losses, for a .451 percentage.

Certainly, this would be far better presented in table format, as in Figure 3.1. Similarly, Figure 3.2 displays employment-related data spanning a ten-year time period.

Team	Won	Lost	Percentage	Behind
St. Louis	90	72	.556	—
Pittsburgh	88	74	.543	2
Milwaukee	82	80	.506	8
Cincinnati	76	86	.469	14
Chicago	73	89	.451	26

FIGURE 3.1 • Table Showing Final 2014 Standings of National League Central Division Baseball Teams

Source: MLB.com

Occupation	Employment in 2010 (in thousands)	Projected Growth 2010–2020 (%)	Median Annual Wage in 2011 ($)	Typical Education Needed for Entry
Computer systems analysts	135.3	43.1	82,160	Bachelor's degree
Computer programmers	116.8	28.8	72,100	Bachelor's degree
Software developers, applications	174.0	57.4	88,120	Bachelor's degree
Software developers, systems	117.8	71.7	94,570	Bachelor's degree
Computer support specialists	107.4	43.1	48,800	Some college, no degree

FIGURE 3.2 • **Table showing employment data 2010–2020**

Source: http://www.bls.gov/news.release/cpi.t01.htm.

Graphs

Graphs are used to display statistical trends, changes, and comparisons. There are essentially two kinds: line graphs and bar graphs.

Line Graphs

The primary purpose of line graphs is to portray change over time. A line graph is created by plotting points along horizontal and vertical axes (the x-axis and y-axis, respectively) and then joining the points using straight lines. The horizontal axis identifies the categories of information that are being compared (the fixed, or independent, variables—usually chronological intervals), whereas the vertical axis identifies the incremental values that are being compared (the dependent variables). Figure 3.3 is a graph of a company's annual profits during a ten-year period.

Additional lines can be added for purposes of comparison, but each line must appear different to avoid confusion. For example, one line can be solid and another broken, or lines can be drawn in contrasting colors, as in Figure 3.4, which compares the annual profits of two competing companies during a ten-year period. Notice the key, which indicates that the darker line represents Company A and the lighter line represents Company B.

FIGURE 3.3 • Line Graph Showing Profits of Company A, 2007–2016

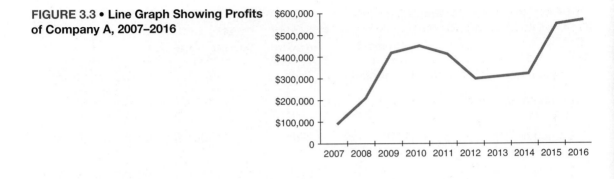

Bar Graphs

Another useful tool for comparing data is the bar graph. Like line graphs, bar graphs consist of horizontal and vertical axes that depict the dependent and independent variables. Which axis depicts which variable is determined by whether the bars are horizontal or vertical. If the bars are vertical, the vertical axis identifies the dependent variables and the horizontal axis identifies the independent variables. Figure 3.5 is a vertical bar graph that portrays productivity in the manufacturing sector during several time periods.

If the bars are horizontal, the arrangement is reversed, with the horizontal axis showing the dependent variables and the vertical axis showing the independent variables. A horizontal bar graph is useful for accommodating many bars and offers the added advantage of permitting the independent variables to be labeled horizontally if those labels are relatively lengthy. This feature is helpful, for example, in Figure 3.6.

To create comparisons within categories of information in a bar graph, each bar can be presented alongside an accompanying bar or two, but the multiple bar(s) must be colored or shaded differently to avoid confusion. Figure 3.7 is illustrative. Notice the key, which shows which color represents which environment.

FIGURE 3.4 • Line Graph Showing Profits of Company A and Company B, 2007–2016

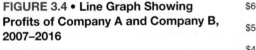
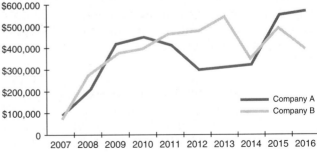

FIGURE 3.5 • Vertical Bar Graph Showing Productivity Change in the Manufacturing Sector, 1987–2013

Source: U.S. Bureau of Labor Statistics

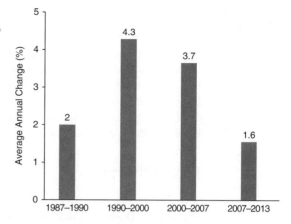

FIGURE 3.6 • Horizontal Bar Graph Showing Projected Employment Growth

Source: U.S. Bureau of Labor Statistics, Employment Projections Program.

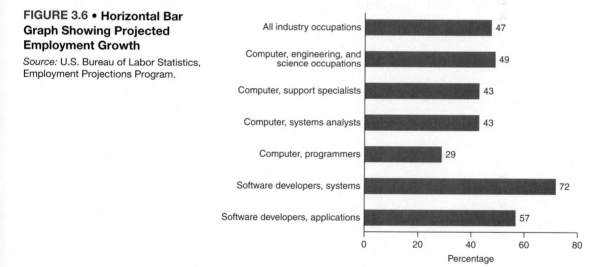

FIGURE 3.7 • Multiple Bar Graph Showing Output and Employment Data

Source: U.S. Bureau of Labor Statistics, Employment Projections Program.

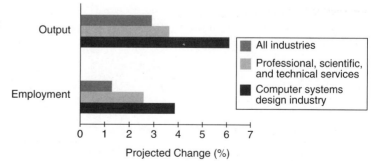

Charts

The purpose of a chart is to portray quantitative, cause-and-effect, and other relationships among the component parts of a unified whole. Comprising squares, rectangles, triangles, circles, and other geometric shapes linked by plain or arrowhead lines, charts can depict the steps in a production process, the chain of command in an organization, and other sequential or hierarchical interactions. Among the principal kinds of charts are flow charts, organizational charts, Gantt charts, and circle charts.

Flow Charts

A flow chart is typically used to portray the steps through which work (or a process) must "flow" to reach completion. The chart clearly labels each step, and arrows indicate the sequence of the steps so that someone unfamiliar with the process can easily follow it. Flow charts are usually read from top to bottom or from left to right, although some depict a circular flow. For example, the chart in Figure 3.8 shows how a successful bill is signed into law.

FIGURE 3.8 • Flow chart Showing How a Bill Is Signed into Law

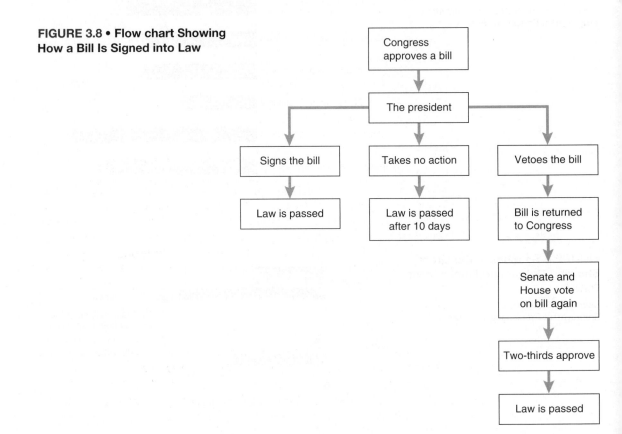

Organizational Charts

Like flow charts, organizational charts consist of labeled boxes linked by lines or arrows. Organizational charts portray chains of command within businesses, agencies, and other collective bodies, indicating who has authority over whom and suggesting the relationships among various functional areas or components within the organization. Not surprisingly, the most powerful positions are placed at the top and the least powerful at the bottom. Those on the same horizontal level are at approximately equal levels of responsibility. For example, Figure 3.9 shows the newsroom organization of a small daily newspaper.

FIGURE 3.9 • Organizational Chart Showing Newsroom Organization for a Small Daily Newspaper

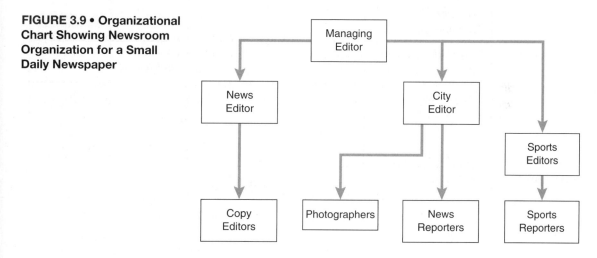

Gantt Charts

Named after the mechanical engineer Henry Gantt (1861–1919), who invented them, Gantt charts are essentially timeline charts that depict the schedule of necessary activities from the beginning to end of a project. Often used in proposals (see Chapter 10), they resemble bar graphs. The y-axis identifies the steps in the project, whereas the x-axis indentifies the chronological milestones. Obviously, some of the horizontal bars representing the various activities may overlap because the multiple phases of projects often do. For this reason, the beginning and end dates of each bar should be specified. Figure 3.10 is a Gantt chart showing the timetable for a company's expansion.

Circle Charts

Among the most familiar of all visual devices, circle (or pie) charts often are used to show the percentage distribution of money. As such, they are helpful in analyzing relative costs and profits. Their more general application is simply to depict relationships among parts within statistical wholes. In that broader context, they facilitate such tasks as risk analysis, needs assessment, and resource allocation.

	March	April	May	June
Purchase Adjacent Building	3/1–31			
Renovate Building		4/1–5/31		
Purchase Equipment & Furnishings			5/1–31	
Install Equipment & Furnishings				6/1–20
Hire Additional Workers			5/1–31	
Train Additional Workers				6/1–20
Open Expansion				6/21

FIGURE 3.10 • Gantt Chart Showing Timetable for Company's Expansion

Each segment of a circle chart resembles a slice of pie and constitutes a percentage. For maximum effectiveness, the pie should include at least three but no more than seven slices. (To limit the number of slices without omitting data, several small percentages can be lumped together under the heading of "Other.") As if the pie were a clock face, the biggest slice usually begins at 12 o'clock, with the slices getting progressively smaller as they continue clockwise around the circle. Each slice is labeled, showing its percentage of the total. (Obviously, the slices must add up to 100 percent.) A key must be provided to identify what each slice represents. Figure 3.11 shows a circle chart presenting the costs of attending a residential community college for one semester.

FIGURE 3.11 • Circle Chart Showing Cost of Attending Residential Community College for One Semester

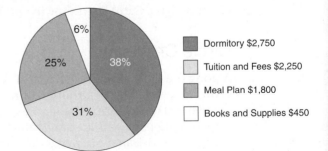

- Dormitory $2,750
- Tuition and Fees $2,250
- Meal Plan $1,800
- Books and Supplies $450

38% / 31% / 25% / 6%

Illustrations

Illustrations—whether photographs, drawings, or diagrams—are another highly effective visual aid. Each type has certain advantages. As with so many aspects of workplace communication, which type you choose depends on your purpose and your audience.

Photographs

A photograph is an exact representation; its main virtue, therefore, is strict accuracy. Of course, Adobe Photoshop and other editing programs can be used to alter images. Nevertheless, photos are often required in certain kinds of documents, such as licenses, passports, accident reports (especially for insurance purposes), and patent applications. Photos are often used in law enforcement, whether to warn the public of fugitive criminals depicted in "Most Wanted" posters or to document the scene of a crime or accident. Figure 3.12, for example, is a photograph documenting vehicle damage following a collision.

Ideally, photos should be taken by trained professionals. Even an amateur, however, can create reasonably useful photos by observing the following fundamental guidelines:

- Ensure that the light source, whether natural (the sun) or artificial (floodlamp or other electrically generated light), is behind you; avoid shooting *into* the light.

- Stand close enough to your subject to eliminate surroundings, or use the appropriate settings to blur them—unless they are relevant.

- Try to focus on the most significant part of your subject to minimize unwanted detail. (By using a photo-editing program, you can crop out unwanted detail and enlarge the remaining image.)

FIGURE 3.12 • Photograph Documenting Vehicle Damage

- To provide a sense of scale in photographs of unfamiliar objects, include a familiar object within the picture. In photos of small objects, for example, a coin or paper clip works well. In photos of very large objects, a human figure is helpful.
- Hold the camera absolutely still while taking the picture. If possible, use a tripod-mounted digital camera with an automatic shutter release.

Drawings

The purpose of most drawings—whether freehand or computer-generated—is to create clear, realistic depictions of objects under discussion. The main advantage is that in a drawing, you can easily omit unwanted detail and portray only what is most relevant (see Figure 3.13). In addition, a drawing can clarify information it depicts by simplifying, enlarging, or otherwise emphasizing key features. One obvious example of this is a type of drawing called a *floor plan,* which—like a map—is much clearer and more informative than an overhead photo (see Figure 3.14).

Other useful applications are the exploded view, which is often used in assembly instructions (see Figure 3.15), and the cross-sectional, or cutaway, view, which provides visual access to the interior workings of mechanisms and other objects (see Figure 3.16). Moreover, drawings can be combined with tables, graphs, and charts to create pictographs that enliven otherwise routine documents. For example, in Figure 3.17, depictions of personal computers have been added to the vertical bar graph to create an attention-getting effect.

American Sign Language Alphabet

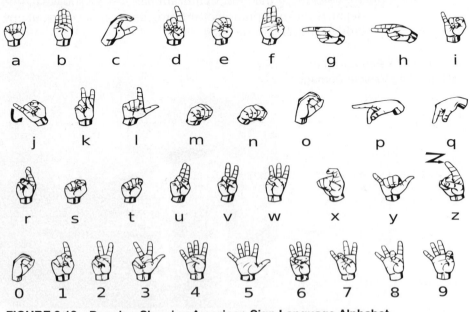

FIGURE 3.13 • Drawing Showing American Sign Language Alphabet

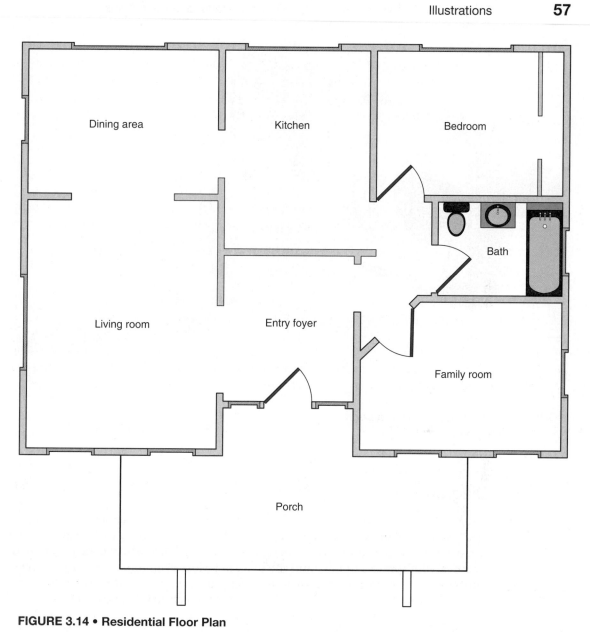

FIGURE 3.14 • Residential Floor Plan

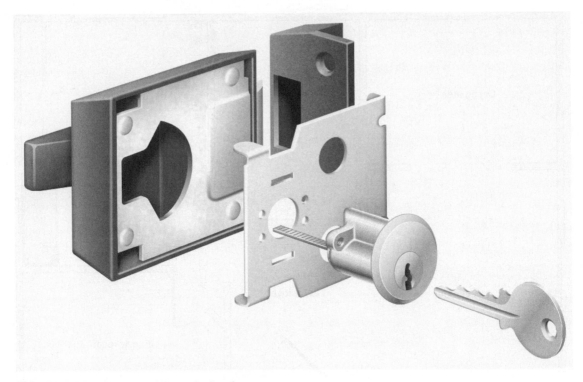

FIGURE 3.15 • Exploded View of a Lock
Source: Peter Bull © Dorling Kindersley

Diagrams

Just as a drawing can be considered a simplified photograph, a diagram can be considered a simplified drawing. For example, Figure 3.18 shows how a three-way switch is wired. Even though this isn't what the actual wiring looks like, anyone conversant with electrical symbols can understand the diagram. Most diagrams—for example, blueprints or engineering graphics—require advanced familiarity on the reader's part and are therefore useful only in documents intended for technicians and other specialists.

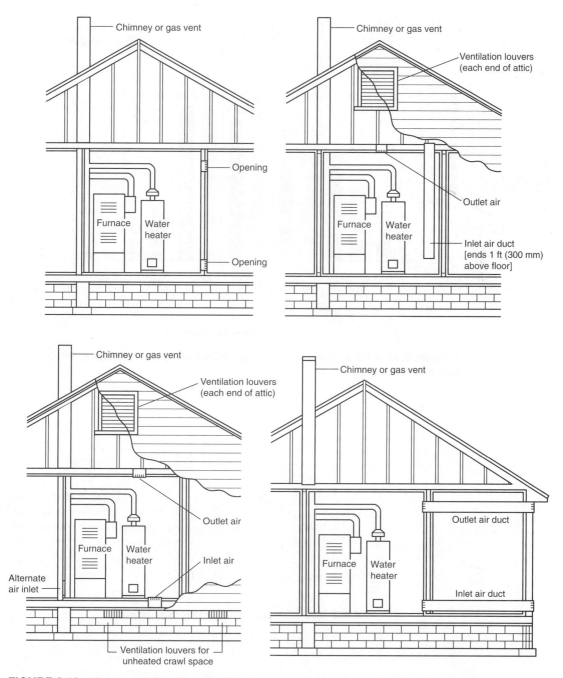

FIGURE 3.16 • Cutaway View Showing Ventilation Requirements for Gas-Fired Boiler

Source: Reprinted with permission from NFPA 54-2012, *National Fuel Gas Code*, Copyright© 2011, National Fire Protection Association. This reprinted material is not the complete and official position of the NFPA on the referenced subject, which is represented only by the standard in its entirety.

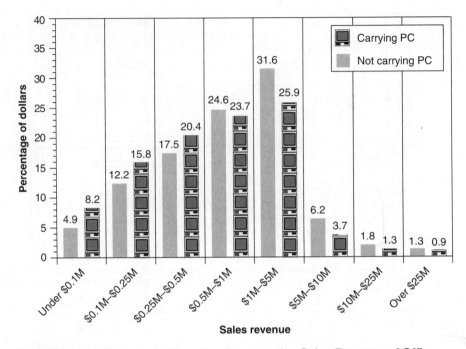

FIGURE 3.17 • Pictograph Showing Comparative Sales Revenue of Office Products Dealers

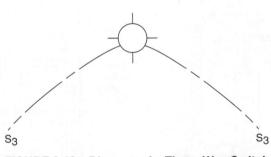
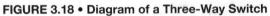

FIGURE 3.18 • Diagram of a Three-Way Switch

Tech**Tips**

At this point, digital clip art has almost completely replaced hard-copy drawings, in part because the digital versions can easily be enhanced, enlarged, reduced, or otherwise modified to suit anyone's needs.

Digital clip art packages sort the images into categories by topic, thereby simplifying the task of finding what you want to insert into documents. Packages intended for use in preparing oral or on-line presentations commonly feature live-action video, sound effects, and music clips.

In the past, clip art was available from mail-order catalogs and local retail stores, as well as from online sources. Today, however, companies rarely ship hard copies, disks, or other formats. Instead, nearly all such art is downloaded from sites such as Microsoft and shutterstock.com.

Using images in a workplace presentation or document is considered non-commercial use, but you may still need to purchase the images. When purchasing, you should select work that's in the public domain to avoid paying royalty fees. Perhaps the most popular of the image-bank Web sites is Google Images, but even there, not all search results are royalty-free. Some are linked to stock websites on which images are watermarked and thereby protected from free use.

Checklist
Evaluating a Visual

A good visual

____ is the most appropriate choice—table, graph, chart, or picture—for a particular communication;

____ is numbered and titled, with the source (if any) identified;

____ occupies the best possible position within the document, immediately after the text it clarifies;

____ does not appear crowded, with enough white space surrounding it to ensure effective page design;

____ includes clear, accurate labels that plainly identify all elements;

____ includes a key if necessary for further clarification;

____ maintains consistency with all relevant text in terms of wording, point of view, and so on;

____ upholds strict standards of accuracy;

____ contains no typos or mechanical errors in spelling, capitalization, punctuation, or grammar.

EXERCISES

EXERCISE 3.1

Choosing from Column B, identify the most appropriate kind of visual for depicting each item in Column A.

Column A	Column B
Registration procedure at your college	Table
Interest-rate fluctuations during the past 10 years	Photograph
Inner workings of a steam boiler	Line graph
Structure of the U.S. executive branch	Bar graph
Average salaries of six selected occupations	Cutaway view
Uniform numbers, names, ages, hometowns, heights/weights, and playing positions of the members of a college football team	Diagram
	Flow chart
House for sale	Exploded view
Percentage distribution of your college's student body by major	Organizational chart
	Pie chart
Automobile steering mechanism	
Circuitry of an electronic calculator	

EXERCISE 3.2

Create a visual showing the current cost per gallon for regular and high octane of three major brands of gasoline.

EXERCISE 3.3

Create a visual showing your favorite professional sports team's place in the league standings for the past 10 seasons.

EXERCISE 3.4

Building on the information in Exercise 3.3, create a visual comparing your favorite professional sports team's place in the league standings for the past 10 seasons with that of one other team.

EXERCISE 3.5

Create a visual showing the total population of the mid-Atlantic states.

EXERCISE 3.6

Write a two- or three-page report explaining a process related to your field of study or employment. Include a visual depicting that process.

EXERCISE 3.7

Write a two- or three-page report about a club or other group to which you belong. Include a visual showing its organizational structure.

EXERCISE 3.8

Create a visual showing how you spend your money in a typical month.

EXERCISE 3.9

Create visuals depicting any three of the following: a flashlight (cutaway view), an electric plug (exploded view), the route from your home to your college (map), three different kinds of hammers (drawings or photos), and the layout of a place where you have worked (floor plan).

EXERCISE 3.10

Collaborating with a classmate or two, find and photocopy or otherwise reproduce an example of each kind of visual discussed in this chapter. Write a brief evaluation to accompany each visual, commenting on its clarity and effectiveness, and present your results to the class.

Short Reports: Page Design, Formats, and Types

Like e-mails and letters, reports are an important form of on-the-job communications, can be internal or external documents, and follow certain standard conventions. In several respects, however, reports are quite different from e-mails and letters.

For example, a report is rarely just a written account of information the reader already knows. Nearly always, the report's subject matter is new information. The reader may be acquainted with the general outline of the situation the report explores but not with the details. Often, in fact, the reader will have specifically requested the report to get those details. Reports exist for the very purpose of communicating needed information that's too complicated for an e-mail or letter. Stated in the simplest terms, there are essentially two kinds of reports: short and long. This chapter focuses on the former, discussing the basic principles of page design, short-report formats, and several common types of short reports. Long reports are covered in Chapter 11.

Page Design

As we have learned, the physical characteristics of memos, e-mails, and letters are largely determined by established guidelines that vary only slightly. But reports, although also subject to certain conventions, are to a much greater degree the creation of individual writers who determine not only their content but also their physical appearance. This is significant because our ability to comprehend what we read is greatly influenced by its physical arrangement on the page or screen. Therefore, a report should never *look* difficult or intimidating. For example, consider Figure 4.1, which has been adapted from a safety manual for railroad employees.

In its present state, the passage is difficult to read. The revised page (Figure 4.2) is much better because the content has been organized into paragraphs, and the ragged right margin further improves legibility.

The use of varied spacing, lists, and boldface headings, as well as some minor editing, will make the content emerge even more clearly. Obviously, Figure 4.3 is easier to read than the earlier versions. Such revision is worthwhile and not particularly difficult if the following fundamental principles of effective page design are observed:

- *Legible type:* Although many different typefaces and type sizes exist, most readers respond best to 12-point type that uses both uppercase and lowercase letters, like this text. Anything smaller or larger is difficult to read, as is the all-capitals approach; such options are useful only in major headings or to emphasize a particular word or phrase.

- *Generous margins:* Text should be framed by white space. The top and bottom margins should both be at least 1 inch and the side margins 1.25 inches. If the report is to be bound, the left margin should be 2 inches. (If the report is to be duplicated back-to-back before binding, the 2-inch margin should be on the *right* side of the even-numbered pages.) The right margin should not be justified; this improves legibility by creating length variation from line to line.

- *Textual divisions:* Long, unbroken passages of text are very difficult to follow with attention, which is why the practice of dividing text into paragraphs was adopted centuries ago. In most workplace writing, paragraphs should not exceed five or six sentences and should be plainly separated by ample white space. If the paragraphs are single-spaced, insert double-spacing between them; if the paragraphs are double-spaced, use triple-spacing between them. To further organize content, group related paragraphs within a report into separate sections that logically reflect the internal organization of the report's information. Like the individual paragraphs, these sections should be plainly separated by proportionately more spacing.

- *Headings:* Separate sections of text should be labeled with meaningful headings that further clarify content and allow the reader to skim the report for specific aspects of its subject matter. Ordinarily, a heading consists of a word or phrase, *not* a complete sentence. (Instructional materials, however, sometimes use *questions* as headings.) The position of a heading is determined by its relative importance.

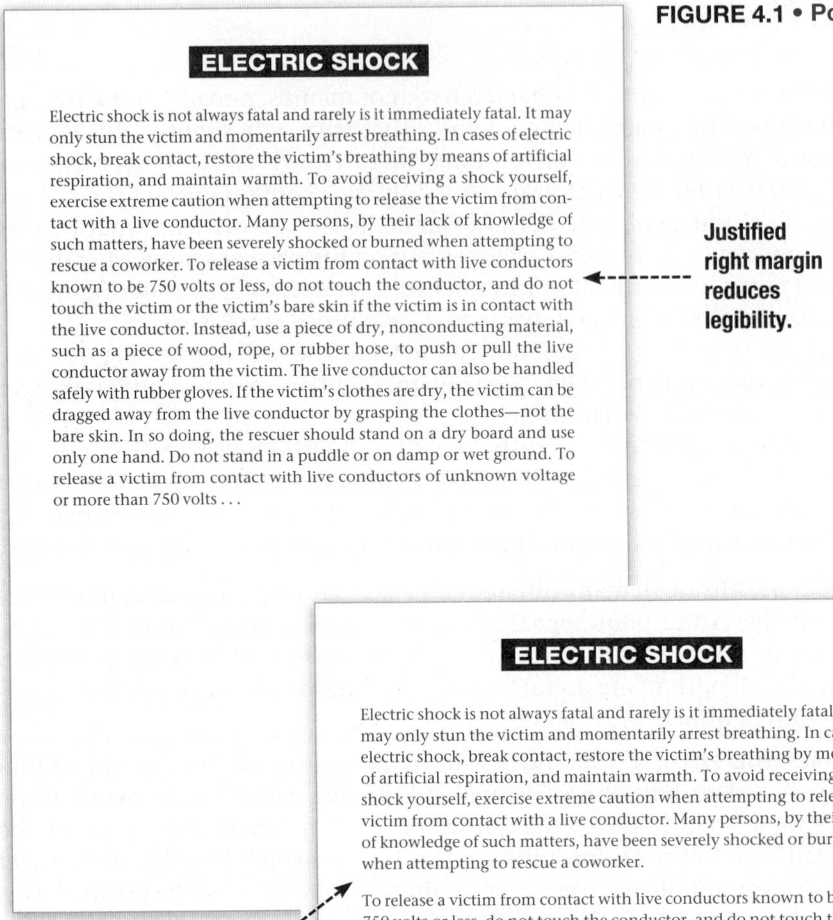

FIGURE 4.1 • Poor Page Design

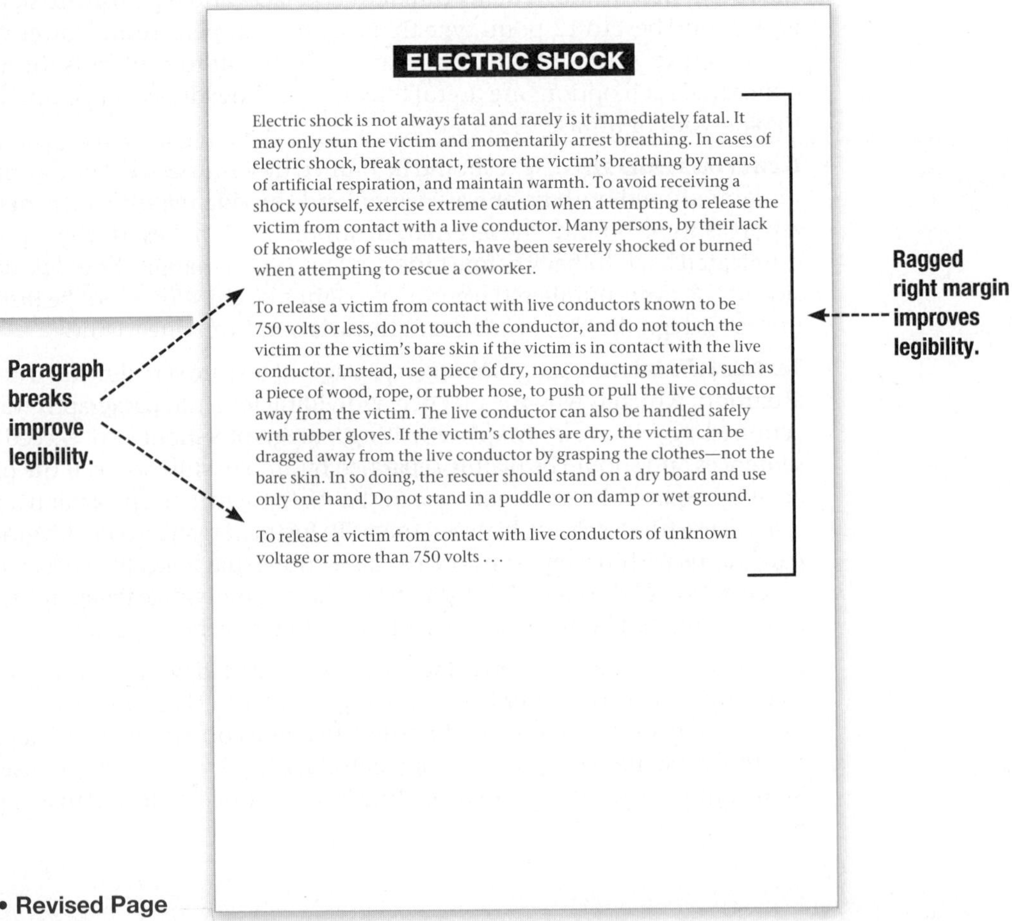

ELECTRIC SHOCK

Electric shock is not always fatal and rarely is it immediately fatal. It may only stun the victim and momentarily arrest breathing. In cases of electric shock, break contact, restore the victim's breathing by means of artificial respiration, and maintain warmth. To avoid receiving a shock yourself, exercise extreme caution when attempting to release the victim from contact with a live conductor. Many persons, by their lack of knowledge of such matters, have been severely shocked or burned when attempting to rescue a coworker. To release a victim from contact with live conductors known to be 750 volts or less, do not touch the conductor, and do not touch the victim or the victim's bare skin if the victim is in contact with the live conductor. Instead, use a piece of dry, nonconducting material, such as a piece of wood, rope, or rubber hose, to push or pull the live conductor away from the victim. The live conductor can also be handled safely with rubber gloves. If the victim's clothes are dry, the victim can be dragged away from the live conductor by grasping the clothes—not the bare skin. In so doing, the rescuer should stand on a dry board and use only one hand. Do not stand in a puddle or on damp or wet ground. To release a victim from contact with live conductors of unknown voltage or more than 750 volts . . .

Justified right margin reduces legibility.

ELECTRIC SHOCK

Electric shock is not always fatal and rarely is it immediately fatal. It may only stun the victim and momentarily arrest breathing. In cases of electric shock, break contact, restore the victim's breathing by means of artificial respiration, and maintain warmth. To avoid receiving a shock yourself, exercise extreme caution when attempting to release the victim from contact with a live conductor. Many persons, by their lack of knowledge of such matters, have been severely shocked or burned when attempting to rescue a coworker.

To release a victim from contact with live conductors known to be 750 volts or less, do not touch the conductor, and do not touch the victim or the victim's bare skin if the victim is in contact with the live conductor. Instead, use a piece of dry, nonconducting material, such as a piece of wood, rope, or rubber hose, to push or pull the live conductor away from the victim. The live conductor can also be handled safely with rubber gloves. If the victim's clothes are dry, the victim can be dragged away from the live conductor by grasping the clothes—not the bare skin. In so doing, the rescuer should stand on a dry board and use only one hand. Do not stand in a puddle or on damp or wet ground.

To release a victim from contact with live conductors of unknown voltage or more than 750 volts . . .

Ragged right margin improves legibility.

Paragraph breaks improve legibility.

FIGURE 4.2 • Revised Page

ELECTRIC SHOCK

Electric shock is not always fatal and is rarely immediately fatal. It may only stun the victim and momentarily arrest breathing. In cases of electric shock, do three things:

Numbered list emphasizes sequence. ----------→

1. Break contact.
2. Restore breathing by artificial respiration.
3. Maintain warmth.

To avoid receiving a shock yourself, exercise extreme caution when attempting to release the victim from contact with a live conductor. Many persons, lacking knowledge of such matters, have been severely shocked or burned attempting to rescue a coworker.

Bold print creates heading. ----------→

Release the victim from contact with live conductors known to be 750 volts or less:

Bulleted list segments information. ----------→

- Do not touch the live conductor.
- Do not touch the victim or the victim's bare skin while the victim is in contact with the live conductor.
- Instead, use a piece of DRY, nonconducting material, such as a piece of wood, rope, or rubber hose, to push or pull the live conductor away from the victim. The live conductor may be handled safely with rubber gloves.
- If the victim's clothes are dry, the victim can be dragged away from the live conductor by grasping the clothing—not the bare skin. In so doing, the rescuer should stand on a dry board and . . .

FIGURE 4.3 • Second Revision

Tech**Tips**

Thanks to word processing, nearly every workplace writer now has access to many page design features. As we've already seen, options such as varied spacing and type size, boldface print, capitalization, italics, and underlining can make your documents appear much more professional. In addition, pages can be formatted in columns or other spatial arrangements.

Used selectively, these features enhance the design of a page not only by signaling major divisions within the content but also by creating emphasis by highlighting key words and phrases. In addition, many software packages are equipped with ready-made report templates and other features such as headers and automatic page numbering for multipage documents, and these can be adapted to suit the individual writer's needs.

Microsoft Word and most other word-processing software include a great many fonts to choose from, but some Web sites provide even more varieties. Dafont.com, for example, offers many free fonts that can be downloaded and installed on your computer, with no permissions or royalty fees.

In addition, there are helpful Web sites that provide assistance with layout. Here are the most popular:

Adobe Framemaker: Available in two versions, Structured and Unstructured. The former can be used to ensure design consistency within multiple documents. The latter is intended for users who want to create a unique format in a single document.

Adobe InDesign: Very useful for creating posters, flyers, brochures, and other print media. Used in conjunction with Adobe Digital Publishing Suite it can produce content suitable for tablet devices.

Quark Xpress: An Apple product that closely resembles Adobe InDesign, it was once the most widely used for creating and editing page layout.

A major heading can be set in boldface caps and centered:

LIKE THIS

A secondary heading can be set either in uppercase letters or in both uppercase and lowercase, is flush with the margin, and can be set in boldface print:

LIKE THIS

or

Like This

A subtopic heading is run into the text, separated by a period or a colon, and is sometimes indented. Set in both uppercase and lowercase letters, it can be set in bold print:

Like This: These recommendations are based on those in *The Gregg Reference Manual,* the most widely recognized authority on such matters.

Obviously, these principles are flexible, and various approaches to heading design and placement are used—some of them quite elaborate. Among the most helpful recommendations in *Gregg* is to limit a report to no more than three levels of headings.

- *Lists:* Sometimes a list is more effective than a conventional paragraph. If the purpose of the list is to indicate a definite order of importance, the items in the list should be *numbered* in descending order, with the most important item first and the least important last. Similarly, if the list's purpose is to indicate a chronological sequence of events or actions (as in a procedures manual), the items should be numbered in sequential order. However, numbers are not necessary in a list of approximately equal items. In those cases, bullets (solid black dots, like those used in this section), asterisks, or dashes suffice.

Report Formats: Memo, Letter, and Booklet

Many companies and organizations prepare short reports on preprinted forms that permit a "fill-in-the-blank" approach. As we have seen, however, computer technology enables individual writers to personally design the pages of their reports. A customized report can usually be categorized into one of three formats: memo, letter, or booklet.

Typically used for in-house purposes and delivered as an e-mail attachment, the **memo report** is similar to a conventional memo but is usually somewhat longer and is therefore divided into labeled sections. The **letter report**—typically sent to an outside reader—is formatted like a conventional business letter except that it's divided into labeled sections, much like the memo report. The **booklet report** resembles a short term paper and includes a title page. Like the other reports, it's divided into labeled sections and—for in-house situations—is delivered as an e-mail attachment. Hard-copy booklet reports sent to outside readers are accompanied by a cover letter. Like the opening paragraph of a memo report or a letter report, the cover e-mail or letter serves to orient the reader by establishing context and explaining the purpose and scope of the booklet report.

Both memo reports and booklet reports often contain visuals; letter reports sometimes do. Figures 4.4–4.11 illustrate the three formats using easily understood subject matter. The three formats can, however, be adapted to any workplace situation simply by changing the headings (and, of course, the text) to suit the subject.

Types of Reports

Like e-mails and letters, workplace reports are written in all kinds of situations for an enormous variety of reasons. Many reports are in a sense unique because they're written in response to one-time occurrences. On the other hand, it's not uncommon for a given report to be part of an ongoing series of weekly, monthly, or annual reports on the same subject. Generally, reports can be classified into several broad categories and are usually transmitted as e-mail attachments. The most common include the following:

- ***Incident report:*** Explains the circumstances surrounding a troublesome occurrence, such as an accident, fire, equipment malfunction, or security breach. Nearly always uses memo report format (with cover e-mail).

- ***Recommendation report:*** Urges that certain procedures be adopted (or rejected). Uses either memo report or booklet report format (with cover e-mail) for in-house situations and either letter report or booklet report format (with cover letter) otherwise.

- ***Progress report:*** Outlines the status of an ongoing project or undertaking. Uses either memo report or booklet report format (with cover e-mail) for in-house situations and either letter report or booklet report format (with cover letter) otherwise.

- ***Travel report:*** Identifies the purpose and summarizes the results of business-related travel. Nearly always uses memo report format (with cover e-mail).

Of course, an individual report can serve more than one purpose; overlap is not uncommon. For example, an incident report may conclude with a recommendations section intended to minimize the likelihood of recurrence. In every situation, the writer must consider the purpose of and intended audience for the report. Content, language, tone, degree of detail, and overall approach must be appropriate to the circumstances, and the report headings, formatting, visuals, and other features must suit the role of the particular report. The following pages discuss in detail the four common report types.

Incident Report

An incident report creates a written record of a troublesome occurrence. The report is written either by the person involved in the incident or by the person in charge of the area where it took place. Such a report may be needed to satisfy government regulations, to guard against legal liability, or to draw attention to unsafe or otherwise unsatisfactory conditions in need of correction. Accordingly, an incident report must provide a thorough description of the occurrence and, if possible, an explanation of the cause(s). In addition, it often includes a section of recommendations for corrective measures.

When describing the incident, always provide complete details:

- Names and job titles of all persons involved, including onlookers
- Step-by-step narrative description of the incident
- Exact location of the incident
- Date and exact time of each major development
- Clear identification of any equipment or machinery involved
- Detailed description of any medical intervention required, including names of ambulance services and personnel, nurses, physicians, hospitals, or clinics
- Reliable statements (quotation or paraphrase) from persons involved
- Outcome of the incident

To avoid liability when discussing possible causes, use qualifiers such as *perhaps, maybe, possibly,* and *it seems.* Do not report the comments of witnesses and those involved as if those observations were verified facts; they often are grossly inaccurate. Attribute all such comments to their sources, and identify them as speculation only. Furthermore, exclude any comments unrelated to the immediate incident. Although you're ethically required to be as complete and accurate as possible, don't create an unnecessarily suspicious climate by relying on secondhand accounts or reporting verbatim the remarks of persons who are obviously angry or distraught, as in this example:

> Ronald Perkins suffered a severed index finger when his left hand became caught in a drill press after he tripped on some wood that another employee had carelessly left on the floor near the machine. According to Perkins, this was "pretty typical of how things are always done around here."

A more objective phrasing might look something like this:

> Ronald Perkins suffered a severed index finger when his left hand became caught in a drill press. Perkins said he had tripped on wood that was lying on the floor near the machine.

Similarly, the recommendations section of an incident report shouldn't seek to assign blame or highlight incompetence but to encourage the adoption of measures that will decrease the likelihood of repeated problems. For example, consider the incident report in Figures 4.4 and 4.5, prepared in memo format.

Recommendation Report

A recommendation report assesses a troublesome or unsatisfactory situation, identifies a solution to the problem, and persuades decision makers to pursue a particular course of action that will improve matters. Such reports are sometimes unsolicited. Generally, however, a recommendation report is written by a knowledgeable employee who has been specifically assigned the task. As with most kinds of reports, the content can vary greatly depending on the nature of the business or organization and on the nature of the situation. In nearly all cases, however, recommendation reports are intended to enhance the quality of products or services, maximize profits, reduce costs, or improve working conditions.

In the case of a solicited report, the writer should attempt to get a written request from the individual who wants the report and then carefully study it to determine the exact parameters of the situation. If unsure of any aspect of the assignment, the writer should seek clarification before continuing. As discussed in Chapter 1, it's vital to establish a firm sense of purpose and audience before you attempt to compose any workplace writing. A clear and focused written request—or the discussion generated by the lack of one—will provide guidance in this regard.

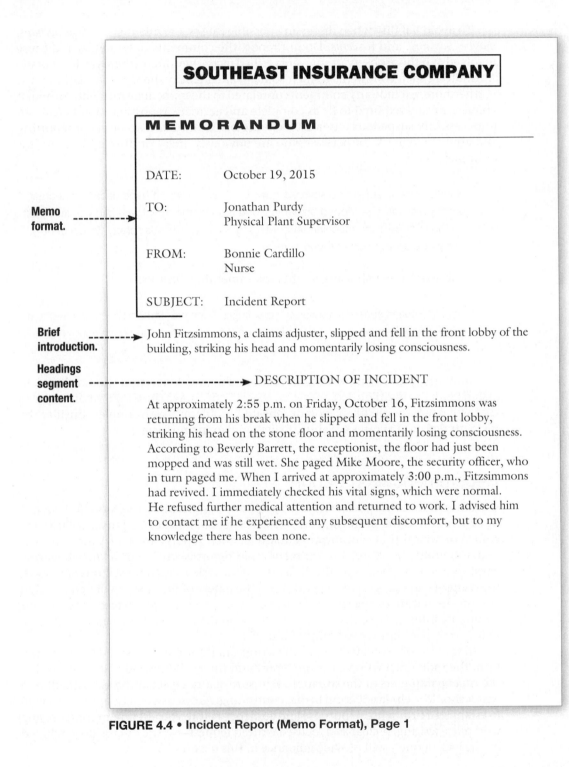

SOUTHEAST INSURANCE COMPANY

MEMORANDUM

DATE: October 19, 2015

TO: Jonathan Purdy
             Physical Plant Supervisor

FROM: Bonnie Cardillo
             Nurse

SUBJECT: Incident Report

John Fitzsimmons, a claims adjuster, slipped and fell in the front lobby of the building, striking his head and momentarily losing consciousness.

DESCRIPTION OF INCIDENT

At approximately 2:55 p.m. on Friday, October 16, Fitzsimmons was returning from his break when he slipped and fell in the front lobby, striking his head on the stone floor and momentarily losing consciousness. According to Beverly Barrett, the receptionist, the floor had just been mopped and was still wet. She paged Mike Moore, the security officer, who in turn paged me. When I arrived at approximately 3:00 p.m., Fitzsimmons had revived. I immediately checked his vital signs, which were normal. He refused further medical attention and returned to work. I advised him to contact me if he experienced any subsequent discomfort, but to my knowledge there has been none.

Memo format.

Brief introduction.

Headings segment content.

FIGURE 4.4 • Incident Report (Memo Format), Page 1

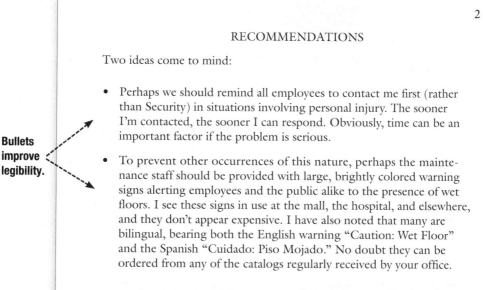

Bullets improve legibility.

FIGURE 4.5 • Incident Report (Memo Format), Page 2

Because recommendation reports are persuasive in nature, they are in several respects trickier to write—and to live with afterward—than reports intended primarily to record factual information. Tact is of great importance. Because your report is essentially designed to bring about an improvement in existing conditions or procedures, you should guard against seeming to be overly critical of the present circumstances. Focus more on what *will be* than on what *is*. Emphasize solutions rather than problems. Do not assign blame for present difficulties except in the most extreme cases. A very helpful strategy in writing recommendation reports is to request input from coworkers whose perspective may give you a more comprehensive understanding of the situation you're assessing.

Recommendation reports are structured in various ways, but almost all include three basic components:

- *Problem:* Identifies not only the problem itself but also, if possible, its causes and its relative urgency.

- *Solution:* Sets forth a recommendation and explains how it will be implemented; also clearly states the advantages of the recommendation, including relevant data on costs, timing, and the like.

- *Discussion:* Summarizes briefly the report's key points and politely urges the adoption of its recommendation.

Figures 4.6 and 4.7 present a recommendation report prepared in letter format. The report focuses on enabling a feed manufacturing company to avert fiscal problems by cutting costs at one of its mills.

FIGURE 4.6 • Recommendation Report (Letter Format), Page 1

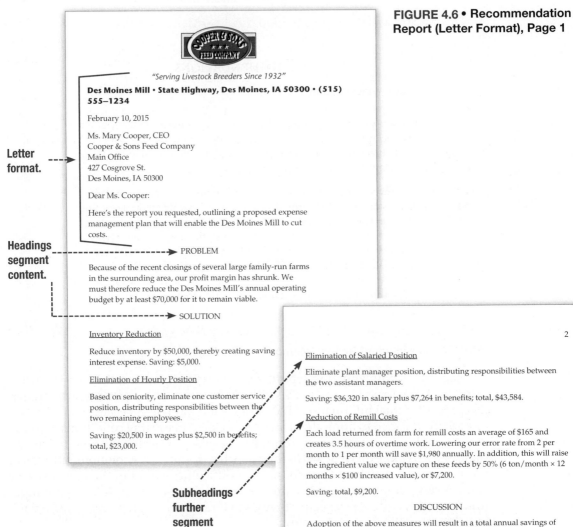

Letter format.

Headings segment content.

Subheadings further segment content.

"Serving Livestock Breeders Since 1932"

Des Moines Mill • State Highway, Des Moines, IA 50300 • (515) 555–1234

February 10, 2015

Ms. Mary Cooper, CEO
Cooper & Sons Feed Company
Main Office
427 Cosgrove St.
Des Moines, IA 50300

Dear Ms. Cooper:

Here's the report you requested, outlining a proposed expense management plan that will enable the Des Moines Mill to cut costs.

PROBLEM

Because of the recent closings of several large family-run farms in the surrounding area, our profit margin has shrunk. We must therefore reduce the Des Moines Mill's annual operating budget by at least $70,000 for it to remain viable.

SOLUTION

Inventory Reduction

Reduce inventory by $50,000, thereby creating saving interest expense. Saving: $5,000.

Elimination of Hourly Position

Based on seniority, eliminate one customer service position, distributing responsibilities between the two remaining employees.

Saving: $20,500 in wages plus $2,500 in benefits; total, $23,000.

2

Elimination of Salaried Position

Eliminate plant manager position, distributing responsibilities between the two assistant managers.

Saving: $36,320 in salary plus $7,264 in benefits; total, $43,584.

Reduction of Remill Costs

Each load returned from farm for remill costs an average of $165 and creates 3.5 hours of overtime work. Lowering our error rate from 2 per month to 1 per month will save $1,980 annually. In addition, this will raise the ingredient value we capture on these feeds by 50% (6 ton/month × 12 months × $100 increased value), or $7,200.

Saving: total, $9,200.

DISCUSSION

Adoption of the above measures will result in a total annual savings of $80,784. This more than meets the requirements.

The principal negative impact will be on personnel, and we regret the necessity of eliminating the two positions. It should be noted, however, that the situation could be much worse. The hourly customer service employee can be rehired after the scheduled retirement of another customer service worker next year. Also, the retrenched plant manager can be offered a comparable position at the Cooper & Sons mill in Northton, where business is booming and several openings currently exist.

Therefore, the above measures should be implemented as soon as possible to ensure the continued cost-effectiveness of the Des Moines Mill.

Thank you for considering these recommendations. I appreciate having the opportunity to provide input that may be helpful in the company's decision-making process.

Sincerely,

John Svenson

John Svenson
Financial Advisor

FIGURE 4.7 • Recommendation Report (Letter Format), Page 2

Progress Report

A progress report provides information about the status of an ongoing project or activity that must be monitored to ensure successful completion within a specified period. Sometimes called status reports or periodic reports, progress reports are submitted either upon completion of key stages of a project or at regular, pre-established intervals—quarterly, monthly, weekly, or sometimes as often as every day. They are written by the individual(s) directly responsible for the success of the undertaking. The readers of these reports are usually in the management sector of the organization, however, and may not be familiar with the technical details of the situation. Rather, their priority is timely completion of the project within established cost guidelines. Therefore, the information in a progress report tends to be more general than specific, and the language tends to be far less technical than that of other kinds of reports.

Most progress reports include the following components:

- **Introduction:** Provides context and background, identifying the project, reviewing its objectives, and alerting the reader to any new developments since the previous progress report.

- **Work completed:** Summarizes accomplishments to date. This section can be organized in either of two ways: If the report deals with one major task, a chronological approach is advisable; if it deals with several related projects, the report should have subdivisions by task.

- **Work remaining:** Summarizes all uncompleted tasks, emphasizing what's expected to be accomplished first.

- **Problems:** Identifies any delays, cost overruns, or other unanticipated difficulties. If all is well or if the problems are of no particular consequence, this section may be omitted.

- **Conclusion:** Summarizes the status of the project and recommends solutions to any major problems.

If properly prepared and promptly submitted, progress reports can be invaluable in enabling management to make necessary adjustments to meet deadlines, avert crises, and prevent unnecessary expense. Figures 4.8–4.11 present a progress report on capital projects, prepared in booklet format with a cover e-mail.

Cover e-mail serves as transmittal document accompanying repot. - - - - - - - - →

Bullets improve legibility. - - - - - - - →

File	Edit	View	Tools	Message	Help

Reply   Reply All   Forward   Print   Delete   Previous   Next   Addresses

From: John Daly, Physical Plant
Date: 11/10/2015
To: Judith Ayres, Accounting Department
Subject: Progress Report on Capital Projects

As requested, here's the progress report on the five capital projects identified as high-priority items at last spring's long-range planning meeting:

- Replacement of front elevator in Main Building
- Replacement of all windows in Main Building
- Installation of new fire alarm system in all buildings
- Installation of emergency lighting system in all buildings
- Renovation of "B" Building basement

Please contact me if you have any questions.

FIGURE 4.8 Progress Report (Booklet Format), Cover E-mail

FIGURE 4.9 • Progress Report (Booklet Format), Title Page

FALLKILL INDUSTRIES, INC.

PROGRESS REPORT

on

CAPITAL PROJECTS

by

John Daly
Physical Plant

Submitted to

Judith Ayres
Accounting Department

November 10, 2015

Headings segment content.

INTRODUCTION

Fallkill Industries, Inc. is currently involved in several major capital projects that were identified as high-priority items at last spring's long-range planning meeting: replacement of the front elevator and all windows in the Main Building, installation of a new fire alarm system and emergency lighting system in all buildings, and renovation of the "B" Building basement. Progress has been made on all of these projects, although there have been a few problems.

WORK COMPLETED

Elevator Replacement

Equipment has been ordered from Uptown Elevator. The pump has arrived and is in storage. We have asked Uptown for a construction schedule.

Window Replacement

Entrance and window wall: KlearVue Window Co. has completed this job, but it is unsatisfactory. See "Problems" section below. Other windows: Architect has approved submittal package, and Cavan Glass Co. is preparing shop drawings. Architect has sent Cavan Glass Co. a letter stating that work must begin no later than April 4, with completion in July.

Fire Alarm System

First submittal package from Alert-All, Ltd was reviewed by architect and rejected. A second package was accepted. The alarm system is on order.

Emergency Lighting System

BriteLite, Inc. has begun installation in the Main Building. They will -proceed on a building-by-building basis, completing one before moving on to another.

Basement Renovation

First submittal package from Innovation Renovation was reviewed by architect and rejected. Innovation Renovation is preparing a second package to reduce HVAC costs. Work will begin in June.

FIGURE 4.10 • Progress Report (Booklet Format), Page 1

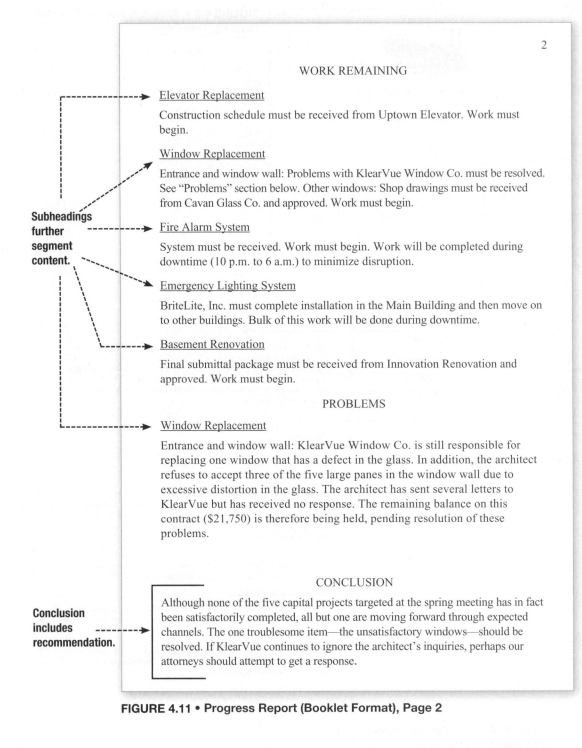

Subheadings further segment content.

2

WORK REMAINING

Elevator Replacement

Construction schedule must be received from Uptown Elevator. Work must begin.

Window Replacement

Entrance and window wall: Problems with KlearVue Window Co. must be resolved. See "Problems" section below. Other windows: Shop drawings must be received from Cavan Glass Co. and approved. Work must begin.

Fire Alarm System

System must be received. Work must begin. Work will be completed during downtime (10 p.m. to 6 a.m.) to minimize disruption.

Emergency Lighting System

BriteLite, Inc. must complete installation in the Main Building and then move on to other buildings. Bulk of this work will be done during downtime.

Basement Renovation

Final submittal package must be received from Innovation Renovation and approved. Work must begin.

PROBLEMS

Window Replacement

Entrance and window wall: KlearVue Window Co. is still responsible for replacing one window that has a defect in the glass. In addition, the architect refuses to accept three of the five large panes in the window wall due to excessive distortion in the glass. The architect has sent several letters to KlearVue but has received no response. The remaining balance on this contract ($21,750) is therefore being held, pending resolution of these problems.

CONCLUSION

Conclusion includes recommendation.

Although none of the five capital projects targeted at the spring meeting has in fact been satisfactorily completed, all but one are moving forward through expected channels. The one troublesome item—the unsatisfactory windows—should be resolved. If KlearVue continues to ignore the architect's inquiries, perhaps our attorneys should attempt to get a response.

FIGURE 4.11 • Progress Report (Booklet Format), Page 2

Travel Report

There are two kinds of travel reports: field reports and trip reports. The purpose of both is to create a record of—and, by implication, justification for—an employee's work-related travel. The travel may be directly related to the performance of routine duties (a field visit to a customer or client, for example) or it may be part of the employee's ongoing professional development (such as a trip to a convention, trade show, or offsite training session). Submitted to the employee's immediate supervisor, a travel report not only describes the employee activity made possible by traveling but also assesses the activity's value and relevance to the organization.

Travel reports are usually structured as follows:

- ***Introduction:*** Provides all basic information, including destination, purpose of travel, arrival and departure dates and times, and mode of travel (personal car, company car, train, plane).

- ***Description of activity/service performed:*** Not an itinerary but rather a selectively detailed account. The degree of detail is greater if readers other than the supervisor will have access to the report and expect to learn something from it. In the case of a field report, any problems encountered should be detailed, along with corrective actions taken.

- ***Cost accounting:*** Usually required for nonroutine travel. The employee accounts for all money spent, especially if the employer provides reimbursement.

- ***Discussion:*** An assessment of the usefulness of the travel and, if applicable, recommendations regarding the feasibility of other such travel in the future. In the case of a field report, suggestions are sometimes made based on the particulars of the situation.

Figures 4.12 and 4.13 present the two kinds of travel reports—both in memo format.

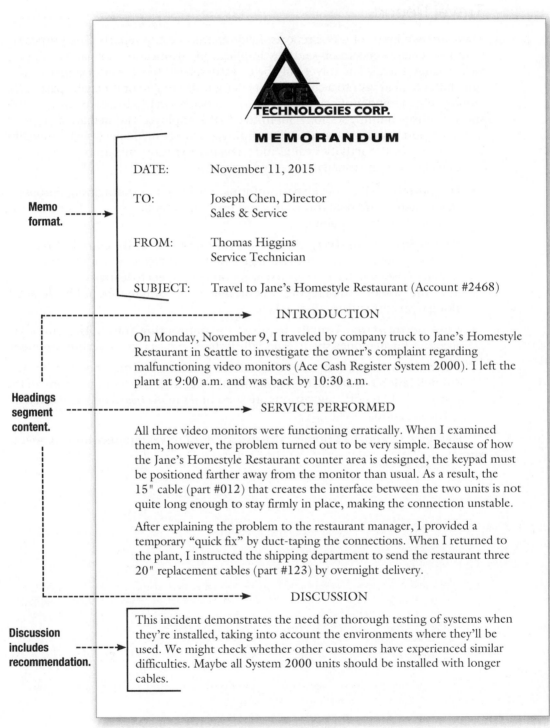

FIGURE 4.12 • Field Report (Memo Format)

$\mathcal{B}$rook $\mathcal{S}$tone
TECHNOLOGIES, INC.
M E M O R A N D U M

Memo format.

DATE: November 17, 2015

TO: Robert Reeves, Director
             Human Resources

FROM: Debra Dickens, Director
             Information Technology

SUBJECT: Travel to Tidewater Conference Center for Seminar

Headings segment content.

INTRODUCTION

On Thursday, November 12, and Friday, November 13, I traveled by company car to the Tidewater Conference Center to attend a seminar entitled "Workplace Communications: The Basics," presented by a corporate training consultant, Dr. George J. Searles. I left the plant at 8 a.m. and was back by 5 p.m. both days.

ACTIVITIES

The seminar consisted of four half-day sessions, as follows:

- Workplace Communications Overview (Thursday a.m.)
- Review of Mechanics (Thursday p.m.)
- E-mail and Letters (Friday a.m.)
- Reports (Friday p.m.)

There were 21 participants from a variety of local businesses and organizations, and the sessions were a blend of lecture and discussion, with emphasis on clear, concise writing. The instructor distributed numerous handouts that illustrated the points under consideration.

Bullets improve legibility.

COSTS

The program cost $1,000, paid by the company. Aside from two days' lunch allowance ($40 total) and use of the company car (38 miles total), there were no other expenses.

DISCUSSION

This was a very worthwhile program. I learned a lot from it. Because it would be quite difficult, however, to summarize the content here, I've appended a complete set of the handouts distributed by the instructor. As you will see when you examine these materials, the focus of the program was quite practical. I recommend that other employees be encouraged to attend the next time this program is offered in our area.

FIGURE 4.13 • Trip Report (Memo Format)

Checklist
Evaluating a Memo Report

A good memo report

___ is accompanied by a cover e-mail;

___ follows the standard memo report format;

___ includes certain features:

    ☐   To line, which provides the name and often the title and/or department of the receiver

    ☐   From line, which provides the name (provided automatically on e-mail) and often the title and/or department of the sender

    ☐   Date line (provided automatically on e-mail)

    ☐   Subject line, which provides a clear, accurate, but brief indication of what the memo report is about

___ is organized into separate, labeled sections, covering the subject fully in an orderly way;

___ includes no inappropriate content;

___ uses clear, simple language;

___ maintains an appropriate tone—neither too formal nor too conversational;

___ uses effective visuals—tables, graphs, charts, and the like—where necessary to clarify the text;

___ contains no typos or mechanical errors in spelling, capitalization, punctuation, or grammar.

EXERCISES

EXERCISE 4.1

Write a report either to your supervisor at work or to the campus safety committee at your college fully describing the circumstances surrounding an accident or injury you've experienced at work or at college and the results of that mishap. Include suggestions about how similar situations might be avoided in the future. Use the memo report format, and include visuals if appropriate.

Checklist
Evaluating a Letter Report

A good letter report

___ follows the full block format;

___ includes certain features:

- ☐ Sender's complete address
- ☐ Date
- ☐ Receiver's full name and complete address
- ☐ Salutation, followed by a colon
- ☐ Complimentary close ("Sincerely" is best), followed by a comma
- ☐ Sender's signature and full name
- ☐ Enclosure notation, if necessary

___ is organized into paragraphs, covering the subject fully in an orderly way:

- ☐ First paragraph establishes context and states the purpose
- ☐ Middle paragraphs constitute the report, separated into labeled sections that provide all necessary details
- ☐ Last paragraph politely achieves closure

___ includes no inappropriate content;

___ uses clear, simple language;

___ maintains an appropriate tone—neither too formal nor too conversational;

___ uses effective visuals—tables, graphs, charts, and the like—where necessary to clarify the text;

___ contains no typos or mechanical errors in spelling, capitalization, punctuation, or grammar.

EXERCISE 4.2

Imagine that you are supervising an employee who is "on loan" from your company's Tokyo office. She is an excellent worker but sometimes absent and often late. Clearly, you must address the situation. You have decided to provide the worker with a report outlining the company's policies regarding attendance and punctuality. But you must be sensitive to cultural differences. Do some Internet research to learn how such issues are approached in Japan. Then write the report, taking those customs into consideration.

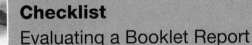

Checklist
Evaluating a Booklet Report

A good booklet report

___ is accompanied by a cover e-mail or letter;

___ includes a title page that contains the following:

- ☐ Title of the report
- ☐ Name(s) of author(s)
- ☐ Name of company or organization
- ☐ Name(s) of person(s) receiving the report
- ☐ Date

___ is organized into separate, labeled sections covering the subject fully in an orderly way;

___ includes no inappropriate content;

___ uses clear, simple language;

___ maintains an appropriate tone—neither too formal nor too conversational;

___ uses effective visuals—tables, graphs, charts, and the like—where necessary to clarify the text;

___ contains no typos or mechanical errors in spelling, capitalization, punctuation, or grammar.

EXERCISE 4.3

Write a report to your communications instructor, outlining your progress in class. List attendance, grades, and any other pertinent information, including an objective assessment of your performance so far and the final grade you anticipate receiving. Use the memo format, and include visuals.

EXERCISE 4.4

Write a report to the academic dean, urging that a particular college policy be modified. Be specific about the reasons for your proposal. Justify the change, and provide concrete suggestions about possible alternative policies. Use the memo format, and include visuals if appropriate.

EXERCISE 4.5

Write a report to your instructor, discussing any recent vacation trip you've taken. Summarize your principal activities during the trip, and provide an evaluation of how successful the vacation was. Use the letter format, and include visuals.

EXERCISE 4.6

Write a report to a classmate, outlining the performance of your favorite sports team over the past three years. Using statistical data, be as factual and detailed as your knowledge of the sport will permit. Attempt to explain the reasons for the team's relative success or lack of it. Use the booklet format, and include visuals.

EXERCISE 4.7

Write a report to the student services director or the physical plant director at your college, evaluating a major campus building with respect to accessibility for individuals who are physically challenged. Discuss the presence or absence of special signs, doors, ramps, elevators, restroom facilities, and the like. Suggest additional accommodations that should be provided if such needs exist. Use the booklet format, and include visuals.

EXERCISE 4.8

Team up with a classmate of the opposite sex and write a report to the physical plant director analyzing the differences, if any, between the men's and women's restroom facilities in the main building on your campus. Suggest any changes or improvements you think might be necessary. Use the booklet format, and include visuals.

EXERCISE 4.9

Have you ever been the victim of or witness to a minor crime on campus? Write a report to the college security director, relating the details of that experience and offering suggestions about how to minimize the likelihood of similar occurrences in the future. Use the letter format, and include visuals if appropriate.

EXERCISE 4.10

Write a report to your classmates in which you evaluate three nearby restaurants featuring similar cuisine (for example, Chinese, Italian, or Middle Eastern) or three nearby stores that sell essentially the same product (for example, athletic shoes, books and music, or clothing). Discuss such issues as selection, quality, price, and service. Use the booklet format, and include visuals.

5

Summaries

LEARNING OBJECTIVES

When you complete this chapter you'll be able to:

- understand the differences among the several kinds of summary.
- write informative descriptive summaries.
- composed detailed informative summaries.
- create convincing evaluative summaries.
- accurately summarize both written and oral sources.

In the broadest sense, *all* writing is a form of summary. Whenever we put words on paper or computer screen, we condense ideas and information to make them coherent to the reader. Ordinarily, however, the term *summary* refers to a brief statement of the essential content of something heard, seen, or read. For any kind of summary, the writer reduces a body of material to its bare essentials. Creating a summary is therefore an exercise in *compression,* requiring logical organization, clear and concrete terminology, and sensitivity to the reader's needs. By that definition, a summary is the same as any other kind of workplace communication. Summary writing, however, demands an especially keen sense of not only what to include but also of what to *leave out.* The goal is to highlight the key points and not burden the reader with unnecessary details. In the workplace context, the most common summary application is in the abstracts and executive summaries that accompany long reports. This chapter explores the main principles governing the writing of summaries—a valuable skill in many work settings.

Types of Summaries: Descriptive, Informative, and Evaluative

In general, summaries can be classified into three categories: descriptive, informative, and evaluative.

A **descriptive summary** states what the original document is about but does not convey any of the document's specific information. It is much like a table of contents in paragraph form. Its main purpose is to help a reader determine whether the document summarized is of any potential use in a given situation. For example, a pamphlet providing descriptive summaries of federal publications on workplace safety may be quite helpful to a personnel director wishing to educate employees about a particular job-related hazard. Similarly, a purchasing agent might consult descriptive summaries to determine the potential relevance of outside studies on needed equipment or supplies. A descriptive summary might look something like this:

> This report discusses a series of tests conducted on industrial-strength coil springs at the TopTech Laboratories in Northton, Minnesota, in January 2015. Three kinds of springs were evaluated for flexibility, durability, and heat resistance to determine their relative suitability for several specific manufacturing applications at Northton Industries.

After reading this summary, someone seeking to become better informed about the broad topic of coil springs might decide to read the report.

An **informative summary,** on the other hand, goes considerably further and presents the document's content, although in greatly compressed form. A good informative summary that includes the document's conclusions and recommendations (if any) can actually enable a busy reader to *skip* the original altogether. Here's an informative version of the previous descriptive summary:

> This report discusses a series of tests conducted on industrial-strength coil springs at the TopTech Laboratories in Northton, Minnesota, in January 2015. Three kinds of springs—all manufactured by the Mathers Spring Co. of Marietta, Ohio—were tested: serial numbers 423, 424, and 425. The springs were evaluated for flexibility, durability, and heat resistance to determine their relative suitability for several specific manufacturing applications at Northton Industries. In 15 tests using a Flexor Meter, #423 was found to be the most flexible, followed by #425 and #424, respectively. In 15 tests using a Duro Meter, #425 proved to be the most durable, followed by #423 and #424, respectively. In 15 tests using a Thermal Chamber, #423 was the most

heat-resistant, followed by #424 and #425, respectively. Although #423 compiled the best overall performance rating, #425 is the preferred choice because the applications in question require considerable durability and involve relatively few high-temperature operations.

The **evaluative summary** is even more fully developed and includes the writer's personal assessment of the original document. The following is an evaluative version of the same summary. Notice that the writer inserts subjective value judgments throughout.

This rather poorly written and finally unreliable report discusses a series of flawed experiments conducted on industrial-strength coil springs at the TopTech Laboratories in Northton, Minnesota, in January 2015. Three kinds of springs—all manufactured by the Mathers Spring Co. of Marietta, Ohio—were tested: serial numbers 423, 424, and 425. The springs were evaluated for flexibility, durability, and heat resistance to determine their relative suitability for several specific manufacturing applications at Northton Industries. In 15 tests using the notoriously unreliable Flexor Meter, #423 was rated the most flexible, followed by #425 and #424, respectively. In 15 tests using the equally outdated Duro Meter, #425 scored highest, followed by #423 and #424, respectively. In 15 tests using a state-of-the-art Thermal Chamber, #423 was found to be the most heat-resistant, followed by #424 and #425, respectively. Although #423 compiled the best overall performance rating, the report recommends #425 on the grounds that the specific applications in question require considerable durability and involve relatively few high-temperature operations. However, these conclusions are questionable at best. TopTech Laboratories has since shut down after revelations of improper procedures. Two of the three test sequences involved obsolete instruments, and #425 proved markedly inferior to #423 and #424 in the only test sequence that can be considered reliable.

Of the three categories, the informative summary is by far the most common. As in a *Reader's Digest* condensed version of a longer original article, the purpose of an informative summary is to convey the main ideas of the original in shorter form. To make an informative summary concrete and to the point rather than vague and rambling, be sure to include hard data—such as names, dates, and statistics—as well as the original document's conclusions and recommendations, if any. Sometimes including a good, well-focused quotation from the original can also be helpful to the reader. Avoid lengthy examples and sidetracks, however, because a summary must always be *brief*—usually no more than a quarter of the original document's length.

In addition, a summary should retain the *emphasis* of the original. For example, a relatively minor point in the source should not take on disproportionate significance in the summary (and perhaps could be omitted altogether). However, crucial information in the original should be equally prominent in the summary, and all information in the summary should spring directly from something in the source. Unless the summary's purpose is to evaluate, no new or additional information should appear, nor should personal opinion or comments be included.

For clarity, all workplace writing should be worded in the simplest possible terms. This is especially important in a summary, which is meant to stand alone. If the reader must go back to the original to understand, the summary is a failure. Therefore, the summary should be coherently organized and written in complete sentences with unmistakably clear meaning. As mentioned before, active verbs are best. They are especially helpful in a summary because they enable you to express ideas in fewer words than passive constructions do.

Depending on its nature, a summary that accompanies a long report is called an *abstract* or *executive summary*. If the summary is intended simply to provide a general overview of the report, it appears near the beginning of the report and is called an *abstract* (for an example of an abstract, see Figure 11.3). If the summary is intended to assist management in making decisions without having to read the report it precedes, it is called an *executive summary*.

Summarizing Written Sources

To summarize information that already exists in a written document, follow these simple steps:

1. Read the entire document straight through to get a general sense of its content. Pay particular attention to the introduction and the conclusion.
2. Watch for context clues (title, subheadings, visuals, boldface print, etc.) to ensure that you have an accurate understanding of the document.
3. Go back and underline or highlight the most important sentences in each paragraph. Write down all those sentences.
4. Now edit the sentences you selected, compressing, combining, and streamlining. When producing a summary of something you've written yourself, it's permissible to *abridge* the material, retaining some of the original wording. This is strictly prohibited, however, when summarizing someone else's work. Instead, you must rephrase the content in your own words. Otherwise, you're guilty of *plagiarism*— a serious offense for which you can incur severe penalties. This issue is discussed at greater length in Chapter 11.
5. Reread your summary to check that it flows smoothly. Insert transitions—such as *therefore, however,* and *nevertheless*—where necessary to eliminate any abrupt jump from one idea to another.
6. Include concrete facts such as names, dates, and statistics, as well as conclusions and recommendations. This is especially important in a summary, which is typically written as one long paragraph incorporating many ideas.
7. Correct all typos and mechanical errors in spelling, capitalization, punctuation, and grammar.

Figures 5.1 through 5.4 depict the major steps in the creation of an effective summary from an existing text—in this case, a NASA press release about new data-gathering technology that provides accurate measurement of snow melt in the western United States.

Summarizing Oral Sources

To summarize a speech, briefing, broadcast, or other oral presentation for which no transcript exists, you must rely on your own notes. Therefore, you should develop some sort of personal system of shortcuts, incorporating abbreviations, symbols, and other notations, to enable you to take notes quickly without missing anything important. Figure 5.5 lists 20 such shortcuts, similar to those that have become so common in text messaging. You will likely develop others of your own. However, this strategy is no help if you have to *think* about it. To serve their purpose, your shortcuts have to become instinctive. Furthermore, you must be able to translate your shortcuts back into regular English as you review your notes. Like anything, this process becomes easier with practice.

To facilitate summarizing from oral sources, you can use a handheld microcassette recorder or download the material to your computer via digital recorder. This will allow you to listen more attentively afterward, at your own pace, under more conducive conditions. But this is a good strategy only if there's no rush or if exact quotation is crucial. And even if recording, it's still important to take good notes—both to maximize understanding through attentive listening and to guard against mechanical failure. Of course, your notes should always highlight the most important points so you can review them later. Searching for those sections on the tape or in audio files can, however, be very time-consuming unless your notes provide orientation. Helpfully, the better cassette recorders are equipped with a counter similar to an automobile's mileage odometer. You can save yourself a lot of frustration by including counter numbers in your notes. If your notes indicate, for example, that point A was discussed when the counter was at 075, point B was discussed at 190, and point C at 250, locating the desired sections of the tape will now be much easier. You can achieve an even higher level of efficiency by using a digital recorder. Even the least expensive ones are available with DSS Player Pro software, which helps you manage and locate recorded files. Higher-end models enable you to navigate through the menu to assign contact points and then easily find and make selections. Some even use voice activation to access specific texts.

May 02, 2013

Steve Cole
Headquarters, Washington
202-358-0918
stephen.e.cole@nasa.gov

Alan Buis
Jet Propulsion Laboratory, Pasadena, Calif.
818-354-0474
alan.buis@jpl.nasa.gov

RELEASE: 13-131

NASA OPENS NEW ERA IN MEASURING WESTERN U.S. SNOWPACK

WASHINGTON—A new NASA airborne mission has created the first maps of the entire snowpack of two major mountain watersheds in California and Colorado, producing the most accurate measurements to date of how much water they hold.

The data from NASA's Airborne Snow Observatory mission will be used to estimate how much water will flow out of the basins when the snow melts. The data-gathering technology could improve water management for 1.5 billion people worldwide who rely on snowmelt for their water supply.

"The Airborne Snow Observatory is on the cutting edge of snow remote-sensing science," said Jared Entin, a program manager in the Earth Science Division at NASA Headquarters in Washington. "Decision makers like power companies and water managers now are receiving these data, which may have immediate economic benefits."

The mission is a collaboration between NASA's Jet Propulsion Laboratory (JPL) in Pasadena, Calif., and the California Department of Water Resources in Sacramento.

A Twin Otter aircraft carrying NASA's Airborne Snow Observatory began a three-year demonstration mission in April that includes weekly flights over the Tuolumne River Basin in California's Sierra Nevada and monthly flights over Colorado's Uncompahgre River Basin. The flights will run through the end of the snowmelt season, which typically occurs in July. The Tuolumne watershed and its Hetch Hetchy Reservoir are the primary water supply for San Francisco. The Uncompahgre watershed is part of the Upper Colorado River Basin that supplies water to much of the western United States.

The mission's principal investigator, Tom Painter of JPL, said the mission fills a critical need in an increasingly thirsty world, initially focusing on the western United States, where snowmelt provides more than 75 percent of the total freshwater supply.

"Changes in and pressure on snowmelt-dependent water systems are motivating water managers, governments and others to improve understanding of snow and its melt," Painter said. "The western United States and other regions face significant water resource challenges because of population growth and faster melt and runoff of snowpacks caused by climate change. NASA's Airborne Snow Observatory combines the best available technologies to provide precise, timely information for assessing snowpack volume and melt." The observatory's two instruments measure two properties most critical to understanding snowmelt runoff and timing. Those two properties have been mostly unmeasured until now.

A scanning lidar system from the Canadian firm Optech Inc. of Vaughan, Ontario, measures snow depth to determine the first property, snow water equivalent with lasers. Snow water equivalent represents the amount of water in the snow on a mountain. It is used to calculate the amount of water that will run off.

An imaging spectrometer built by another Canadian concern, ITRES of Calgary, Alberta, measures the second property, snow albedo. Snow albedo represents the amount of sunlight reflected and absorbed by snow. Snow albedo controls the speed of snowmelt and timing of its runoff.

By combining these data, scientists can tell how changes in the absorption of sunlight cause snowmelt rates to increase. The Airborne Snow Observatory flies at an altitude of 17,500 feet–22,000 feet (5,334 to 6,705 meters) to produce frequent maps that scientists can use to monitor changes over time. It can calculate snow depth to within about 4 inches (10 centimeters) and snow water equivalent to within 5 percent. Data are processed on the ground and made available to participating water managers within 24 hours. Before now, Sierra Nevada snow water equivalent estimates have been extrapolated from monthly manual ground snow surveys conducted from January through April. These survey sites are sparsely located, primarily in lower to middle elevations that melt free of snow each spring, while snow remains at higher elevations. Water managers use these survey data to forecast annual water supplies. The information affects decisions by local water districts, agricultural interests and others. The sparse sampling can lead to large errors. In contrast, the NASA observatory can map all the snow throughout the entire snowmelt season.

"The Airborne Snow Observatory is providing California water managers the first near-real-time, comprehensive determination of basin-wide snow water equivalent," said Frank Gehrke, mission co-investigator and chief of the California Cooperative Snow Surveys Program for the California Department of Water Resources. "Integrated into models, these data will enhance the state's reservoir operations, permitting more efficient flood control, water supply management and hydroelectric power generation."

Gehrke said the state will continue to conduct manual surveys while it incorporates the Airborne Snow Observatory data. "The snow surveys are relatively inexpensive, help validate observatory data and provide snow density measurements that are key to reducing errors in estimating snow water equivalent," he said.

Painter plans to expand the airborne mapping program to the entire Upper Colorado River Basin and Sierra Nevada. "We believe this is the future of water management in the western United States," he said.

For more information about the Airborne Snow Observatory, visit: http://aso.jpl.nasa.gov/

-end-

FIGURE 5.1 • News Release with Most Important Sentences Underlined

Source: http://www.nasa.gov/topics/earth/features/earth20130502.html

A new NASA airborne mission has created the first maps of the entire snowpack of two major mountain watersheds in California and Colorado.

The data from NASA's Airborne Snow Observatory mission will be used to estimate how much water will flow out of the basins when the snow melts. The data-gathering technology could improve water management.

The mission is a collaboration between NASA's Jet Propulsion Laboratory (JPL) in Pasadena, Calif., and the California Department of Water Resources in Sacramento.

"Changes in and pressure on snowmelt-dependent water systems are motivating water managers, governments and others to improve understanding of snow and its melt," Painter said. "The western United States and other regions face significant water resource challenges because of population growth and faster melt and runoff of snowpacks caused by climate change."

A scanning lidar system . . . measures . . . snow water equivalent . . . to calculate the amount of water that will run off.

An imaging spectrometer . . . measures . . . snow albedo . . . the amount of sunlight reflected and absorbed by snow. Snow albedo controls the speed of snowmelt and . . . runoff.

By combining these data, scientists can tell how changes in the absorption of sunlight cause snowmelt rates to increase.

Before now, Sierra Nevada snow water equivalent estimates have been extrapolated. . . .

The sparse sampling can lead to large errors.

These data will enhance the state's reservoir operations, permitting more efficient flood control, water supply management and hydroelectric power generation.

Painter plans to expand the airborne mapping program to the entire Upper Colorado River Basin and Sierra Nevada.

FIGURE 5.2 • Compilation of Release's Most Important Sentences

For the purpose of better water management, NASA's new Airborne Snow Observatory mission has mapped two major mountain watersheds in California and Colorado to predict the volume of runoff that will result from melting snow.

"Changes in and pressure on snowmelt-dependent water systems are motivating water managers, governments and others to improve understanding of snow and its melt," said Tom Painter of NASA's Jet Propulsion Laboratory, which is jointly coordinating the effort with the California Department of Water Resources.

"The western United States and other regions face significant water resource challenges because of population growth and faster melt and runoff of snowpacks caused by climate change," Painter added.

A laser scanner measures the snow's depth to estimate the amount of water runoff, while an imaging spectrometer calculates the role of sunlight in speeding up the rate of snowmelt and ensuing runoff.

By combining these data, scientists can tell how changes in the absorption of sunlight cause snowmelt rates to increase.

In the past, such predictions were based on extrapolation from small data samples, resulting in major miscalculations.

But these new, more reliable data will lead to better reservoir operations, flood control, water supply management, and power generation.

Painter said that this program will be expanded to include the whole Upper Colorado River Basin and Sierra Nevada.

FIGURE 5.3 • Release's Most Important Sentences, Edited and Revised

COUNTY COMMUNITY COLLEGE

MEMORANDUM

DATE: March 24, 2015

TO: Professor Mary Ann Evans, Ph.D.

FROM: George Eliot, Student

SUBJECT: Summary

In fulfillment of the "summary" assignment in English 110, Workplace Communications, here is a memo report. I have summarized a NASA news release, "NASA Opens New Era in Measuring Western U.S. Snowpack." A copy of the release is attached.

NASA Opens New Era in Measuring Western U.S. Snowpack

For the purpose of better water management, NASA's new Airborne Snow Observatory mission has mapped two major mountain watersheds in California and Colorado to predict the volume of runoff that will result from melting snow.

"Changes in and pressure on snowmelt-dependent water systems are motivating water managers, governments and others to improve understanding of snow and its melt," said Tom Painter of NASA's Jet Propulsion Laboratory, which is jointly coordinating the effort with the California Department of Water Resources.

"The western United States and other regions face significant water resource challenges because of population growth and faster melt and runoff of snowpacks caused by climate change," Painter added.

A laser scanner measures the snow's depth to estimate the amount of water runoff, while an imaging spectrometer calculates the role of sunlight in speeding up the rate of snowmelt and ensuing runoff.

These data enable scientists to determine how sunlight absorption increases the rate of snowmelt.

In the past, such predictions were based on extrapolation from small data samples, resulting in major miscalculations.

But these new, more reliable data will lead to better reservoir operations, flood control, water supply management, and power generation.

Painter said that this program will be expanded to include the whole Upper Colorado River Basin and Sierra Nevada.

FIGURE 5.4 • Summary (Memo Report Format)

Notation	Meaning	Explanation
=	Is	Symbol instead of word
#	Number	Symbol instead of word
&	And	Symbol instead of word
∴	Therefore	Symbol instead of word
2	To, too, two	Numeral instead of word
4	For, four	Numeral instead of word
B	Be, bee	Letter instead of word
C	See, sea	Letter instead of word
U	You	Letter instead of word
Y	Why	Letter instead of word
R	Are	Letter instead of word
R̸	Are not	Slash to express negation
w.	With	Abbreviation
w̸	Without	Slash to express negation
bcs	Because	Elimination of vowels
2B	To be	Blend of numeral and letter
B4	Before	Blend of letter and numeral
rathan	Rather than	Blend of two words
rite	Right	Phonetic spelling
turn handle	Turn the handle	Elimination of obvious

FIGURE 5.5 • Note-Taking Shortcuts

Checklist
Evaluating a Summary

A good summary

___ is no more than 25 percent as long as the original;

___ accurately reports the main points of the original;

___ includes no minor or unnecessary details;

___ includes nothing extraneous to the original;

___ preserves the proportion and emphasis of the original;

___ is well-organized, providing transitions to smooth the jumps between ideas;

___ maintains an objective tone;

___ uses clear, simple language;

___ contains no typos or mechanical errors in spelling, capitalization, punctuation, or grammar.

EXERCISES

EXERCISE 5.1

Here are three summaries of the same article, Ted Cushman's "The Science of Kitchen Ventilation," in the February 2015 issue of *JLC: The Journal of Light Construction*, a trade magazine aimed at building contractors. Identify each of the three as descriptive, informative, or evaluative.

Summary A

At a 2014 building trades conference in San Francisco, scientists from the Lawrence Berkeley National Laboratory presented findings about the importance of kitchen ventilation, specifically range hoods and exhaust fans. Scientists agree that kitchen pollutants are different from outdoor pollutants such as diesel exhaust. Because of recently increased environmental regulations on outdoor pollutants, however, indoor levels are sometimes actually higher. Researchers had been investigating air pollution produced by both gas-burning and electrical ranges, and concluded that gas-burning ranges are more hazardous than electrical ones. But cookware and even food itself release harmful particles into the environment. Therefore, range hoods and exhaust fans should always be used when stovetop food is being prepared. Studies have shown that units achieving 150 CFM (cubic feet per minute) of exhaust are effective, especially when cooking is done on the back burners. Ductwork should be no smaller than six inches and should be installed to avoid bends or transitions. The article concludes by urging contractors to advise homeowners about these findings.

Summary B

Although intended for building trades professionals, this well-written article would be clear to general readers as well. It outlines the findings of scientists from the prestigious Lawrence Berkeley National Laboratory, who addressed a 2014 San Francisco conference and stressed the importance of kitchen ventilation, specifically range hoods and exhaust fans. Scientists agree that kitchen pollutants are different from outdoor pollutants such as diesel exhaust. Because of recently increased environmental regulations on outdoor pollutants, however, indoor levels are sometimes actually higher. Researchers had been investigating air pollution produced by both gas-burning and electrical ranges, and concluded that gas-burning ranges are more hazardous than electrical ones. But cookware and even food itself release harmful particles into the environment. Therefore, range hoods and exhaust fans should always be used when stovetop food is being prepared. Studies have shown that units achieving 150 CFM (cubic feet per minute) of exhaust are effective, especially when cooking is done on the back burners. Ductwork should be no smaller than six inches and should be installed to avoid bends or transitions. The article concludes by urging contractors to advise homeowners about these findings. But some of the article's recommendations may encounter resistance, especially among "foodies," who prefer gas ranges and would undoubtedly feel restricted if told to use only their back burners.

Summary C

Studies done by the Lawrence Berkeley National Laboratory and presented at a 2014 building trades conference in San Francisco identified harmful concentrations of nitrogen dioxide and carbon monoxide produced by gas and electrical ranges. Scientists concluded that electrical ranges are far safer, and that contractors should alert homeowners to the importance of effective kitchen ventilation systems (range hoods and fans) that will exhaust pollutants from the kitchen and prevent their spread to other living spaces.

EXERCISE 5.2

Write a one-hundred-word descriptive summary of a recent article from a reputable periodical or Web site in your field of study or employment. Submit the article along with the summary.

EXERCISE 5.3

Write a 250-word informative summary of the same article mentioned in Exercise 5.2. Submit the article along with the summary.

EXERCISE 5.4

Write a 300-word evaluative summary of the same article mentioned in Exercises 5.2 and 5.3. Submit the article along with the summary.

EXERCISE 5.5

Write a 200-word informative summary of the plot of a recent episode of your favorite television show.

EXERCISE 5.6

Write a 250-word informative abstract of a term paper you've completed in the past for another course. Submit the term paper along with the abstract.

EXERCISE 5.7

Write an informative summary of an article from a popular periodical (for example, *Time, Rolling Stone,* or *Sports Illustrated*). Make the summary no more than 20 percent as long as the article, and submit the article along with the summary.

EXERCISE 5.8

Summcarize a lecture given by the instructor of one of your other classes. Limit the summary to roughly 500 words.

EXERCISE 5.9

Write a seventy-five-word informative summary of an article from your local newspaper. Select an article at least 300 words long. Submit the article along with your summary.

EXERCISE 5.10

Write a fifty-word descriptive abstract of the sample report in Chapter 11.

Fliers, Brochures, Newsletters, and Web Sites

LEARNING OBJECTIVES

When you complete this chapter you'll be able to:

- use text and visuals to create eye-catching fliers.
- design focused, informative brochures.
- apply proven journalistic principles to produce impressive newsletters.
- write concise, targeted Web site content.

Virtually all successful businesses rely on advertising to improve their bottom line. Obviously, increased visibility most likely results in a larger customer base. That's the whole point of advertising: to bring a business or organization to people's attention. Advertisements come in many forms. Some of the most common are newspaper, magazine, radio, and television ads, along with Yellow Pages displays, product catalogs, billboards, and Internet pop-ups. This chapter, however, deals with three forms of *collateral* advertising—more low-key and less expensive but also highly effective forms of promotion: fliers, brochures, and newsletters. In addition, it discusses the increasing importance of Web sites.

Fliers

A flier is simply a one-page, 8½″ × 11″ poster that can be folded and mailed to potential customers or, more typically, exhibited on a public bulletin board or kiosk in a high-traffic area such as a supermarket, launderette, or shopping mall.

As with so many forms of workplace communication, the key to an effective flier is *simplicity*. If a flier is read at all, it's read quickly, so it has to make its points immediately. Like a PowerPoint slide, a flier works best if it uses no more than two easily legible typefaces and short, bulleted phrases highlighting the most important points without overburdening the reader with unnecessary detail. It should also include a strong visual component to catch the eye of anyone passing by. Colored paper is helpful in this regard, as are capitalization, bold print, and simple illustrations. Notice how the flier shown in Figure 6.1 uses clip art drawings of a motorcycle, boat, and vintage auto to attract attention.

Checklist
Evaluating a Flier

A good flier

____ is simple in design;

____ integrates visuals to attract attention and reinforce content;

____ uses no more than two easily legible typefaces;

____ uses capitalization and bold print to increase legibility;

____ includes only key details;

____ implements short, direct, bulleted phrases rather than complete sentences;

____ presents information in logical sequence;

____ provides complete contact information;

____ contains no typos or mechanical errors in spelling, capitalization, punctuation, or grammar.

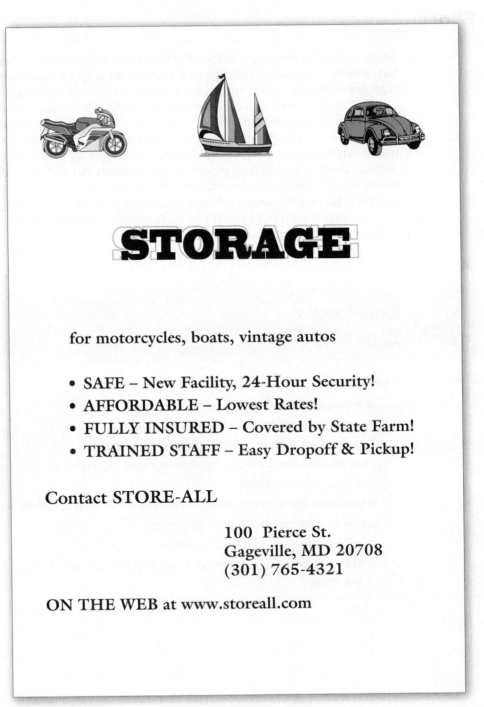

FIGURE 6.1 • Flier

Brochures

Another effective advertising medium is the brochure. A typical brochure is printed on both sides of 8½" × 11" or 8½" × 14" (legal size) paper in landscape (rather than portrait) orientation and folded to create vertical panels on which to display information. The smaller version, folded twice to create six panels, is the most common. See Figure 6.2.

The front panel of a brochure serves as its cover and therefore is seen first when the brochure lies flat on a table or is inserted in a display rack. It should feature an attention-getting visual and should prominently identify the business, agency, or organization it profiles, and it certainly may include a logo. That is all that needs to appear on the cover, except perhaps for an appropriate slogan or keyword that reinforces the content inside.

Once inside, the reader should find all relevant information presented in an easily digestible format. As explained in Chapter 1, effective workplace communication depends on careful analysis of audience, purpose, and tone. Therefore, when writing a brochure, it's important to remember who will be reading it and what you're attempting to accomplish. For example, a lawn care business would be wasting its time and money placing brochures under the windshield wipers of cars parked outside apartment buildings, whose residents would have no need for such services. Far better to target neighborhoods of single-family homes largely populated by the elderly. They would value the convenience and labor-saving advantages of hiring the company, and those are the points the brochure should certainly emphasize.

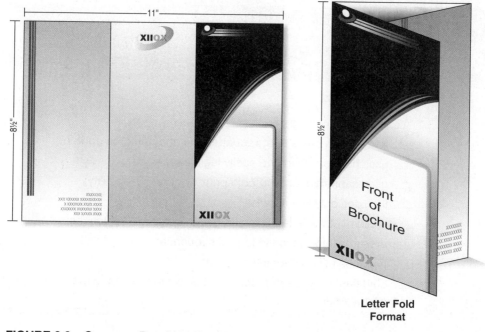

FIGURE 6.2 • Common Brochure Design

A common error in brochure-writing is to overload the panels with *unnecessary* information that competes with—and thereby obscures—what should be the main points. Indeed, one useful strategy is to design each panel as if it were a mini-flier, using text and visuals in a manner that facilitates easy reading and comprehension. As in flier design, use no more than two fonts and take advantage of such options as centering, bold print, underlining, and bulleted lists. Often, one middle panel is left completely blank except for a return address, so the brochure can be taped shut, addressed, and mailed. Again, see Figure 6.2.

Because a brochure creates what is often a potential customer's first impression of a business, it's obviously very important that the brochure project a professional image. Therefore, if possible, brochures should be printed in color on heavier, glossy paper. Microsoft Word includes brochure templates that ensure a reasonably polished appearance when a high-quality laser printer is used. (The templates can be found by typing "brochure" in the Help drop-down menu at the top of your screen.) So desktop publishing may indeed be the way to go, although it's more economical to enlist a commercial copying service to actually print large numbers of copies rather than using up expensive ink cartridges of your own. But if more than 1,000 copies are needed, it's probably better to have the brochure designed and produced by an actual print shop. Although this involves greater expense, the cost-to-benefit ratio justifies the additional outlay because—as in most situations—price goes down as quantity increases.

Checklist
Evaluating a Brochure

A good brochure

___ is simple in design;

___ integrates visuals to attract attention and reinforce content;

___ uses no more than two easily legible typefaces;

___ uses capitalization and bold print to increase legibility;

___ includes only key details;

___ implements bulleted lists along with complete sentences;

___ presents information in logical sequence;

___ provides full contact information;

___ contains no typos or mechanical errors in spelling, capitalization, punctuation, or grammar.

Newsletters

A company newsletter, published monthly or quarterly, serves two purposes. First, it fosters a sense of community among employees by updating them on trends and developments within their own workplace and elsewhere and by recognizing their accomplishments both on and off the job. In addition to this morale-boosting function, it also serves as a form of advertising because company newsletters are routinely sent to customers and other outside readers—elected officials and community leaders, for example. Furthermore, newsletters informally find their way into the larger community. For example, when an employee takes the newsletter home, it's seen by relatives, friends, and neighbors, thereby creating still greater visibility for the company. In recent years, online newsletters have become increasingly popular, largely because they can be distributed even more widely without incurring postage costs.

Many newsletter formats exist, but here we focus only on the standard 8½″ × 11″ version, which surveys have identified as the most effective. Such a newsletter is printed on both sides of an 11″ × 17″ sheet of paper that's then folded in the middle. The resulting four pages—with three vertical columns on each—afford ample space for the content without overwhelming a busy reader. (See Figure 6.3.) Online newsletters can include as many "pages" as the editor wishes at no added expense.

Here's a selection of what a company newsletter might contain:

- The newsletter's name and issue date, prominently displayed on the front page, along with the company name and location.
- Company news—anything of particular interest to that specific workplace, such as information about a new product, for example—also on page 1, with a large headline and an accompanying photo or other visual.
- General news stories relevant to the field, usually on page 1.
- Table of contents, usually in one of the bottom corners of page 1 or page 2.
- Personnel news: hirings, promotions, accomplishments, awards, and the like.
- Profiles (e.g., company president, "Employee of the Month").
- News of retirees, obituaries of former employees.
- Health/safety/benefits news (e.g., weight-loss seminar, adoption of new vision plan).
- Local interest features (e.g., coverage of a regional attraction or historically significant event, site, or person).
- Seasonal/topical features (e.g., daylight saving time or tax deadline reminder).
- Mailer (on the bottom of page 4, so the newsletter can be folded, taped shut, and mailed to outside readers).

As we have seen throughout this book, workplace writing should always be simple and direct. This is especially true in a newsletter, which is a form of journalism. Perhaps more than any other kind of writing, journalism prizes concision. But it also involves some other characteristics that are unique to that kind of writing.

For one thing, paragraphs in journalism are very short—usually no more than two or three sentences and often only one. This is because the writing appears in narrow columns. "Normal" five- or six-sentence paragraphs would be very long vertically, depriving the reader of necessary visual breaks. In addition, a journalism story's opening sentence (called the "lead") must fully summarize the story's main points in just twenty or thirty words. This is done by using the "Five W's" approach (Who/What/Where/When/Why) mentioned in Chapter 1. But in a newspaper, people's *names* do not appear until the second or third paragraph unless they are well-known. For example, if "some guy" is arrested for drug possession, that's essentially all the lead will say because the individual's specific identity is probably not that important to the majority of readers. His name will appear later, but the lead will be phrased like this:

WHO   **WHAT**

A Stratford motorist was arrested for heroin possession after a routine traffic stop

WHERE   **WHEN**   **WHY**

on Elm Street Thursday night turned up an envelope of the drug in his car.

If the motorist happened to be the mayor, a prominent defense attorney, or some other well-known local figure, however, the name would appear right away. In any case, the story would then go on to narrate the specifics of the situation, revealing the facts in *reverse* order of importance. Indeed, you can usually skip the last few paragraphs of a conventionally structured newspaper story without missing anything very important. Newspaper stories are deliberately set up this way so busy readers can skim the first few paragraphs and move on, reading in their entirety only those stories that particularly interest them. Newsletter stories should also follow that pattern of development.

On the other hand, in newsletters, it's appropriate to "name names" right away because anyone mentioned will be known to the in-house readership. Besides, in company journalism, the person's identity is usually the point of the story. For this reason, names are often used, even in headlines.

This brings us to another specialized area unique to journalism: headlines. Much like the subject line of a memo or e-mail, the headline is crucial because it serves to orient the reader, providing a clear sense of what's in the story. In fact, the headline is simply a condensation of the lead. Created in the mid-nineteenth century to highlight Civil War news, headlines allow busy readers to exercise selectivity, picking and choosing what to read and what to ignore.

It's sometimes said that good headlines have something in common with poetry. That's not as far-fetched as it seems; headline writing is an art and, like any specialized skill, can be mastered only through practice. But certain rules are helpful:

- Use all capital letters. Although a mix of uppercase and lowercase letters takes less space, an all-caps approach is better because it allows the writer to avoid wrestling with tricky decisions about when and what to capitalize.

- Use *sans serif* type. Simply put, *serif* type has little lines at the tops and/or bottoms of the letters, like most of the type in this book; *sans serif* type does not (*sans* is the French word for "without"), and its use helps reinforce the separation between head and story.

Serif: **A**   Sans Serif: **A**

- Leave out all articles (a, an, the) and unnecessary words. For example:

WRONG: **THE THIRD QUARTER SALES FIGURES ARE IMPRESSIVE**

RIGHT: **THIRD QUARTER SALES IMPRESSIVE**

- Never use past tense. For example:

SALES IMPROVE rather than **SALES IMPROVED**

- Use active rather than passive verbs. For one thing, the active approach requires fewer words, as in this example:

CAT CHASES RAT (three words) vs. **RAT CHASED BY CAT** (four words)

Use passive only for good reason. For example, the passive head shown above might be preferable in a newsletter intended to be read by rats rather than cats.

- Now here's the trickiest headline rule of all: Try not to create awkward and unnatural line breaks in a multiline head. As far as possible, try to keep related words together. For example:

QUICK BROWN FOX
JUMPS OVER
LAZY DOG

is much better than:

QUICK BROWN
FOX JUMPS
OVER LAZY DOG

- Always use the shortest word, provided it's well-known. There exists a whole specialized vocabulary of words rarely used except in headlines. For example, nobody would ever say, "Hey, the Yanks topped the Bosox last night," yet that's exactly what the head might say:

YANKS TOP BOSOX

- Leave out most punctuation. Use only commas, apostrophes, and single quotation marks (which require less space than double quotation marks). Even periods are unnecessary. The colon, however, can substitute for "says," and the comma can substitute for the word "and," as in this example:

SALES MANAGER: LATEST NUMBERS 'SURPRISING, GREAT'

On a related note, let's consider photo captions. There are really only two rules. First, no photo or other illustration should appear without a brief caption *beneath* it. Second, the caption should be written in conventional English, not in the compressed style appropriate for headlines.

Checklist
Evaluating a Newsletter

A good newsletter

___ provides the company name and location along with the newsletter's name and publication date;

___ observes the principles of good layout design, presenting stories in column format with frequent paragraph breaks;

___ uses no more than three readily legible typefaces;

___ includes photos or other visuals, with captions, on every page;

___ has clear, concise headlines that reflect the stories' content;

___ is written in journalistic style, with a sharp lead and reverse order of importance in each story;

___ includes appropriate categories of information;

___ maintains strict standards of accuracy;

___ contains no typos or mechanical errors in spelling, capitalization, punctuation, or grammar.

HEALTHCO NEWS

Newsletter of HealthCo, Inc., Stratford, NY
Providing Medical Supplies Since 1960
Vol. 51, No. 1   Spring 2015

SALES TOP PROJECTIONS, STOCK VALUE DOUBLES

xxxxxxxxxxxxxxxxxxxxx
xxxxxxxxxxxxxxxxxxxxx
xxxxxxxxxxxxxxxxxxxxx
xxxxxxxxxxxxxxxxxxxxx
xxxxxxxxxxxxxxxxxxxxx
xxxxxxxxx

xxxxxxxxxxxxxxxxxxxxx
xxxxxxxxxxxxxxxxxxxxx
xxxxxxxxxxxxxxxxxxxxx
xxxxxxxxxxxxxxxxxxxxx
xxxxxxxxxxxxx

xxxxxxxxxxxxxxxxxxxxx
xxxxxxxxxxxxxxxxxxxxx
xxxxxxxxxxxxxxxxxxxxx
xxxxxxxxxxxxxxxxxxxxx
xxxxxxxxx

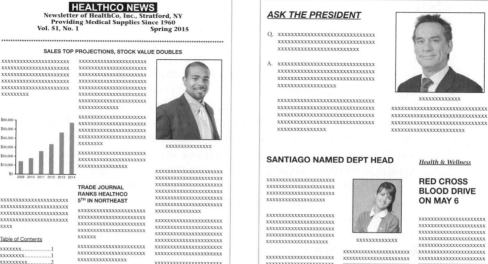

xxxxxxxxxxxxxx

TRADE JOURNAL RANKS HEALTHCO 5TH IN NORTHEAST

xxxxxxxxxxxxxxxxxxxxxx
xxxxxxxxxxxxxxxxxxxxxx
xxxxxxxxxxxxxxxxxxxxxx
xxxxxxxxxxxxxxxxxxxxxx
xxxx

xxxxxxxxxxxxxxxxxxxxx
xxxxxxxxxxxxxxxxxxxxx
xxxxxxxxxxxxxxxxxxxxx
xxxxxx

xxxxxxxxxxxxxxxxxxxxx
xxxxxxxxxxxxxxxxxxxxx
xxxxxxxxxxxxxxxxx

xxxxxxxxxxxxxxxxxxxxx
xxxxxxxxxxxxxxxxxxxxx
xxxxxxxxxxxxxxxxxxxxx
xxxxxxxxxxxxx

xxxxxxxxxxxxxxxxxxxxxxx
xxxxxxxxxxxxxxxxxxxxxxx
xxxxxxxxxxxxxxxxxxxxxxx
xxxxxxxxxxxxxxxxxxxxxxx
xxxxxxxxxxxxxxxxxxxxxxx
xxxxxxxxxxxxxxxxx

xxxxxxxxxxxxxxxxxxxxxxx
xxxxxxxxxxxxxxxxxxxxxxx
xxxxxxxxxxxxxxxxxxxxxxx
xxxxxxxxxxxxxxxxxxxxxxx
xxxxxxxxxxxxxxxxxxxxxxx
xxxxxxxxxxxxxxxxxxxxxxx

xxxxxxxxxxxxxxxxxxxxxxx
xxxxxxxxxxxxxxxxxxxxxxx
xxxxxxxxxxxxxxxxxxxxxxx
xxxxxxxxxxxxxxxxxxxxxxx
xxxxxxxxxxxxxxxxxxxxxxx
xxxxxxxxxxxxxxx

ASK THE PRESIDENT

Q. xxxxxxxxxxxxxxxxxxxxxxxxxxxxx
xxxxxxxxxxxxxxxxxxxxxxxxxxxxx
xxxxxxxxxxxxxxxxxxxxxxxx

A. xxxxxxxxxxxxxxxxxxxxxxxxxxxxx
xxxxxxxxxxxxxxxxxxxxxxxxxxxxx
xxxxxxxxxxxxxxxxxxxxxxxxxxxxx
xxxxxxxxxxxxxxxxxx

xxxxxxxxxxxxxxxxxxxxxxxxxxxxx
xxxxxxxxxxxxxxxxxxxxxxxxxxxxx
xxxxxxxxxxxxxxxxxxxxxxxxxxxxx
xxxxxxxxxxxxxxxxxxxxxxxxxxxxx
xxxxxxxxxxxxxxxxx

xxxxxxxxxxxxxx

xxxxxxxxxxxxxxxxxxxxxxxxxxx
xxxxxxxxxxxxxxxxxxxxxxxxxxx
xxxxxxxxxxxxxxxxxxxxxxxxxxx
xxxxxxxxxxxxxxxxxxxxxxx

SANTIAGO NAMED DEPT HEAD

Health & Wellness

xxxxxxxxxxxxxxxxxxxxxxx
xxxxxxxxxxxxxxxxxxxxxxx
xxxxxxxxxxxxxxxxxxxxxxx
xxxxxxxxxxxxxxxxxxxxx

RED CROSS BLOOD DRIVE ON MAY 6

xxxxxxxxxxxxxxxxxxxxx
xxxxxxxxxxxxxxxxxxxxx
xxxxxxxxxxxxxxxxxxxxx
xxxxxxxxxxxxxxxxxxxxx
xxxxxxxxxxxxxxxxxxxxx

xxxxxxxxxxxxxx

xxxxxxxxxxxxxxxxxxxxxxx
xxxxxxxxxxxxxxxxxxxxxxx
xxxxxxxxxxxxxxxxxxxxxxx
xxxxxxxxxxxxxxxxxxxxxxx

xxxxxxxxxxxxxxxxxxxxxxx
xxxxxxxxxxxxxxxxxxxxxxx
xxxxxxxxxxxxxxxxxxxxxxx
xxxxxxxxxxxxxxxxxxxxx

xxxxxxxxxxxxxxxxxxxxxxx
xxxxxxxxxxxxxxxxxxxxxxx
xxxxxxxxxxxxxxxxxxxxxxx
xxxxxxxxxxxxxxxxxxxxx

SPORTS UPDATE

xxxxxxxxxxxxxxxxxxxxxxxxxx

HOOP SQUAD WINS CITY REC LEAGUE TITLE

xxxxxxxxxxxxxxxxxxxxxxxxxxxxxxxxxx
xxxxxxxxxxxxxxxxxxxxxxxxxxxxxxxxxx
xxxxxxxxxxxxxxxxxxxxxxxxxxxxxxxxxx
xxxxxxxxxxxxxxx

xxxxxxxxxxxxxxxxxxxxxxxxxxxxxxxxxx
xxxxxxxxxxxxxxxxxxxxxxxxxxxxxxxxxx
xxxxxxxxxxxxxxxxxxxxxxxxxxxxxxxxxx
xxxxxxxxxxxxxxxxxxxxxxxxxxxxxxxxxx

xxxxxxxxxxxxxxxxxxxxxxxxxxxxxxxxxxxx
xxxxxxxxxxxxxxxxxxxxxxxxxxxxxxxxxxxx
xxxxxxxxxxxxxxxxxxxxxxxxxxxxxxxxx
xxxxxxxxxxxxxxxxxxxxxxxxxxxxx

xxxxxxxxxxxxxxxxxxxxxxxxxxxxxxxxxxxx
xxxxxxxxxxxxxxxxxxxxxxxxxxxxxxxxxxxx
xxxxxxxxxxxxxxxxxxxxxxxxxxxxxxxxxxxx
xxxxxxxxxxxxxxxxxxxxxxxxxxxxxxxxxxxx
xxxxxxxxxxxxxxxxxxxxxxxxxxxxxxxx

JASTREBSKI BOWLS 300 GAME

xxxxxxxxxxxxxxxxxxxxxxxxxxxxxxxxxx
xxxxxxxxxxxxxxxxxxxxxxxxxxxxxxxxxx
xxxxxxxxxxxxxxxxxxxxxxxxxxxxxxxxxx
xxxxxxxxxxxxxxxxxxxxxxxxxxxxxxxxxx
xxxxxxxxxxxxxxxxxxxxxxxxxxxxxxxxxx
xxxxxxxxxxxxxxxxxxxxxxxxxxxxxxxxxx
xxxxxxxxxxxxxxxxxxxxxxxxxxxxxxxxxx
xxxxxxxxxxxxxxxxxxxxxxxxxxxxxxxxxx

LEE RUNS BOSTON MARATHON

xxxxxxxxxxxxxxxxxxxxxxxxxxxxxxxxxx
xxxxxxxxxxxxxxxxxxxxxxxxxxxxxxxxxx
xxxxxxxxxxxxxxxxxxxxxxxxxxxxxxxxxx
xxxxxxxxxxxxxxxxxxxxxxxxxxxxxxxxxx
xxxxxxxxxxxxxxxxxxxxxxxxxxxxxxxxxx
xxxxxxxxxxxxxxxxxxxxxxxxxxxxxxxxxx

EMPLOYEE OF THE YEAR

SHANIQUA JAMES

xxxxxxxxxxxxxxxxxxxxxxxxxxxxxxxx
xxxxxxxxxxxxxxxxxxxxxxxxxxxxxxxx
xxxxxxxxxxxxxxxxxxxxxxxxxxxxxxxx
xxxxxxxxxxxxxxxxxxxxxxxxxxxxxxxx
xxxxxxxxxxxxxxxxxxxxxxxxxxxxx

xxxxxxxxxxxxxxxxxxxxxxxxxxxxxxxx
xxxxxxxxxxxxxxxxxxxxxxxxxxxxxxxx
xxxxxxxxxxxxxxxxxxxxxxxxxxxxxxxx
xxxxxxxxxxxxxxxxxxxxxxxxxxxxxxxx
xxxxxxxxxxxxxxxxxxxxxxxxxxxxxxxx

xxxxxxxxxxxxxx

xxxxxxxxxxxxxxxxxxxxxxxxxxxxxx
xxxxxxxxxxxxxxxxxxxxxxxxxxxxxx
xxxxxxxxxxxxxxxxxxxxxxxxxxxxxx
xxxxxxxxxxxxxxxxxxxxxxxxxxxxxx
xxxxxxxxxxxxxxxxxxxxxxxxxxxxxx
xxxxxxxxxxxxxxxxxxxxxxxxxxxxxx
xxxxxxxxxxxxxxxxxxxxxxxxxx

xxxxxxxxxxxxxxxxxxxxxxxxxxxxxxxxx
xxxxxxxxxxxxxxxxxxxxxxxxxxxxxxxxx
xxxxxxxxxxxxxxxxxxxxxxxxxxxxxxxxx
xxxxxxxxxxxxxxxxxxxxxxxxxxxxxxxxx
xxxxxxxxxxxxxxxxxxxxxxxxxxxxxxxxx
xxxxxxxxxxxxxxxxxxxxxxxxxxxxxxxxx

HealthCo, Inc.
1101 Goodman Ave.
Stratford, NY 13501

FIGURE 6.3 • Newsletter

Web Sites

Virtually every successful business, agency, or other organization maintains an Internet presence to create visibility and provide information to current or prospective clients or customers. This is accomplished through a variety of media, including Facebook pages, Twitter sites, and blogs. By far the most common such vehicle, however, is the Web site. Practically cost-free compared to traditional forms of advertising, a good Web site conveys a positive image and an aura of polished professionalism, thereby creating greater consumer confidence and increased market share. Indeed, a well-designed, continuously updated Web site is essential for credibility—and survival—in today's electronically oriented environment.

But Web site design is a complex matter. Therefore, most sites are created not by individuals but by teams of coworkers collectively competent in a range of highly specialized fields. Among these are graphic design, advertising, marketing, computer science, and writing. To ensure accuracy and sufficient breadth of content, the members of every such team must not only collaborate effectively among themselves but also solicit, secure, and process input from all other sectors of their workplace.

Given the rather compressed nature of this book, the more technical aspects of Web site construction are beyond its scope. However, there's something to be said here about Web site *writing*. Of course, all writing is governed by certain basic principles that almost never change. But how those principles are applied does change depending on the writing situation. As we have already seen, different genres of writing—memo, e-mail, business letter, report, and so on—require somewhat different approaches. Web site content is yet another genre. As such, it's governed by certain principles specific to the unique manner of its delivery.

Ordinarily, we read sequentially, in linear progression. We start at the upper left part of the page or screen and read from there, left to right, top to bottom, until we reach the end. Not so with a Web site, which we skim and scan, jumping from one topic to another, one page to another, not necessarily in any particular order. The very design of a Web site enables—indeed, encourages—such an approach. In addition, Web sites are accessed not only by desktop computers but also by various portable devices including smartphones, laptops, and tablets, all with varying screen sizes. Accordingly, a system called *Responsive Web Design* has been developed. The browser recognizes the screen size of the device calling up the site and displays content in the layout most appropriate for that screen. The result is a mobile-friendly site that's equally content-rich in all configurations.

Figure 6.4 depicts the home page of Mohawk Valley Community College, as configured for viewing on a desktop computer. "Buttons" at the top of the screen enable visitors to navigate the site spatially. Each is geared to the needs of a particular category of visitor: Future Students, Current Students, Faculty & Staff, Alumni & Friends, Community & Business. After the visitor clicks on one of these, a navigation bar on the left side of the screen provides hyperlinks to various nodes within the site. Both the buttons and the navigation bar function rather like headlines in a newspaper, allowing site visitors to be selective in choosing what to read. But the similarity to print journalism ends there. Whereas most newspaper stories are structured in compliance with one uniform formula, information on a Web site can be presented in many different

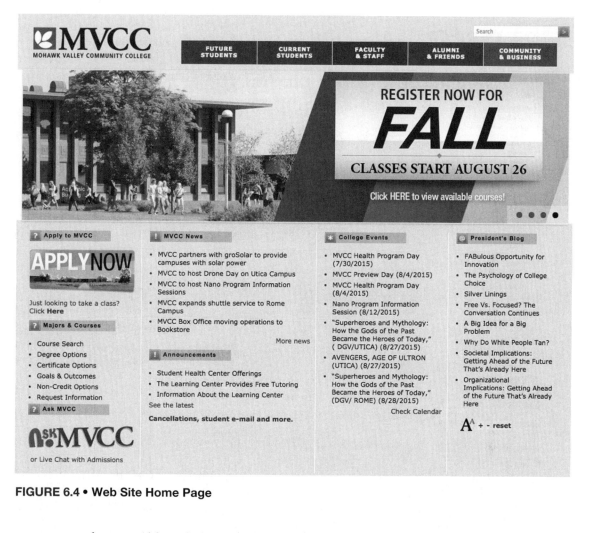

FIGURE 6.4 • Web Site Home Page

formats. Although the overall page design of the various nodes is usually fairly consistent, the design of the links within each node can vary greatly. This is not surprising because different kinds of information require different kinds of presentation.

As Figure 6.5 illustrates, the Current Students page provides links to a range of topics, and each is structured in a manner consistent with its content. "About MVCC," for example, brings the site visitor to a page of conventional narrative prose describing the history and mission of the institution, followed by nine additional links. However, a click on "Academics" brings the visitor directly to a long menu of subheadings, each with its own distinct personality. The second of these, "Academic Calendar," is simply a link to several four-column PDF files highlighting significant dates and deadlines during the current and future semesters. By contrast, a click on the navigation bar's "Athletics" node leads to the Physical Education Department's own colorfully elaborate home page, replete with schedules, scores, write-ups, action photos, and even a further link to an "apparel" page.

FIGURE 6.5 • "Current Students" page with Pull-Down Menu

Clearly, writing Web site content can be challenging. But adherence to certain basic principles—some of which have already been mentioned in this text—make it more manageable.

- Keep purpose and audience foremost in mind when composing *every page*; these considerations may change from link to link.

- Organize the content sensibly, with first things first, second things second, and so on, sequencing information in the most logical order.

- Use bulleted lists.

- Provide concrete, specific details to fully convey the information required by the visitor to the site.

- But don't overdo it. Repeating yourself or overloading the screen with unnecessary clutter may cause the reader to lose interest and jump to a different link or abandon the site altogether.

- Say precisely what you mean. Always choose the exact right word, rather than one that means something a bit different from—or opposite to—the one you intend.

- Avoid clichés, metaphors, slang, and figures of speech. These are often generation- or culture-specific and may not be understood by all visitors to the site.

- Stick to simple, plainspoken language, using short sentences and familiar, everyday vocabulary your reader can process with minimum effort—nothing elaborate or fancy.

- Carefully proofread to ensure mechanical correctness.

Perhaps the most overriding principle when writing for a Web site is to strive for compression. In most situations, information should be chunked into short segments—no more than two or three sentences or phrases at a time. If there's a need for in-depth discussion, that kind of coverage should be accessed via links to downloadable sources of such information.

Checklist
Evaluating a Web Site

A good Web site

____ clearly identifies the sponsor of the site, and provides full contact information;

____ includes all appropriate content categories, each plainly labeled;

____ makes effective use of white space, headings, and other design features to create an uncluttered, welcoming layout on the screen;

____ Uses complementary colors that highlight rather than obscure content;

____ reinforces content by achieving a visually pleasing interplay between text and images;

____ maintains consistent design from page to page within the site;

____ provides a home page link on every page within the site;

____ does not make the reader scroll too much; limits each page to no more than 1½ screens, except for pages configured for viewing on the smaller screens of mobile devices;

____ maintains strict standards of up-to-date accuracy;

____ contains no typos or mechanical errors in spelling, capitalization, punctuation, or grammar.

EXERCISES

EXERCISE 6.1

Create a flier advertising a business for which you have worked in the past or are working for now.

EXERCISE 6.2

Create a flier advertising a business of your own, either real or imaginary (e.g., snow removal, appliance repair, computer troubleshooting, babysitting).

EXERCISE 6.3

Create a flier announcing an upcoming event, such as a concert, party, or contest. Again, this can be real or imaginary.

EXERCISE 6.4

Create a flier advertising the Workplace Communications course in which you are currently enrolled.

EXERCISE 6.5

Expand the flier created in response to Exercise 6.1 to a brochure.

EXERCISE 6.6

Expand the flier created in response to Exercise 6.2 to a brochure.

EXERCISE 6.7

Expand the flier created in response to Exercise 6.3 to a brochure.

EXERCISE 6.8

Expand the flier created in response to Exercise 6.4 to a brochure.

EXERCISE 6.9

Go online and access the newsletter of a local business, agency, or organization. Referring to the "Evaluating a Newsletter" checklist on pg. 106, write a memo report in which you evaluate the newsletter.

EXERCISE 6.10

Go online and access the Web site of a local business, agency, or organization. Referring to the "Evaluating a Web Site" checklist on pg. 111, write a memo report in which you evaluate the site.

Instructions
and Procedure
Descriptions

7

LEARNING OBJECTIVES

When you complete this chapter you'll be able to:

- write both general and specific instructions.
- create helpful trouble-shooting guidelines.
- write accurate, informative procedure descriptions.
- maintain parallel structure to facilitate understanding.
- provide timely hazard alerts to protect readers and avoid liability.

Instructions and procedure descriptions serve a wide variety of functions. You might write instructions for coworkers to enable them to install, operate, maintain, or repair a piece of equipment or to follow established policies such as those explained in employee handbooks. You might also write instructions for customers or clients to enable them to assemble, use, or maintain a product (as in owner's manuals, for example) or to follow mandated guidelines. As in procedure description writing, the broad purpose of instructions is to inform. However, the more specific purpose is to enable the reader to *perform* a particular procedure rather than simply understand it.

Clearly, instructions must be closely geared to the needs of the intended reader. The level of specificity will vary greatly, depending on the procedure's complexity and context and the reader's level of expertise or preparation. For example, computer documentation intended for a professional programmer is very different from documentation written for someone with little experience in such matters. In addition, it's important to remember that in the global economy your reader may not be a native speaker of English. Therefore, just as when writing for Web sites, you must exercise great care to avoid expressions that may not be readily understood by readers from other cultures. Obviously, audience analysis is crucial to writing effective instructions and procedure descriptions.

Instructions

Just as there are different kinds of summaries, there are also different kinds of instructions: general and specific. *General instructions* explain how to perform a generic procedure—trimming a hedge, for example—and can be adapted to individual situations. *Specific instructions* explain how to perform a procedure under conditions involving particular equipment, surroundings, or other such variables—operating a 22-inch Craftsman Bushwacker electric hedge trimmer, for instance.

Like other kinds of workplace writing, instructions appear in diverse contexts, from brief notes—such as the reminder that "Employees must wash hands before returning to work" that appears in many restaurant bathrooms—to lengthy manuals and handbooks. However, regardless of context, most instruction writing follows a basic format resembling that of a recipe in a cookbook. This format includes the following features:

- Brief introduction explaining the purpose and importance of the procedure. *Note:* An estimate of how much time is required to complete the procedure may be included, as well as any unusual circumstances that the reader must keep in mind throughout the procedure, such as safety considerations.
- Lists of materials, equipment, tools, and skills required, enabling the reader to perform the procedure uninterrupted.
- Actual instructions: a numbered, step-by-step, detailed explanation of how to perform the procedure.
- In most cases, one or more visuals for clarification.

Although they *look* very easy, instructions are actually among the most difficult kinds of writing to compose. The slightest error or lapse in clarity can badly mislead—or even endanger—the reader. Instructions should always be read in their entirety before the reader attempts the task. However, many readers read the instructions a bit at a time, on the fly, while already performing the procedure. This puts an even greater burden on the writer to achieve standards of absolute precision and clarity.

The best approach is to use short, simple commands that start with verbs and are arranged in a numbered list. This enables the reader to follow the directions without confusion and also fosters consistent, action-focused wording, as in this example:

1. Push the red "On" button.
2. Insert the green plug into the left outlet.
3. Push the blue "Direction" lever to the right.

Notice that instructions are not expressed in "recipe shorthand." Small words such as *a*, *an*, and *the*, which would be omitted in a recipe, are included in instructions.

Although it's usually best to limit each command to one action, sometimes closely related steps can be combined to prevent the list from becoming unwieldy. Consider the following example:

1. Hold the bottle in your left hand.
2. Twist off the cap with your right hand.

These steps should probably be combined as follows:

1. Holding the bottle in your left hand, twist off the cap with your right hand.

When a procedure is very complicated, requiring a long list, a good strategy is to use subdivisions under major headings, like this:

1. Prepare the solution:
    a. Pour two drops of the red liquid into the vial.
    b. Pour one drop of the blue liquid into the vial.
    c. Pour three drops of the green liquid into the vial.
    d. Cap the vial.
    e. Shake the vial vigorously for 10 seconds.
2. Pour the solution into a beaker.
3. Heat the beaker until bubbles form on the surface of the solution.

However, if two actions *must* be performed simultaneously, present them together. For example, do not write something like this:

1. Push the blue lever forward.
2. Before releasing the blue lever, push the red button twice.
3. Release the blue lever.

Instead, write this:

1. While holding the blue lever in the forward position, push the red button twice.
2. Release the blue lever.

Frequently, the conclusion to a set of instructions takes the form of a trouble-shooting section, in which possible causes of difficulty are identified, along with remedies. This example is from a bank's instructions on how to balance a checkbook:

> Subtract Line 4 from Line 3. This should be your present register balance. If not, the most common mistakes are either an error in arithmetic or a service charge not listed in your register. If you need further assistance, please bring this statement to your banking office.

Sometimes, the troubleshooting guide is in the form of a three-column "fault table" like the one in Figure 7.1, which appeared in an automobile owner's manual.

Another helpful feature of good instructions is effective visuals. Photographs, line drawings (especially cutaway and exploded views), and flow charts can clarify concepts that might otherwise be difficult to understand. However, as explained in

Symptom	Probable Cause	Solution
Starter motor won't work	1. Loose connections 2. Weak battery 3. Worn-out motor	1. Tighten connections 2. Charge battery 3. Replace motor
Starter motor works but engine won't start	1. Wrong starting procedure 2. Flooded engine 3. No fuel 4. Blown fuse 5. Ignition defect, fuel-line blockage	1. Correct procedure 2. Wait awhile 3. Refuel 4. Replace fuse 5. Contact dealer
Rough idle, stalling	1. Ignition defect, fuel-line blockage	1. Contact dealer

FIGURE 7.1 • Fault Table

Chapter 3, you must choose the right type of visual for each situation, and this is certainly true with respect to writing instructions. Different kinds of instructions are best illustrated by different kinds of visuals. For example, a precise operation involving the manipulation of small parts may be best rendered by a close-up photograph or line drawing of someone's hands performing the operation. On the other hand, instructions emphasizing the correct sequence of the steps in a less delicate task may be best illustrated by a conventional flow chart.

Increasingly, instructions designed to accompany products feature visuals alone or with minimal text. The principal reason for this development is that manufacturers wish to target the broadest possible market by accommodating consumers from various countries and cultures. This trend is likely to grow as we move ever closer to a fully global economy.

A good way to determine the effectiveness of a set of instructions you have created—whether with text and visuals or with visuals alone—is to field-test them by observing while someone unfamiliar with the procedure attempts to perform it using your directions. For the test to be valid, however, you must resist the temptation to provide verbal assistance if the person expresses uncertainty. This will enable you to detect any unclear sections within the instructions and to determine the cause of the confusion. Another effective test is to ask someone who *is* familiar with the procedure to critique your instructions. Even better, subject your instructions to both forms of evaluation.

Figure 7.2 and Figure 7.3 illustrate the two main types of instructions: general and specific. Figure 7.2 explains how to perform a very basic workplace procedure: preparing a business letter. Figure 7.3, adapted from an owner's manual, relates to a specific product: a two-burner electric range. Note the hazard alert in that document.

HOW TO COMPLETE A BUSINESS LETTER

The business letter is an essential form of written workplace communication. To ensure that a letter is as professional as possible, the writer must not only be familiar with standard letter-writing principles (the three-part structure, for example) but should also follow these fundamental guidelines:

1. Type the letter in full block format.

2. Proofread the letter before printing.

3. Make corrections if necessary.

4. Print the letter on workplace letterhead.

5. Proofread the hard copy.

6. Make corrections if necessary.

7. Print again if necessary.

8. Save the letter to the appropriate folder.

9. Sign the letter.

10. Insert the letter in an envelope, folded as shown.

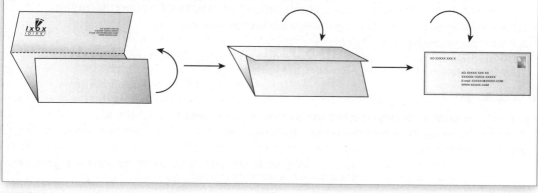

FIGURE 7.2 • General Instructions

INSTRUCTIONS
TWO-BURNER ELECTRIC RANGE

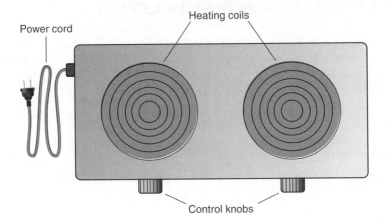

Before Using Range

1. Read ALL of these instructions!
2. Remove your two-burner electric range from its box.
3. Discard all packaging materials; tear up the plastic bag, which can pose a safety risk to children.
4. Place the range on a firm, heat-resistant table or other completely flat surface within easy reach of a polarized electrical outlet.
5. Gently clean the heating coils with a damp sponge or soft cloth.

Choosing Cookware

1. Choose cookware made only of stainless steel, heat-proof glass, or heat-proof ceramic.
2. Choose cookware with FLAT bottoms only.
3. Choose cookware with a bottom diameter no more than one inch larger than the diameter of the heating coil.

Using Range

1. Plug in the range; do not use an extension cord.
    WARNING: TO ENSURE THAT THE RANGE REMAINS SAFELY IN PLACE, DO NOT ALLOW THE CORD TO DANGLE WITHIN REACH OF HOUSEHOLD PETS OR YOUNG CHILDREN!
2. Put the food in the cookware, following all recipe and food package instructions.
3. Place the cookware on the heating coils.
4. Use the control knobs to adjust the temperature of the heating coils. Turn the knobs clockwise to raise the temperature, counter-clockwise to lower the temperature.

After Using Range

1. Turn the range off by rotating the control knobs fully counter-clockwise.
2. Using pot holders, remove the cookware from the heating coils.
3. Unplug the range.
4. Wait until the heating coils are completely cool before cleaning the range. Do not use abrasive cleaners or scouring pads and do not submerge the stove in water or other liquid.

FIGURE 7.3 • Specific Instructions

Procedure Descriptions

Although closely related, a procedure description differs sharply from instructions because it enables the reader to understand a procedure but not necessarily to perform it. The purpose of a procedure description is simply to inform. Accordingly, it usually includes the following features:

- Brief introduction explaining the nature, purpose, and importance of the procedure.

- List of materials, tools, and other equipment that might be needed.

- Stage-by-stage explanation of how the procedure occurs, with all necessary details; transitions are helpful here.

- One or more visuals for purposes of clarification; flow charts are often useful in this context (see Chapter 3).

- Brief conclusion.

As in other kinds of workplace writing, use *parallel structure* when phrasing the stage-by-stage explanation. For example, don't say:

1. Customer drops off the clothing.
2. Clothing is sorted and marked.
3. Clothes you want washed go to washing machines, and clothes to be dry-cleaned go to dry-cleaning machines.

Instead, be consistent by phrasing the description as follows:

1. Clothing is dropped off.
2. Clothing is sorted and marked.
3. Clothing to be washed is sent to washing machines, and clothing to be dry-cleaned is sent to dry-cleaning machines.

The revision is better because the emphasis is now on the same word ("clothing") in each of the three stages, and the verbs are now all passive. Because the focus in this kind of description is on the procedure itself rather than on a human agent, this is one of the few situations in which passive verbs rather than commands or other active constructions are preferable.

As with so many kinds of workplace communication, the level of detail and technicality in procedure descriptions depends on the needs and background of the audience. In any case, the sequential, cause-and-effect, action-and-reaction nature of the information must be conveyed clearly to ensure the reader's understanding. For example, don't say:

1. X happens.
2. Y happens.
3. Z happens.

Instead, use transitions to reveal the relationships among the stages of the process or procedure, like this:

1. X happens.
2. Meanwhile, Y happens.
3. As a result, Z happens.

Avoiding Liability

Remember that what may seem obvious to you is not necessarily apparent to the reader. Include all information, and provide the reason for each step if the reason is important to enhance performance or prevent error. Sometimes this is best done as a note, as in this example:

- **Note:** Lubricate the axle now because it will be much more difficult to reach after the housing is in place.

Often, as in the preceding example, the reason for doing something a certain way is simply to avoid inconvenience. But if a serious hazard exists, you must alert the reader by using LARGE PRINT, underlining, **boldface,** or some other attention get-ter *before* the danger point is reached. By law, any such alert must identify the hazard, specify the consequences of ignoring it, and explain how to avoid it. Although there's some variation in the use of these terms, there are basically three levels of hazard alerts:

- **Caution:** Alerts the reader to the risk of equipment failure or damage, as in this example:

  CAUTION: The cutter blades are not designed to cut metal. To prevent damage to the blades, never put tools or other metal objects on the conveyor belt.

- **Warning:** Alerts the reader to the possibility of equipment damage, serious injury, or death, as in this example:

  WARNING: The drill press bit can shred your fingers. To avoid injury, keep your hands far away from the bit.

- **Danger:** Alerts the reader to the probability of serious injury or death, as in this example:

  DANGER: This machine is powered by high-voltage electricity. To avoid death by electrocution, turn the power off before removing the cover plate.

Hazard alerts are commonly accompanied by attention-getting icons like the one in Figure 7.4, which represents the danger of electrical shock. These are often displayed in red for added impact.

Hazard alerts are now more important than ever, not only to avoid malfunc-tion and physical danger but also to minimize legal liability in case of a mishap. The

FIGURE 7.4 • Hazard Icon

number of product liability lawsuits has skyrocketed in recent years, with the majority of suits alleging not that the products themselves are defective but that manufacturers have failed to provide sufficient warnings about dangers inherent to their use. As a result, even obvious precautions must be spelled out in very explicit terms. For example, McDonald's coffee cups now include a warning that the beverage is hot. This is in response to losing $2.7 million in a lawsuit brought by a customer who had been scalded by a spill. Another recent example is the superhero costume that actually carried the following message on its packaging:

> FOR PLAY ONLY: Mask and chest plates are not protective; cape does not enable user to fly.

Of course, these are extreme cases. But they underscore the importance of providing ample warning in your instructions about any potential hazard. Similarly, if malfunction can occur at any point, you should explain corrective measures, as in these examples:

- If the belt slips off the drive wheel, disengage the clutch.
- If any of the solution splashes into the eyes or onto exposed skin, wash immediately with cold water.
- If the motor begins to whine, immediately turn off the power.

Checklist
Evaluating Instructions and Procedure Descriptions

Good instructional writing or procedure description

___ opens with a brief introduction that identifies the procedure and explains its function;

___ lists the materials, equipment, tools, and skills required to perform the procedure;

___ provides a well-organized, step-by-step explanation of how to perform the procedure;

___ provides any appropriate warnings, cautions, or notes to enable the reader to perform the procedure without unnecessary risk;

___ is clear, accurate, and sufficiently detailed to enable the reader to understand and/or perform the procedure without unnecessary difficulty;

___ uses helpful comparisons and analogies to clarify difficult concepts;

___ uses clear, simple language;

___ concludes with a brief summary with troubleshooting guidelines;

___ integrates effective visuals (photographs and line drawings—exploded and/or cutaway views) to clarify the text;

___ contains no typos or mechanical errors in spelling, capitalization, punctuation, or grammar.

EXERCISES

EXERCISE 7.1

As discussed in the text and mentioned on the checklist, written instructions should open with a brief introduction that identifies the procedure and explains its purpose. Write such introductions for three of the following procedures:

- Creating a new file in Microsoft Word
- Creating a playlist on an MP3 player
- Measuring a person's blood pressure
- Programming a digital wristwatch
- Hemming a pair of pants

EXERCISE 7.2

Write instructions (and include visuals) explaining how to perform a common procedure related to your field of study or employment—for example, welding a lap joint, administering a bed bath, or restraining a potentially troublesome person.

EXERCISE 7.3

Write a description of a process related to your field of study or employment—for example, interviewing, stock rotation, or safety check.

EXERCISE 7.4

Write instructions (and include visuals) explaining how to perform a common outdoor household chore—for example, mowing a lawn, sealing a blacktop driveway, or installing a rain gutter.

EXERCISE 7.5

Write a description of a procedure that occurs in the world of sports—for example, the annual National Basketball Association (NBA) draft, the way in which points are awarded in diving competitions, or the way the starting line is organized at the Boston or New York Marathon.

EXERCISE 7.6

Write instructions (and include visuals) explaining how to perform a common procedure related to automobile maintenance and repair—for example, changing the engine oil and filter, using jumper cables, or washing and cleaning a vehicle.

EXERCISE 7.7

Write instructions (and include a map) explaining how to travel from your home to your college.

EXERCISE 7.8

Write instructions (and include visuals) explaining how to perform one of these procedures:

- Cooking a favorite meal
- Laying track on a model railroad
- Building a doghouse
- Changing a baby's diaper
- Waterproofing a pair of work boots

EXERCISE 7.9

Although you may be inclined to use them when writing instructions, common clichés like the following may be puzzling to non-native speakers of English. Replace them with more literal expressions.

- At the end of the day _____

- Back to the drawing board _____

- Believe it or not _____

- Be that as it may _____

- Bite off more than you can chew _____

- Don't count your chickens _____

- First and foremost _____

- Go around in circles _____

- Goes without saying _____

- Last but not least _____

EXERCISE 7.10

Team up with two classmates. One of you will focus on books, one on periodicals, and one on Web sites. Each of you must find three examples of visuals that illustrate instructions. Then, as a team, produce a booklet report that evaluates the accuracy and helpfulness of the visuals.

Job Application Process: On-Line Search, Letter, Résumé, Interview, and Follow-Up

8

LEARNING OBJECTIVES

When you complete this chapter you'll be able to:

- use the Web to network and locate employment opportunities.
- compose an effective application letter.
- craft an impressive résumé.
- interview successfully.
- produce a timely follow-up.

The employment outlook today is quite challenging, with many qualified applicants vying for every available position, and all indicators suggest that the competition will continue to get even tougher. Therefore, it's now more important than ever to understand fully the process of finding and applying for a job. Essentially, it involves five components: a productive search, an effective application letter, an impressive résumé, a strong interview, and a timely follow-up.

Some job announcements (especially in print media) provide only a phone number or an address, with no mention of a written response. In such cases you'll probably complete a "fill-in-the-blanks" questionnaire instead of submitting a letter and résumé. In general, however, these are not the most desirable positions. The better openings—those that pay more and offer greater opportunity for advancement—typically require you to respond in writing, either by mail or on-line. This enables employers to be more selective by automatically eliminating applicants who are unable or too unmotivated to compose a letter and résumé, or too unskilled with technology.

You must understand the basic principles governing a job search and the preparation of application correspondence. This chapter provides you with that information, along with guidance about how to interview and follow up successfully.

Job Search

Traditionally, job seekers would consult the classified section of a newspaper or perhaps enlist the assistance of a private or public employment agency. But the most successful candidates have always been those who could network productively, relying on word-of-mouth tips from associates, friends, and relatives. In short, it's always been helpful to "know somebody." Truthfully, though, there's something a bit unfair about this. For starters, people who are fortunate enough to occupy the upper rungs of society's ladder are far more likely to be acquainted with others who can provide this kind of assistance.

But now the game has changed. With the rise of the Internet, a more level playing field has emerged. While contacts are still a major factor, individuals who are savvy about social media can bring themselves to the attention of hiring managers much more easily than in the past. Indeed, it's beneficial to maintain an on-line presence on one or more of the professional networking sites regularly consulted by human resources offices seeking qualified employees. LinkedIn is the most prominent of these, enabling job seekers to create professional profiles, post their résumé, provide links to other credentials, and apply for advertised positions. In addition, personal sites such as Facebook are often used the same way now that there's less of a distinction between personal and professional sites. In short, networking is now done electronically, allowing us all to maintain up-to-the-minute contact with a vastly greater number of potentially helpful "friends" than before.

It's important to remember, however, that your on-line presence can easily become a liability rather than an asset if there's anything inappropriate on your Facebook or other Internet site. Employers routinely conduct Google searches for any job candidate they're seriously considering hiring. Clearly, it's important to ensure there's nothing objectionable to be found.

In addition, it's advisable to acquaint yourself with at least some of the many other employment-related Web sites. These too allow you to post your résumé and other links, but their main function is to enable you to inspect job announcements posted by employers. Most of these sites help you to focus efficiently, searching by job title, geographical location, company name, keyword(s), and other factors. The sites often feature company profiles, on-line job fairs and newsletters, links to other sites, résumé tutorials, and other kinds of career development advice. FlexJobs.com and some other sites even enable job seekers to verify their expertise by taking skills tests and posting the results. Here are ten more well-known sites:

Bestjobsusa.com	Job-hunt.org
CareerBuilder.com	Monster.com
Dice.com	SimplyHired.com
Idealist.com	SnagAJob.com
Indeed.com	usajobs.gov

Application Letter

It's important to understand that if employers require a written response, they do so in part to see a representative sample of your *best* work. Therefore, the physical appearance of your job application correspondence is crucially important. You may be well-qualified, but if your letter and résumé are sloppy, poorly formatted, or marred by mechanical errors, they'll probably be rejected immediately.

Prepared in full block format and three-part organization, a job application letter is no different from any other business letter (see Chapter 2). As such, it should be neatly printed on 8½-by-11″ white paper and should be framed by ample (1 to 1½″) margins. In nearly every case, the letter should be no longer than one page. The writer's address, the date, the reader's name and address, the salutation, and the complimentary close appear just as they would in any other letter, and all punctuation is included.

Ideally, the job posting—whether in print or on-line—will provide the name and title of the contact person, as in this example:

> **ELECTRICIAN:** Permanent, full-time. Associate's degree, experience preferred. Good salary, benefits. Cover letter and résumé to: Maria Castro, Director of Human Resources, Senior Citizens' Homestead, 666 Grand Blvd, Belford, CT 06100. Equal opp'ty employer.

Sometimes, however, the ad doesn't mention an individual's name but provides only a title—Human Resources Manager, for example—or simply the company's name. If so, you should phone the employer and explain that you're interested in applying for the job and would like to know the name and title of the contact person. Be sure to get the correct spelling and, unless the name plainly reveals gender, determine whether the individual is a man or a woman. This ensures that your letter will be among the only personalized ones received, thereby creating a more positive first impression. For various reasons, some ads reveal almost nothing—not even the name of the company—and provide only a box number or e-mail address. In such an instance, set up your letter without the inside address and use "Dear Employer" as your salutation. This is somewhat more original than such unimaginative greetings as the impersonal "To Whom It May Concern," the gender-biased "Dear Sir," and the old-fashioned "Dear Sir or Madam." Again, your letter will stand out from the others received, suggesting you're more resourceful than the other applicants.

In your opening paragraph, directly state your purpose: that you're applying for the job. Strangely, many applicants fail to do this. Wordy and ultimately pointless statements—for example, "I read with great interest your classified advertisement in my hometown newspaper, the *Daily Gazette*"—invite the reader to respond, "So? Do you *want* the job or what?" Instead, compose a one-sentence opening that comes right to the point: "As an experienced sales professional, I am applying for the retail position advertised in the *Daily Gazette*." This approach suggests that you're a confident, focused individual—and therefore a desirable applicant.

Always mention the job *title* because the employer may have advertised more than one. Also indicate how you learned of the opening. Most employers find this information helpful in monitoring the productivity of their various advertising efforts, and they appreciate the courtesy. However, if you learned of the opening by word of mouth, do *not* mention the name of the person who told you about it, even if you've been given permission to do so. The individual may not be well-regarded by the employer, and because you have no way of knowing this, you should not risk the possibility of an unfortunate association. In such a situation, use a sentence such as *"It has come to my attention that you have an opening for an electrician,* and I am applying for the job."

In the middle section, which can be anywhere from one to three paragraphs, provide a narrative summary of your experience, education, and other qualifications. Go into some depth, giving sufficient information to make the employer want to read your résumé, which you should refer to specifically. But avoid *excessive* detail. Dates, addresses, and other particulars belong in the résumé, not the letter. However, be sure to mention any noteworthy attributes—specialized licenses, security clearances, computer skills, foreign language fluency—that may set you apart from the competition. Do not pad the letter with vague claims that you can't document. "I have five years of continuous experience as a part-time security guard" scores a lot more points than "I am friendly, cooperative, and dependable." Never mention weaknesses, and always strive for the most upbeat phrasing you can devise. For example, "I'm currently unemployed" creates a negative impression; the more positive "I am available immediately" turns this circumstance to your advantage.

Of course, the purpose is to make the employer recognize your value as a prospective employee. Using the "you" approach explained in Chapter 1, gear your letter accordingly. Without indulging in exaggeration or arrogant self-congratulation, explain why it would be in the employer's best interests to hire you. Sometimes a direct, straightforward statement such as this can be quite persuasive: "With my college education now completed, I am very eager to begin my career in hospitality management and will bring a high level of enthusiasm and commitment to this position."

Your closing paragraph—no longer than two or three sentences—should briefly thank the employer for considering you and request an interview. Nobody has ever received a job offer on the strength of a letter alone. The letter leads to the résumé, the résumé (if you're lucky) secures an interview, and the interview (if you're *really* lucky) results in a job offer. By mentioning both the résumé and the interview in your letter, you indicate that you're a knowledgeable person familiar with conventions of the hiring process.

However, understand that even one mechanical error in your letter may be enough to knock you out of the running. You must make absolutely certain that there are no typos, spelling mistakes, faulty punctuation, or grammatical blunders—none whatsoever! Check and double-check to ensure that your letter (along with your résumé) is mechanically perfect.

Figure 8.1 is an effective hardcopy application letter in response to the classified ad for an electrician on page 127. Figure 8.2 depicts a transmittal e-mail accompanying the applicant's letter and résumé files.

32 Garfield Ave.
Belford, CT 06100
April 3, 2015

Ms. Maria Castro
Director of Human Resources
The Senior Citizens' Homestead
666 Grand Blvd.
Belford, CT 06100

Dear Ms. Castro:

Opening paragraph creates context, asks for the job.

As an experienced electrician about to graduate from County Community College with an AOS degree in electrical engineering technology, I am applying for the electrician position advertised in the *Daily Herald*.

Middle paragraph summarizes credentials.

In college I have maintained a 3.60 grade point average while serving as vice president of the Technology Club and treasurer of the Minority Students' Union. In keeping with my ongoing commitment to community service, last year I joined a group of volunteer workers renovating the Belford Youth Club. Under the supervision of a licensed electrician, I helped rewire the building and acquired a great deal of practical experience during the course of this project. The combination of my academic training and the hands-on knowledge gained at the Youth Club equips me to become a valued member of your staff. Past and current employers, listed on the enclosed résumé, will attest to my strong work ethic. I can provide those individuals' names and phone numbers upon request.

Closing paragraph thanks the reader, mentions interview.

Thank you very much for considering my application. I am hoping to visit the Senior Citizens' Homestead for an interview at your convenience.

Sincerely,

James Carter

James Carter
Enclosure: Résumé

FIGURE 8.1 • Application Letter

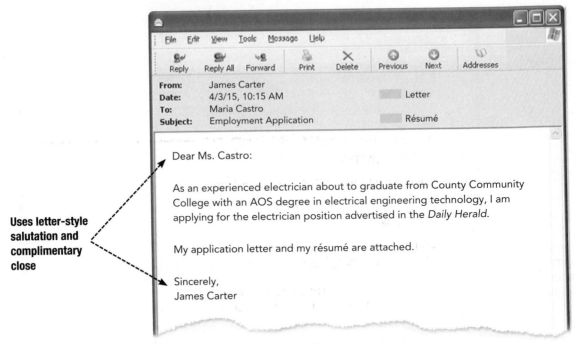

Uses letter-style salutation and complimentary close

FIGURE 8.2 • E-mail Application

Résumé

As Figure 8.3 illustrates, a résumé is basically a detailed list or outline of a job applicant's work history and other qualifications. The following categories of information typically appear:

- Contact Information
- Career Objective
- Education
- Work Experience
- Military Service
- Computer Literacy
- Specialized Skills or Credentials
- Honors and Awards
- Community Activities

Of course, few résumés include *all* these categories. For example, not everyone has served in the military or received awards. Not everyone is active in the community or possesses special skills. But practically anyone can assemble an effective résumé. The trick is to carefully evaluate your own background, identify your principal strengths, and emphasize those attributes. For example, a person with a college degree but little relevant experience would highlight the education component.

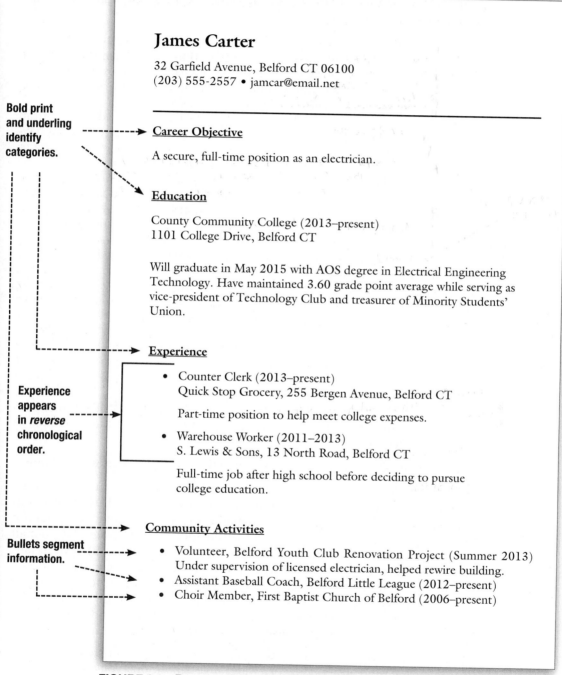

Bold print and underling identify categories.

James Carter

32 Garfield Avenue, Belford CT 06100
(203) 555-2557 • jamcar@email.net

<u>**Career Objective**</u>

A secure, full-time position as an electrician.

<u>**Education**</u>

County Community College (2013–present)
1101 College Drive, Belford CT

Will graduate in May 2015 with AOS degree in Electrical Engineering Technology. Have maintained 3.60 grade point average while serving as vice-president of Technology Club and treasurer of Minority Students' Union.

<u>**Experience**</u>

Experience appears in *reverse* chronological order.

- Counter Clerk (2013–present)
  Quick Stop Grocery, 255 Bergen Avenue, Belford CT

  Part-time position to help meet college expenses.

- Warehouse Worker (2011–2013)
  S. Lewis & Sons, 13 North Road, Belford CT

  Full-time job after high school before deciding to pursue college education.

<u>**Community Activities**</u>

Bullets segment information.

- Volunteer, Belford Youth Club Renovation Project (Summer 2013)
  Under supervision of licensed electrician, helped rewire building.
- Assistant Baseball Coach, Belford Little League (2012–present)
- Choir Member, First Baptist Church of Belford (2006–present)

FIGURE 8.3 • Reverse Chronological Résumé

Conversely, someone with a great deal of experience but relatively little formal schooling would emphasize the employment history. However, both individuals would follow these well-established guidelines:

1. The résumé, like the application letter, should be visually attractive. It should be printed on 8½-by-11″ white paper. Use capitalization, boldface, and white space skillfully to create an inviting yet professional appearance. Unless you're applying on-line, you can lay out your résumé in any number of ways, but it must *look* good. Experiment with a variety of layouts until it does.

2. The various categories of information must be clearly labeled and distinct from one another so the employer can quickly review your background without having to labor over the page or screen. Indeed, most employers are unwilling to struggle with a confusing résumé and simply move on to the next one.

3. All necessary details must appear—names, addresses, dates, and so on—and must be presented in a consistent manner throughout. For example, do not abbreviate words like *Avenue* and *Street* in one section and then spell them out elsewhere. Adopt one approach to abbreviation, capitalization, spacing, and other such matters.

4. Use reverse chronological order in categories such as Education and Work Experience. List the most recent information first and then work backward through time.

5. A printed résumé should be no longer than one page unless your background and qualifications truly warrant a second. This isn't usually the case except among applicants with ten or more years of work experience. If your résumé does have two pages, include your name at the top of the second page.

6. Some employers and Web sites provide on-line "fill-in-the-blanks" résumé forms for electronic submission. The design of the form governs the length of your online résumé. Rather than providing online forms, some employers request that you submit a scannable résumé online. This type of résumé is discussed in detail later in the chapter.

7. Like your letter, your résumé must be mechanically perfect, with absolutely no errors in spelling, punctuation, or grammar. Edit for careless blunders such as typos and inconsistent spacing.

Here are some detailed pointers concerning the various categories of a résumé:

- ***Contact Information:*** Irrelevant personal details such as birth date, religion, marital status, and Social Security number simply waste space. Include *only* your name, address, phone number, and e-mail address. Your contact information should appear at the top of the page and need not be labeled. *Note:* Many e-mail addresses are somewhat silly (for example, bigsexydood@aol.com). If yours falls into this category, you should set up a "professional" e-mail account specifically for job search purposes. Similarly, you should ensure that the message on your answering machine or cell phone also conveys an appropriate impression. If you maintain a Facebook or other social networking site, it should contain absolutely nothing that potential employers might find juvenile or irresponsible.

- ***Career objective:*** A brief but focused statement of your career plans can be useful. But if you wind up applying for a wide range of positions, you must revise it to suit each occasion. Whether to include this category depends on your individual circumstances and whether you have room for it.

- **_Education:_** Provide in reverse chronological order the name and address of each school you've attended, and mention your program of study and any degrees, diplomas, or certificates received, along with dates of attendance. You may wish to list specific classes completed, but this consumes a lot of space and isn't necessary. Don't list any schooling earlier than high school—and high school itself should be omitted unless you're attempting to "beef up" an otherwise skimpy résumé.

- **_Work experience:_** Besides the Education section, this is the most important category in a résumé. For each position you've held, provide your job title, dates of employment, the name and address of your employer, and—if they are not evident from the job title—the duties involved. Some résumés also include the names of immediate supervisors. As in the Education section, use reverse chronological order. If you have worked at many different jobs (perhaps some for short periods), you may list only your most important positions, omitting the others or lumping them together in a one-sentence summary like this: "At various times, I also held temporary and part-time positions as service station attendant, retail clerk, and maintenance worker."

- **_Military service:_** If applicable, list the branch and dates of your service, the highest rank you achieved, and any noteworthy travel or duty. Some applicants, especially those with no other significant employment history, list military activity under the Work Experience category.

- **_Computer literacy:_** This is a highly valued attribute—indeed, a necessary one—in today's technology-driven workplace. Mention specific word-processing and other software with which you're familiar (for example, Microsoft Word and Excel or Adobe Photoshop).

- **_Specialized skills or credentials:_** Include licenses, certifications, security clearances, foreign language competency, proficiency with certain machines—any "plus" that doesn't fit neatly elsewhere.

- **_Honors and awards:_** These can be academic or otherwise. In some cases—for example, if you received a medal while in the military or made the college honor roll—it's best to include such distinctions under the appropriate categories. But if the Kiwanis Club awarded you its annual scholarship or you were cited for heroism by the mayor, these honors would probably be highlighted in a separate category.

- **_Community activities:_** Volunteer work or memberships in local clubs, organizations, or church groups are appropriate here. Most helpful are well-known activities such as Scouting, Little League, 4-H, PTA, and the like. Include full details: dates of service or membership, offices held, if any, and special projects or undertakings you initiated or coordinated. Obviously, community activities often bear some relationship to applicants' pastimes or hobbies. Employers are somewhat interested in this because they are seeking individuals who can not only perform the duties of the job but also "fit in" easily with coworkers. But don't claim familiarity with an organization or activity you actually know little about. You're likely to get caught because many interviewers like to open with some preliminary conversation about an applicant's interests outside the workplace.

- ***References:*** Employers no longer require applicants to list the names of references on their résumés or even to include a "References available on request" line. Nevertheless, you'll probably be asked for references if you become a finalist for a position, so you should mention near the end of your application letter that you're ready to provide them. But never name someone as a reference without the person's permission. Before beginning your job search, identify at least three individuals qualified to write recommendation letters for you, and ask them whether they'd be willing to do so. Select persons who are familiar with your work habits and who are likely to comment favorably. Teachers and former supervisors are usually the best choices for recommendations because their remarks tend to be taken the most seriously. However, you must be absolutely certain that anyone writing on your behalf has nothing but good things to say. Tentative, halfhearted praise is worse than none at all. If someone seems even slightly hesitant to serve as a reference, you should find somebody more agreeable. One way to determine whether someone is indeed willing to compose an enthusiastic endorsement is to request that a copy of the recommendation be sent to you as well as to the employer. Anyone reluctant to comply with such a request is probably not entirely supportive. In any case, securing copies of recommendation letters enables you to judge for yourself whether any of your references should be dropped from your list. Better to suffer the consequences of a lukewarm recommendation once than to be undermined repeatedly without your knowledge. Usually, however, anyone consenting to write a letter on your behalf (and provide you with a copy) will give an affirmative evaluation that will work to your advantage.

Traditional Résumé

Most traditional résumés can be described as either *reverse chronological* or *functional* in nature.

A **reverse chronological résumé** (sometimes called an *archival résumé*) is the most common and the easiest to prepare. Figures 8.3 and 8.4 typify this style. Schooling and work experience are presented in reverse chronological order, with the names and addresses of schools and employers indicated, along with the dates of attendance and employment. Descriptions of specific courses of study and job responsibilities are provided as part of the Education and Work Experience categories. This style is most appropriate for persons whose education and past experience are fairly consistent with their future career plans or for those seeking to advance within their own workplace.

A **functional résumé,** on the other hand, highlights what the applicant has done rather than where or when it has been done. The functional résumé is skills-based, summarizing in general terms the applicant's experience and potential for adapting to new challenges. Specific chronological details of the person's background are included but are not the main focus. Moreover, the list of competencies occupies considerable space on the page and may therefore crowd out other categories of information. In Figure 8.5, for example, the Service category has necessarily been

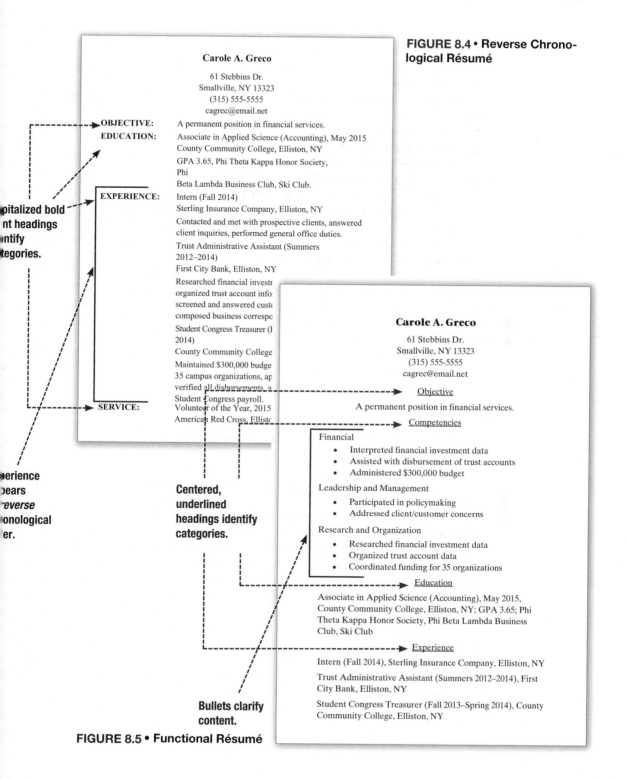

Carole A. Greco

61 Stebbins Dr.
Smallville, NY 13323
(315) 555-5555
cagrec@email.net

OBJECTIVE: A permanent position in financial services.

EDUCATION: Associate in Applied Science (Accounting), May 2015
County Community College, Elliston, NY

GPA 3.65, Phi Theta Kappa Honor Society, Phi

Beta Lambda Business Club, Ski Club.

EXPERIENCE: Intern (Fall 2014)
Sterling Insurance Company, Elliston, NY

Contacted and met with prospective clients, answered client inquiries, performed general office duties.

Trust Administrative Assistant (Summers 2012–2014)

First City Bank, Elliston, NY

Researched financial investr
organized trust account info
screened and answered custo
composed business correspo

Student Congress Treasurer (I 2014)

County Community College

Maintained $300,000 budge
35 campus organizations, ap
verified all disbursements, a
Student Congress payroll.

SERVICE: Volunteer of the Year, 2015
American Red Cross, Ellisto

pitalized bold
nt headings
ntify
tegories.

erience
bears
reverse
onological
er.

**Centered,
underlined
headings identify
categories.**

**Bullets clarify
content.**

FIGURE 8.5 • Functional Résumé

FIGURE 8.4 • Reverse Chrono-logical Résumé

Carole A. Greco

61 Stebbins Dr.
Smallville, NY 13323
(315) 555-5555
cagrec@email.net

Objective

A permanent position in financial services.

Competencies

Financial
- Interpreted financial investment data
- Assisted with disbursement of trust accounts
- Administered $300,000 budget

Leadership and Management
- Participated in policymaking
- Addressed client/customer concerns

Research and Organization
- Researched financial investment data
- Organized trust account data
- Coordinated funding for 35 organizations

Education

Associate in Applied Science (Accounting), May 2015, County Community College, Elliston, NY; GPA 3.65; Phi Theta Kappa Honor Society, Phi Beta Lambda Business Club, Ski Club

Experience

Intern (Fall 2014), Sterling Insurance Company, Elliston, NY

Trust Administrative Assistant (Summers 2012–2014), First City Bank, Elliston, NY

Student Congress Treasurer (Fall 2013–Spring 2014), County Community College, Elliston, NY

omitted. This style is most appropriate for applicants wishing to emphasize their actual proficiencies rather than their work history.

In addition to the variations in the ways the two styles of résumés present a candidate's credentials, there are also *layout* differences. In Figure 8.4, the category headings are in capitals and are flush with the left margin; in Figure 8.5, they're underlined and centered. These differences don't derive from the fact that the two résumés are in reverse chronological and functional style, respectively. Rather, the variations simply reflect the open-ended nature of résumé design.

For many applicants, this flexibility is liberating, allowing them to experiment and exercise creativity. But for others, it can pose problems. For example, someone who's not visually oriented may find it difficult to choose among the many possible options. For this reason, some applicants prefer to use the predesigned résumé templates that accompany most word-processing programs. But one obvious drawback to this is that these templates are clearly generic. If you use one, your résumé will not stand out because it will so closely resemble many of the others received. Therefore, some job seekers choose to pay for on-line services that custom design their résumé or provide access to templates that are more creative than the ones typical of Microsoft Word and other software. Often these résumés include a photo of the applicant and are characterized by nonlinear layouts that make them resemble Web pages. Three of these businesses—sometimes called "personal branding" services—are Loft Resumes (loftresumes.com), MyOptimalCareer (myoptimalcareer.com), and Splash Resumes (splashresumes.com).

Scannable Résumé

Rapid advances in computer technology have greatly changed every aspect of workplace communications. The hiring process is an obvious example. Many companies now advertise job openings only on the Internet, inviting applicants to submit résumés electronically to be read on the screen rather than as hard copy. One problem with this development is that, depending on which software is used, a creatively formatted résumé may appear confusingly jumbled or downright illegible on the receiving end. Format enhancements such as bold print, italics, underlining, bullets, and the like can dress up a résumé on paper, but in the online environment, they can create havoc. For this reason, many career counselors now urge applicants to greatly simplify the design of their résumés by adopting a no-frills, flush-left format. An online résumé should always be sent as a Word document or RTF file, not as a compressed (zip) or PDF file, which might create problems for the recipient. To enable the employer to quickly locate your résumé, the file name should begin with your last name, like this: Smith_2015 apr.19.doc. Also, resist the urge to attach pictures, graphics, or URLs. Most employers will not bother to access these. Figure 8.6 depicts the same résumé as shown in Figure 8.4 but in a readily scannable format.

CAROLE A. GRECO

61 Stebbins Drive
Smallville, NY 13323
(315) 555-5555
cagrec@email.net

PROFILE

Experienced financial services professional with accounting degree
and expertise in customer service, data retrieval, and budget, payroll,
and investment analysis and management. Administrative and
research skills, along with computer proficiency in Micrsoft Word,
Adobe Photoshop, and PowerPoint.

EDUCATION

Associate in Applied Science (Accounting), May 2015, County
Community College, Elliston, NY: GPA 3.65; Phi Theta Kappa Honor
Society, Phi Beta Lambda Business Club, Ski Club.

EXPERIENCE

Intern (Fall 2014), Sterling Insurance Company, Elliston, NY:
Contacted and met with prospective clients, answered client inquiries,
performed general office duties.

Trust Administrative Assistant (Summers 2012–2014), First City
Bank, Elliston, NY: Researched financial investment data, organized
trust account information, screened and answered customer
inquiries, composed business correspondence.

Student Congress Treasurer (Fall 2013–Spring 2014), County
Community College, Elliston, NY: Maintained $300,000 budget
funding 35 campus organizations, approved and verified all
disbursements, administered Student Congress payroll.

SERVICE

Volunteer of the Year (2015), American Red Cross, Elliston, NY.

Profile includes numerous keywords.

All content is flush with left margin.

FIGURE 8.6 • **Scannable Résumé**

Streamlining for the computer's sake is probably a positive development. Simpler is generally better in workplace communications, and the trend toward a less complicated résumé layout serves to counterbalance the tendency to overbuild such documents. Indeed, most people who have created scannable versions of their résumés eventually tone down their hard-copy originals. An incidental benefit of the simpler format is that more information can be included because limited space is used more effectively. Because scannable résumés are rapidly becoming the norm, many employers now use a strategy called the *keyword search*. Computerized scanning programs check all résumés received to identify those that include certain terms (that is, keywords) the employer considers particularly relevant. Of course, the computer can detect keywords wherever they may appear in a résumé, but many job-seekers are now creating a separate, keyword-loaded section—sometimes called the *profile*—in place of the job objective. Notice that the scannable résumé in Figure 8.6 includes this feature.

Tech**Tips**

For optimal results, you should create and save a résumé only as a Word document, not online. Save the document in hypertext markup language (HTML) so you can easily post your résumé to the Web. You should adhere to several important rules:

- Create the résumé in "text-only" or "rich-text" format, using a conventional font in 12-point size throughout.
- Set 1.2" side margins.
- Position all text flush with the left margin.
- Enter your name and the category headings in uppercase letters.
- Insert only one space after periods and other end punctuation.
- Do not use the ampersand (&), bold print, centering, indentations, italics, line justification, the percent sign (%), ruling lines, the slash (/), bullets, or underlining.
- Limit each line to six inches on your computer screen, and advance down the screen by hitting the Enter key before reaching the end of the line rather than allowing the lines to wrap around automatically.
- If you've posted your résumé to the Web, reference the URL in the body of your message so employers can click on it and go directly to your site.

Interview

If your letter and résumé result in an interview, you can assume you're in the running for the position; no personnel office deliberately wastes time interviewing applicants who aren't. But now you must outperform the other finalists by excelling in the interview. For this to happen, you must have three assets going for you: preparation, composure, and common sense.

To prepare, find out everything you can about the position and the workplace. Read any existing literature about the employer (Web site, annual reports, promotional materials, and product brochures). Consult some of the employment-related Web sites mentioned earlier in this chapter. If possible, talk to past and current employees or to persons in comparable jobs elsewhere. For generic information about the job title, consult the Department of Labor's *Occupational Outlook Handbook* (available online at *www.bls.gov/oco*). By familiarizing yourself with the nature of the job and the work environment, you'll be better equipped to converse intelligently with the interviewer. You'll *feel* more confident, a major prerequisite to successful interviewing.

If the interview will be in person (rather than by phone or Skype), locate the interview site beforehand and determine how much time you'll need to get there punctually. Be sure to get enough sleep the night before. Take a shower. Eat a light breakfast. Dismiss from your mind all problems or worries. All this may seem like obvious and rather old-fashioned advice, but it goes a long way toward ensuring that you'll be physically and mentally at ease and ready to interact smoothly. Of course, you shouldn't be *too* relaxed; an employment interview is a fairly formal situation, and you should conduct yourself accordingly.

Stand up straight, firmly shake the interviewer's hand, establish eye contact, and speak in a calm, clear voice. Sit down only when invited to or when the interviewer does. Don't chew gum, and—needless to say—*never* attend an employment interview with tobacco or alcohol on your breath or while under the influence of any controlled substance.

Whether you have applied by mail or online, be sure to bring several crisp, unfolded copies of your résumé, preferably in a professional-looking portfolio folder. It doesn't hurt to have a tablet with you as well, to demonstrate that you're tuned in to current modes of communication. In that vein, it's probably wise to say something about the company's Web site or mention something that caught your eye on their Twitter feed. But do not place anything on the interviewer's desk and by all means turn off your phone and put it away, out of sight. Nothing is more irritating to an interviewer than being interrupted by an applicant's incoming calls or noticing the applicant glancing down in anticipation of new texts.

Anticipate key questions. As mentioned earlier, the interviewer might begin by asking you about your interests and hobbies or perhaps by remarking about the weather or some other lightweight topic. From there, however, the conversation will become more focused. Expect discussion of your qualifications, your willingness to work certain hours or shifts, your long-range career plans, your desired salary, your own questions about the job, and so on. Here's a list of 20 typical questions often asked by interviewers:

1. Tell me about yourself. (A common variation is, If you had to describe yourself in just one word, what would it be?)
2. What do you do in your spare time?
3. Why did you choose your particular field of study?
4. What do you think you've learned in college?
5. How much do you know about information technology?
6. Why aren't your grades higher?
7. Do you plan to further your education?
8. What are your long-range goals?
9. What kind of work do you like best? Least?
10. What was the best job you ever had? Why?
11. How do you explain the "gaps" on your résumé?
12. Can you provide three solid references?
13. Why do you think you're qualified for this position?
14. Why do you want to work for this particular company?
15. Are you willing to work shifts? Weekends? Overtime?
16. Are you willing to relocate?
17. If hired, when could you start work?
18. How much do you expect us to pay you?
19. Why would you be a valuable employee?
20. Do *you* have any questions?

Interviewers ask questions such as these partly because they want to hear your answers but also because they want to determine how poised you are, how clearly you express yourself, and how well you perform under pressure. For the same reason, interviewers sometimes even ask seemingly hostile or confrontational questions. Try to formulate some responses to such queries beforehand so you can reply readily without having to grope for intelligent answers. Just as important, try to settle on several good questions of your own. Gear these to matters of importance, such as the employer's training and orientation procedures, the job description and conditions of employment, performance evaluation policies, likelihood of job stability, opportunities for advancement, and the like. You want the employer to know you're a serious candidate with a genuine interest in the job. But don't talk *too* much or attempt to control the interview. Answer questions fully—in three or four sentences—but know when to stop talking. Stay away from jokes or controversial topics. Avoid slang. Don't try to impress the interviewer with "big words" or exaggerated claims. Maintain a natural but respectful manner. In short, just be yourself, but be your *best* self.

Many applicants are unsure about how to dress for an interview. The rule is actually quite simple: Wear approximately what you would if you were reporting for work. If you are applying for a "dress-up" job, dress up. For a "jeans and sweatshirt" job, dress casually. Some employment counselors advise applicants to dress just a step above the position for which they are interviewing. In any case, make sure your interview clothing fits properly, is neat and clean, and is not too outlandishly "stylish." Minimize jewelry. Small earrings are acceptable (two or three for a woman, one for a man), but nose and eyebrow rings, tongue studs, chains, or any other such adornments are better left at home. The same is true for shower flip-flops, crocs, sweatpants, hats, and any clothing imprinted with sports logos or "clever" slogans. If you have been tattooed, do your best to cover your ink. Just as the physical appearance of your letter and résumé influences whether you're invited to an interview, your *own* appearance influences whether you get hired. As mentioned at the beginning of this section, *common sense* is a major factor in interviewing well. You must "use your head" and "put your best foot forward." As threadbare as these well-known clichés may seem, they really are good advice.

Follow-Up

The follow-up to an interview is another exercise in common sense. Although it requires very little effort, many applicants neglect it. This is unfortunate because a timely follow-up (within a day or two) can serve as a tie-breaker among several comparably qualified candidates. Every employer wants to hire someone willing to go a bit beyond what's required. Your follow-up is evidence that you are such a person, so it can enable you to get a step ahead of the other applicants.

In the form of a brief letter, the follow-up expresses gratitude for the interview and assures the employer that you're still interested in the job. There's no need to compose anything elaborate. Keep it simple. For an example, see Figure 8.7. In the interest of timeliness, you may be inclined to follow up via e-mail or text instead. Many career counselors advise against this, however, because some hiring managers prefer the greater formality of a letter. But send it immediately after the interview to ensure its arrival within a day or two.

32 Garfield Ave.
Belfield, CT 06100
April 22, 2015

Ms. Maria Castro
Director of Human Resources
The Senior Citizens' Homestead
666 Grand Blvd.
Belford, CT 06100

Dear Ms. Castro:

Thank you for meeting with me to discuss the electrician position.

Having enjoyed our conversation and the tour of The Senior Citizens' Homestead, I am still very interested in the job and will be available immediately after my graduation from college next month. I can also start sooner (on a part-time basis) if necessary.

Please contact me if you have any further questions about my background or credentials, and thanks again for your time.

Sincerely,

James Carter

James Carter

FIGURE 8.7 • Follow-Up Letter

Checklist
Evaluating an Application Letter, Résumé, and Follow-Up

A good application letter

—— follows a standard letter format (full block is best);

—— is organized into paragraphs:

☐ First paragraph asks for the job by name and indicates how you learned of the opening

☐ Middle paragraphs briefly outline your credentials, emphasize your potential value to the employer, and draw attention to your résumé

☐ Last paragraph closes on a polite note, mentioning that you would like an interview

—— does not exceed one page;

—— uses simple language, maintains appropriate tone, and contains no typos or mechanical errors in spelling, capitalization, punctuation, or grammar.

A good résumé

—— *looks* good, making effective use of white space, capitalization, boldface type, and other format features;

—— includes no irrelevant personal information;

—— includes separate, labeled sections for education, experience, and other major categories of professional qualifications;

—— maintains a consistent approach to abbreviation, spacing, and other elements;

—— does not exceed one page;

—— contains no typos or mechanical errors in spelling, capitalization, punctuation, or grammar.

A good follow-up letter

—— follows a standard format (full block is best);

—— is organized into paragraphs:

☐ First paragraph thanks the employer for the interview and mentions the job by name

☐ Middle paragraph restates your interest and availability

☐ Last paragraph politely invites further contact

—— does not exceed one page or screen;

—— uses simple language, maintains appropriate tone, and contains no typos or mechanical errors in spelling, capitalization, punctuation, or grammar.

EXERCISES

EXERCISE 8.1

Read the classified advertisements in a recent Sunday edition of your local newspaper and write a booklet report about what you find there. Include information not only about what kinds of jobs are listed but also about the qualifications required. Provide a breakdown of how many jobs require written responses as opposed to telephone or personal contact. Indicate whether there seems to be any correlation between the type of job and the likelihood that a written response will be requested.

EXERCISE 8.2

Explore the employment-related Web sites CareerBuilder, Monster.com, and Work-Tree.com, then write a memo report about what you discover. Compare and evaluate these sites. Which one is best for your purposes? Why? Which is the *least* useful to you? Why?

EXERCISE 8.3

Using the Internet along with print resources, such as the Department of Labor's *Occupational Outlook Handbook,* research a particular job title and then write a booklet report discussing your findings. What are the principal responsibilities of the position? What qualifications are typically required? What is the salary range? Are there more openings for this job in certain geographical areas?

EXERCISE 8.4

Using the Internet along with print resources, such as Standard & Poor's Ratings Services, research a particular employer and then write a booklet report discussing your findings. What are the employer's main products or services? How long has the employer been in business? Where is the corporate headquarters? How large is the workforce? What kinds of skills or credentials are required to work for this company?

EXERCISE 8.5

Interview someone currently employed in a job related to your field of study, then write a memo report summarizing the conversation. Why did the person choose this kind of work? How long has the person been in the position? What kind of education and other qualifications does the individual possess? What was said about the best and worst features of the job? Does he or she find the work challenging, interesting, and rewarding?

EXERCISE 8.6

Find an actual advertisement for an opening in your field that specifically requests a written response. Compose a job application letter and a reverse chronological résumé. Imagine you have been successful in getting an interview and have met with the Human Resources director. Compose a follow-up letter.

EXERCISE 8.7

Trade résumés with two or three classmates and provide constructive feedback to one another, making recommendations about how the résumés could be improved.

EXERCISE 8.8

Find an actual advertisement for an opening in some field other than your own but related to it that specifically requests a written response. Compose a job application letter and a functional résumé. Imagine you have been successful in getting an interview and have met with the human resources manager. Compose a follow-up letter.

EXERCISE 8.9

Design scannable versions of the reverse chronological and functional résumés you created in response to Exercises 8.6 and 8.8.

EXERCISE 8.10

Three application letters accompanied by résumés follow. For a variety of reasons, all are badly flawed. Rewrite each to eliminate its particular weaknesses.

Carla Zogby
2400 Front St., Apt. 32
Kansas City, MO
64100

February 23, 2015

Diversified Services, Inc.
500 Tower Street
Kansas City, Missouri 64100

Dear Sirs:

I am writting this letter in reply to your recent add in the Innernet.

As you can see from the enclosed resume, I have all the qualifications for which you are looking for.

Thank you for your time.

Your's Truely,

Carla Zogby

Carla Zogby

EXERCISE 8.10 *Continued*

NAME: Carla Zogby
ADDRESS: 2400 Front St., Apt. 32, Kansas City, MO 64100
TELEPHONE NUMBER: 816-555-4370
DATE OF BIRTH: October 1, 1991
RELIGION: Catholic
MARITAL STATUS: Single
HEIGHT: 5"3' WEIGHT: 110 lbs.

EXPERIENCE 9/2012–2/2013 Receptionist	St. Aedan's Church Answered phones, greeted visitors, handled weekly collection deposits, prepared and distributed weekly bulletin.
3/2012–8/2013 Store Trainer, Waitress	Friendly's Corporation Trained all new waitstaff, took food orders, cleared tables, washed dishes, helped cook.
11/2014–present Insurance Processor	City Bank Process disability and death claims, work with insurance companies to pay accounts.
EDUCATION 9/2008–6/2012	St. Aedan's High School • Honor Roll 3, 4 • Student Council 2
8/2015–present	Kansas City Technical College Secretarial Science

SKILLS
Personal computer systems, software proficiency with spreadsheets, word processing and database programs.

EXERCISE 8.10 *Continued*

Thomas Logan
105 Lincoln Ave.
Lincoln, Nebraska 68500
July 17, 2015

Conklin's Department Stores, Inc.
1400 West Carroll Street
Chicago, Illinois 60600

Gentlemen,

I am responding to an employment ad of yours that I found via the Internet for the Store Security position. I am sure that you will find that I am highly qualified for this job.

As a military policeman in the United States Army from July 2010 until April 2015 I had over six years experience in law enforcement. My job responsibilities included public relations, emergency vehicle operations, weapons handling, equipment maintenance and personnel management. My training included interpersonal communication skills, radio communications procedures, weapons safety, police radar operations, unarmed self-defense and riot and crowd control operations. I enforced traffic regulations by monitoring high traffic areas, being visible to the public, and issuing citations as necessary. I performed law enforcement investigations as needed, as well as prepared, verified, and documented police reports to include sworn statements and gathering and processing evidence. I conducted foot and motorized patrols of assigned areas and applied crime prevention measures by maintaining control and discipline through ensuring that all laws and regulations were obeyed at all times. I also performed basic first aid as first responder when needed.

Earlier I served as a parachute rigger, rigging, assembling, and repairing several of the military parachutes used in Airborne operations. I rigged various vehicles, weapons, and supplies to be air-dropped as well as hold airborne status for the duration. I also trained in combat operations.

At present I have just enrolled in the Criminal Justice program at Lincoln (Nebraska) Community College, and I have also completed a Human Relations course at Texas Central College, a Combat Lifesaver course, a ten-week course at the United States Army Military Police School, as well as studies at the United States Army Airborne and Pararigger Schools and the United States Army Basic Training and Infantry Schools.

Additional Skills include knowledge of first aid, knowledge of conversational Spanish, an accident-free driving record (nine years (civilian and military), and a United States Army Secret Security Clearance.

Sincerely,

Thomas Logan

EXERCISE 8.10 *Continued*

Résumé of

Thomas Logan, Jr.

105 Lincoln Avenue
Lincoln, Nebraska

Career Objective
Full-time position in law enforcement or security.

Education
Dickinson High School
Jersey City, NJ (Class of 2010)

Lincoln Community College
Lincoln, Nebraska (Currently enrolled)

Armed Forces
United States Army (2010–2015)

Interests
Fishing, Hunting, Snowmobiling

References
Professor John Dhayer
Sgt. Warren Landis
Mr. Thomas Logan, Sr.

EXERCISE 8.10 *Continued*

July 17, 2015

Superior Steel, Inc.
c/o NYS Department of Labor
121 North Main Street
Herkimer, NY 13350

Dear Superior Stell;

I am applying for the machinist/production assembler position you have
posted with the Department of Labor. I have been a machinist at the
Curtis Arms Co. for two years with experience in the manufacture of
low tolerance parts from blueprints. I also have eight years experience
as a self-employed general contractor, and additional experience as a
tree service worker. I am now continuing my education at Proctor Technical College. I have completed 12 credits towArd an AOS degree and
have maintained a 4.0 GPA. I am looking forward to meeting with you
for an interview as soon as possible. Thank you for your consideration.

Sincerely;

Roland Perry

Roland Perry

EXERCISE 8.10   *Continued*

Roland Perry
30 East Street
Proctor, NY 13500
(315)555-3806
e-mail: rolper30@aol.com

OBJECTIVE

To obtain a full-time position as a machinist with Superior Steel.

WORK HISTORY

Curtis Arms Company, Inc., Utica, NY

Machine operation/set-up on CNC, Pratt-Whitney bore reamers, NAPCO
black oxide color line, neutral and hardening furnaces. (January 2015–present)

DUTIES

- machining gun parts to tolerances of $+/-.005$ inch
- metal fabricating from blue prints
- hardening parts to Rockwell hardness specifications
- maintaining quality standards

Larry's Tree Service, Kingston, NY

Ground crew member. (July 2014–January 2015)

DUTIES

- operated chain saws, chippers, stump machine
- controlled lowering lines and climbers lifeline
- operated and maintained trucks and machinery

EXERCISE 8.10 *Continued*

- page 2 -

Perry Construction, Inc., Poughkeepsie, NY

Self-employed general contractor. (August 2001–February 2011)

DUTIES

* carpentry, masonary, plumbing, electrical work
* contracts, book-keeping, customer service

EDUCATION

Proctor Technical College, Proctor, NY (August 2015–present)

COURSES COMPLETED

* Air Conditioning Technology 101–A
* Technical English 101–A
* Technical Math 101–A
* Public Speaking 101–A

COMMUNITY ACTIVITIES

Volunteer Fire Department
American Legion Post Secretary
Community Band (Tuba Player)

Oral Presentations: Preparation and Delivery

LEARNING OBJECTIVES

When you complete this chapter you'll be able to:

- apply rehearsal techniques to build confidence for public speaking.
- devise effective introductions and conclusions.
- master vocal and physical qualities to engage your audience.
- use PowerPoint and other presentation aids productively.
- provide helpful evaluations of other students' presentations.

If you're like most people, you dread the prospect of having to stand in front of an audience and make a speech. You feel unsure of yourself and fear you'll appear awkward or foolish. Nevertheless, you should make a real effort to overcome such misgivings. The ability to present your ideas clearly and forcefully to a group of listeners is a valuable skill that equips you for leadership in the workplace, where it's often necessary to address groups of supervisors, coworkers, clients, or customers. The skill is also quite useful in community contexts, such as club gatherings, town meetings, school board hearings, and other public forums. It's certainly helpful in the college setting too, where oral reports are becoming a requirement in more and more courses.

A good speech is the result of three elements: preparation, composure, and common sense. If that sounds familiar, it should; in Chapter 8, the same was said of the employment interview. In many respects, the two endeavors are similar. Both are examples of oral communication, both are fairly formal speaking situations, and both place essentially the same demands on you. Of course, the main difference is that in a job interview, you're usually speaking to one or two listeners, whereas an oral presentation generally involves addressing a group. After reading this chapter, you should be able to prepare and deliver successful oral presentations.

Preparation

A successful oral presentation is nearly always based on thorough preparation. This involves some preliminary activities followed by actual rehearsal of the speech.

Preliminaries

Preparing for an oral presentation is much like preparing to write. Just as if you were about to compose an e-mail, letter, or written report, you must first identify your purpose. Are you simply trying to inform your listeners or are you attempting to entertain them? Are you perhaps seeking to persuade them of something or motivate them to action? In any case, you need a plan that enables you to achieve your goal.

It's crucial to assess your audience. What are your listeners' backgrounds and interests? How about their perspective on your topic? In short, what might influence their expectations or responses? Unless you gear your remarks to your audience, you probably won't connect with them satisfactorily. For example, a mayoral candidate addressing a gathering of senior citizens would be foolish to focus a campaign speech on long-range outcomes the listeners may never live to see. Such a group would respond better to a presentation of the candidate's short-term goals, particularly those related to that audience's immediate concerns—crime prevention, perhaps, or health care. Just as you do in written communications, you must always bear in mind the nature of your audience when preparing your remarks.

It's also helpful to get a look in advance at the room where you'll be speaking. This ensures that you'll be somewhat more at ease during the presentation because you'll be on familiar turf. If you're planning to use electronic presentation aids, you should also acquaint yourself with them. Nothing is more embarrassing than suddenly discovering that expected equipment is defective or unavailable. Guard against such setbacks by checking everything when you visit the site beforehand.

Of course, you must be thoroughly familiar with your subject matter. Gather information about the topic and assemble an arsenal of facts, figures, and examples to support your statements. This requires some research and homework—an essential part of your preparation. You must know not only how to approach and organize the material but also how to *develop* it. Nobody wants to listen to a speaker who has nothing to say or who rambles on and on with no apparent direction or focus.

Therefore, the opening of your speech must include a clear statement of purpose, informing the audience about what to expect. From there you must follow a logical path, covering your material in a coherent, step-by-step fashion, dealing with one main idea at a time, in an orderly sequence. And, as in written communication, you should provide effective transitions to facilitate progress from point to point. For all this to happen, you must write out your entire speech ahead of time. However, because it's best to actually *deliver* the speech from notes or note cards, a finely polished, letter-perfect piece of writing is not absolutely necessary. But you do need to have a well-developed and well-organized draft from which you can select key points and supporting details for your notes or note cards. You must also ensure that your notes or cards are plainly legible so you can glance down and easily see them on the lectern as you deliver the speech. Prepare your notes or cards using a bold, felt-tipped pen, and write substantially larger than you normally do. Another strategy is to prepare your notes or cards on the computer and print them out, using large, bold print. It's very damaging to your presentation if you have to pause to decipher your own handwriting or if you have to bend over or pick up your notes or cards to see them clearly. Figure 9.1 depicts note cards for a speech about radar technology.

Rehearsal

Although preliminaries are important, rehearsal is the most important part of your preparation. Many people skip this step, figuring they'll "wing it" when the time comes and rely on their wits. However, unless you're a very experienced speaker, this almost never works. Before attempting to deliver an oral presentation, you *must* practice it. You need not recruit a practice audience (although it certainly helps), but you should at least recite the speech aloud several times. This reveals which parts of the presentation seem the most difficult to deliver and establishes how *long* the speech really is. You don't want to run noticeably shorter or longer than the allotted time because that would violate the audience's expectations. Remember that speeches tend to run shorter in actuality than in rehearsal; the pressures of live performance generally speed up the delivery. If you're aiming for a five-minute presentation, you need seven or eight minutes in rehearsal. If you're expected to speak for half an hour, your rehearsal might take forty to forty-five minutes.

In addition to preparing your speech, you must prepare *yourself*. All the common-sense advice presented in Chapter 8 concerning the employment interview applies equally here. Get a good night's sleep. Shower. Eat, but do not consume any alcoholic beverages. Dismiss any troubling thoughts from your mind. Wear clothing appropriate for the occasion. All this preparation will contribute to your general sense of confidence and well-being, thereby helping you develop composure and deliver the presentation to the best of your ability.

Delivery

The key to successfully delivering your oral presentation in public is to relax. Admittedly, this is more easily said than done but not as difficult as it may seem. Most audiences are at least reasonably receptive, so you need not fear them. For example, in the classroom setting, all your listeners will soon be called on to present their own speeches or will have done so already. This usually makes them empathetic and supportive. It's simply not true that everyone in the room is scrutinizing your every word and gesture, hoping you'll perform poorly. (In fact, at any given moment, a certain percentage of the audience is probably not paying attention at all!) Nevertheless, you may wish to consider several areas of concern when delivering an oral presentation.

Permanent Ballistic Missile Early Warning

Systems (BMEWS):

   Clear, Alaska

      Thule, Greenland

         Fylingdale Moor, England

Relocatable Over-the-Horizon Radar (ROTHR):

bounces high-frequency signals off ionosphere;

can scan areas 500–1,800 naut. miles away.

FIGURE 9.1 • Note Cards

Introductions and Conclusions

Because first impressions are so important, a good oral presentation must begin with an effective introduction. Here are four useful strategies for opening your speech:

- *Ask the audience a pertinent question:* This is an effective introduction because it immediately establishes a connection between you and your listeners, especially if somebody responds. But even if no one does, you can provide the answer yourself, thereby leading smoothly into your discussion. For example, in a presentation titled "Tourist Attractions in New York City," you might open with the query, "Does anyone here know the name of the street the Empire State Building is on?"

- *Describe a situation:* There's something in human nature that makes us love a story, especially if it involves conflict. The enduring appeal of fairy tales, myths and legends, and even soap operas and sentimental country-western lyrics proves the point. You can capitalize on this aspect of your listeners' collective psychology by opening your presentation with a *brief* story that somehow relates to your subject. For example, a speaker attempting to explore the dangers of tobacco might begin like this: "My friend Jane, a wonderful young woman with a bright future, had been smoking a pack a day since tenth grade. Finally, at age twenty-five, she decided to quit. But when she went to the doctor for her annual physical, she learned that it was already too late. Tragically, Jane died of lung cancer less than a year later."

- *Present an interesting fact or statistic:* This will help you grab the audience's attention by demonstrating that you're familiar with your topic. The annual editions of *The Statistical Abstract of the United States* and the *World Almanac and Book of Facts* are both excellent sources of statistical information on diverse topics, but there are many other resources. Librarians can direct you to government documents, corporate reports, Internet sites, and other useful resources. Even though statistics can be deceptive, people like what they perceive as the hard reality of such data and therefore find numbers quite persuasive. For example, a speech intended to demonstrate the need for stricter gun control legislation might open with the observation, "Every year, there are more than 10,000 handgun-related murders in the United States." The Internet is a good source of statistics if used judiciously. Useful Internet sites include the University of Michigan's Web site (www.lib.umich.edu/govdocs/stats.html) the U.S. Department of Labor's Bureau of Labor Statistics (www.bls.gov/), and the U.S. Census Bureau (www.census.gov).

- *Use a quotation:* Get a "Big Name"—Shakespeare, Martin Luther King Jr., the Bible—to speak for you. Find an appropriate saying that will launch your own remarks with flair. Many useful books of quotations exist, but *Bartlett's Familiar Quotations* (available in virtually any good bookstore or library) is the best known—and for good reason. For example, *Bartlett's* includes nearly a hundred quotes on the subject of money alone. It is also available—along with the *Columbia World of Quotations*—on the Web.

The conclusion to your talk is as important as the introduction. Always sum up when you reach the end of an oral presentation. Repeat your key points and clearly show how they support your conclusion. Like an airplane rolling smoothly to a stop on the runway rather than crashing to the ground after reaching its destination, you should not end abruptly. You can accomplish this by returning the audience to the starting point. When you reach the end of your speech, refer to the question, scenario, fact, statistic, or quotation with which you opened. This creates in your listeners the satisfying sense of having come full circle, returning them to familiar territory.

Another common concluding tactic is to ask whether members of the audience have any questions. If so, you can answer them, and then your work is done. If no questions are forthcoming, the audience has in effect ended the speech for you. Because this creates the sense of a letdown, however, you can instead have an accomplice or two in the audience ask questions to which you have prepared responses in advance. Although staged, this is a common practice among professional speakers. Whatever form of conclusion you choose, always close by thanking the audience for their time and attention.

Vocal Factors

Obviously, the *voice* is the principal instrument of any oral presentation. Therefore, pay attention to your vocal qualities. Speak at a normal rate of speed, neither too fast nor too slow, and at a normal volume, neither too loud nor too soft. Pronounce each word clearly so the audience can understand your entire speech without straining. When using a microphone, be sure it's approximately one foot away from your mouth—any farther and it may not pick up your voice adequately; any closer and your overly amplified *b*s and *p*s may create an annoyingly explosive sound. In addition, try to maintain the normal rhythms of everyday conversation. Nothing is more boring than listening to a speech delivered in an unvarying monotone. Conversely, it's irritating to be subjected to an overly theatrical delivery characterized by elaborate gestures or exaggerated vocal effects. The key is to be natural, as if you were speaking to one or two people rather than a whole group.

At the same time, however, an oral presentation is certainly a more formal speaking situation than a social conversation. Therefore, you should provide more examples and illustrations than you ordinarily might, along with more transitional phrases than usual. In addition, make a conscious effort to eliminate verbal "ticks," those distracting little mannerisms that characterize everyday speech: *um, y'know, okay?, right?,* and the like. Listening to a tape recording of your oral presentation enables you to assess the degree to which you need to work on your vocal mannerisms. Although you don't want to sound stiffly artificial, you should stay away from the more colorful vernacular. Avoid slang, expletives, and conspicuously substandard—"I ain't got no"—grammar. Achieving the right level of formality can be challenging, but practicing the presentation helps.

Physical Factors

Although your voice is obviously important, your audience *sees* you as well as hears you. They respond to your body language as much as to your words. As you would in an employment interview, you must create a favorable physical impression. Get rid of any chewing gum or tobacco long before stepping up to the lectern. Stand up straight behind the lectern; don't slump or lean over it. Control your hand motions. Don't fold your arms, bury your hands in your pockets, drum with your fingertips, click a pen, or cling rigidly to the lectern with a stiff-armed, white-knuckled grip. Refrain from touching your face or hair, tugging at your clothes, or scratching your body. You can gesture occasionally to make a point—but only if such movements are spontaneous, as in casual conversation. In short, your hands should not distract the audience from what you're saying. Your feet can also create problems. Resist the tendency to tap your feet, shift from one leg to the other, or stray purposelessly from the lectern. Plant your feet firmly on the floor and stay put unless the speech is long.

In the academic setting, your professors (much like many workplace supervisors) may impose certain regulations concerning proper attire for oral presentations. Baseball caps, for example, are sometimes prohibited, along with various other style and dress affectations such as those mentioned in the "Interview" section of Chapter 8. Whether in a college classroom or on the job, you should observe any such guidelines, even if you feel they're overly restrictive.

Eye Contact

As much as possible, *look at* your audience. This is probably the hardest part of public speaking, but it's imperative. Unless you maintain eye contact with audience members, you'll lose their attention. Keep your head up and your eyes directed forward. If you find it impossible to actually look at your listeners, fake it. Look instead at desktops, chair legs, or the back wall. You must create at least the *illusion* of visual contact.

Holding your listeners' attention is one—although certainly not the only—reason you should absolutely avoid the dreadful error of simply reading to your audience from the text of your speech. Few practices are more boring, more amateurish, or more destructive of audience–speaker rapport. As mentioned in the section on preparation, you should deliver your presentation from notes or note cards rather than from a polished text to force yourself to adopt a more conversational manner. But keep your papers or cards out of sight, lying flat on the lectern. Do not distract the audience by nervously shuffling them. To prevent your cards from getting out of order, number them sequentially.

Presentation Aids

To greatly enhance your speech, consider using presentation aids in conjunction with the various visuals (tables, graphs, charts, pictures) discussed in Chapter 3. Such tools can be helpful to both you and your audience by illustrating key points throughout your talk. If the room where you're speaking is equipped with a chalkboard or dry-erase board, take advantage of it as appropriate. A flip chart—a giant, easel-mounted pad of paper that you write on with markers—is another useful option. You may also choose to use large display posters prepared in advance, but you must remember to bring along tape or thumbtacks to secure them for viewing.

Whether using a chalkboard, flip chart, or poster to make your point, remember to position yourself *next to* it, not in front; you must not block the audience's view. Remember to face the audience rather than the display. Be sure your writing is plainly legible from a distance; write in large, bold strokes, using color for emphasis and incorporating the other design principles outlined in Chapter 4. Make sure your drawings and text are easy to see even from the back of the room.

For lettering, use the following chart:

Distance	Size of Lettering
Up to 10 ft.	¾ in.
20 ft.	1 in.
30 ft.	1¼ in.
40 ft.	1½ in.
50 ft.	1¾ in.
60 ft.	2 in.

Depending on the duration, scope, and topic of your speech, you may decide to supplement your remarks with video or sound recordings, provided they're of good quality. Relevant physical objects can also be displayed or passed around. For example, if you were explaining how to tune a guitar, you would certainly want to demonstrate the procedure on an actual instrument. Similarly, if you were explaining the workings of a particular tool or other device, ideally you would provide one (or more) for the audience to examine.

To lend your remarks an impressive aura of professionalism, you may decide to use presentation software such as Microsoft PowerPoint. Images are exhibited by a liquid crystal display (LCD) projector connected to a laptop or other computer that you control. This technology provides a wide range of type sizes, fonts, colors, clip art, backgrounds, three-dimensional effects, and other format features, as well as sound and animation. In addition, static images and streaming video can be imported from the Web to create multimedia presentations. Although some training is required to fully exploit this technology's potential, anyone can easily learn the fundamentals. Here are a few basic rules governing the creation of PowerPoint slides:

- Don't include too much information on any one slide. Keep it simple, using brief phrases instead of full sentences, and limiting each screen to no more than four or five main points.

- Don't use more than two type sizes, fonts, or styles on a given slide.

- Maintain consistency throughout the presentation, using capitalization, underlining, spacing, and other elements (including fonts) the same way on each slide.

- Include no more than twenty-five slides in any one presentation.

Notice how the PowerPoint slides depicted in Figure 9.2 reflect these principles.

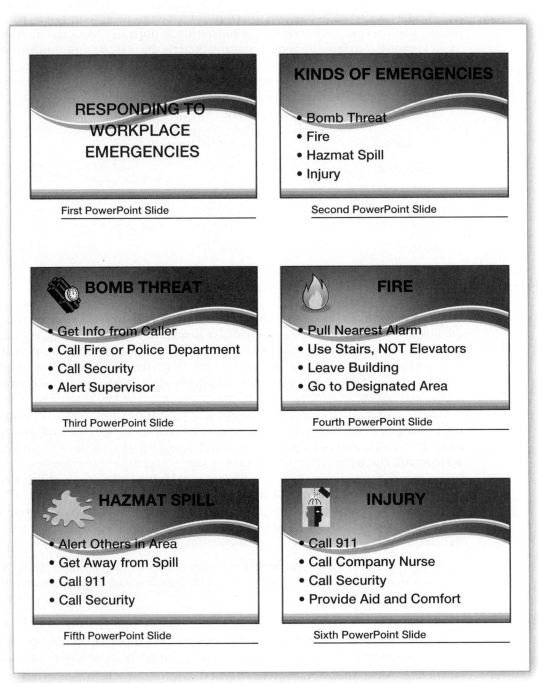

FIGURE 9.2 • PowerPoint Slides

PowerPoint affords a speaker many useful features, which include an array of techniques borrowed from Hollywood filmmakers. To move from one slide to the next, for example, PowerPoint is able to "wipe" the screen as if it were a windshield; one image is pushed from view while another moves in behind it. Similarly, the Dissolve option causes the slow fading out of one image and the gradual appearance of its successor, sometimes with a superimposition of images midway through the transition. Among the most common features is the Fly In, whereby a word or image seems airborne, "landing" on the screen like a lobbed dart, often accompanied by a sound effect.

A well-crafted PowerPoint component adds a high degree of polish to any oral presentation, revealing that the speaker is up-to-date and knowledgeable about current practices. However, you should use PowerPoint not simply to appear tech-savvy but to genuinely enrich your performance. A common mistake is to overload the presentation with special effects, creating a jumpy, hyperactive quality that deflects the audience's attention from the content. An opposite but equally unproductive error is to outline the entire speech and then read aloud from these too-numerous slides while facing the screen rather than the audience. This can literally put listeners to sleep. Instead, you should use PowerPoint slides simply as background, greatly expanding on their content by presenting a fully developed speech in accordance with the established principles of effective public performance. PowerPoint is not a substitute for the speech but rather a tool for better delivery of it. The purpose of any audiovisual aid is to reinforce and clarify, rather than overshadow, the speaker's remarks.

Remember also that electronic delivery systems can malfunction or present other unexpected difficulties. If you plan to use PowerPoint in an upcoming presentation, rehearsal (actually using the technology) is even more crucial than it would be otherwise. And even if everything seems to be ready, you should always have a backup plan. Bring printed copies of your slides to distribute to the audience in case of equipment failure or other last-minute problems.

Enthusiasm

Try to deliver your oral presentations in a lively, upbeat, enthusiastic manner. This actually makes your job easier because a positive attitude on your part will help foster a more receptive attitude on the part of the audience. If your listeners sense that you'd rather be elsewhere, they'll probably "tune out." When that occurs, you receive no encouraging feedback, and knowing you've lost your audience makes it even more difficult to continue. On the other hand, if you sense that the audience is following along, this reinforcement in turn fuels your performance. But that can't happen unless you project in an engaging way. From the start, *you* establish the tone. Therefore, it makes sense to adopt a positive attitude when giving an oral presentation, not only for the audience's sake but also to serve your own purposes.

TechTips

Here are some basic guidelines for creating an effective PowerPoint presentation:

- Don't get carried away with all the options at your disposal; exercise restraint. As with so many aspects of workplace communications, less is often more.

- Don't allow a patterned, textured, or incompatibly colored background to obscure your text. Use a dark background with light text for projection in a lighted room; use a light background with dark text for projection in a darkened room.

- Use relatively large print for increased legibility: 30 to 34 point for text; 44- to 50-point bold for headings.

- Use consistent formatting features on all slides.

- Avoid large segments of running text. Use lists and outlines instead.

- Include no more than five items of information and no more than fifteen words per slide.

- Include no more than twenty-five slides in any presentation.

- To guard against technical difficulties, have a backup plan that provides several options. Because not all computers have a CD drive, some may not be compatible with your flash drive, and some don't have Internet access, e-mail your PPT presentation to yourself and bring an electronic version on CD and/or flash drive.

The many factors that contribute to a good delivery may seem like a lot to keep track of. But if you're like most speakers, you probably have real difficulty in only one or two areas. An especially useful strategy is to videotape your rehearsal to determine what you should work on to improve your delivery. As stated at the start of this chapter, a successful oral presentation is the result of preparation, composure, and common sense. If you take seriously the recommendations offered in this chapter and practice the strategies and techniques suggested, your performance as a public speaker will improve greatly.

Evaluation of a Presentation

When you deliver an oral presentation in response to a college assignment, your professor will judge (and grade) your efforts. But it's quite common for classmates to provide feedback as well. This can be tricky because in any class the quality of the speeches will vary. Some will be very good, but others may be rather unsatisfactory. It's important to exercise tact and sensitivity when commenting on other students' performances. Although the purpose of peer evaluation is not to heap undeserved praise on weak speeches, it's certainly not to tear them apart either. Nothing is gained by harsh, destructive criticism.

Instead, try to comment on your classmates' efforts in a positive, encouraging manner, identifying strengths before weaknesses. When weaknesses are mentioned, they should be described gently, in a considerate way. The goal is to work productively to improve everyone's skills, not to ridicule, deflate, or discourage anyone. For example, if a speaker failed to provide enough detail about some feature of the topic, it would be unhelpful to respond with remarks such as, "I didn't know what he was talking about. He didn't give us anywhere near enough information to understand what he was trying to say." A far better response would be something such as, "This topic was such an interesting one and was presented with such obvious enthusiasm that I would've liked to hear about it in greater depth. Maybe more details would've given us a better understanding of the speaker's perspective."

In a sense, though, peer evaluation begins as soon as the speech does. Without even realizing it, audience members often send the speaker signals—both positive and negative—right from the first moment. When the speaker looks at the audience, their level of interest and engagement is clearly communicated by their body language and other nonverbal cues. If they're slumping in their seats, examining their fingernails, gazing out the window, giggling or chatting with one another, or sneakily checking their text messages, it's clear that they're ignoring the speech. This will have an extremely discouraging effect on any speaker. If, on the other hand, audience members are sitting up straight, looking at the speaker, listening attentively, and nodding in agreement at appropriate points along the way, this positive feedback reinforces the speaker psychologically and always results in better performance. A speaker must deliver in an upbeat way that encourages audience involvement, but the opposite is also true: The audience has an equal responsibility to support the speaker by behaving attentively and courteously.

Many professors use a checklist system for grading oral presentations, and some require the audience to complete the checklist as well. This is productive because each speaker then receives multiple evaluations and can check the results to identify patterns of response. If one person gives the speaker low marks for eye contact, that assessment can probably be ignored. But if eight or nine listeners mention eye contact as a weakness (even if the professor doesn't), that's obviously something the speaker should take seriously and try to improve. The checklist that follows is a representative example.

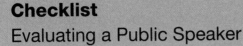

Checklist
Evaluating a Public Speaker

A good public speaker

____ opens with an interesting, attention-getting introduction;

____ follows a clear and logical pattern of organization;

____ provides enough detail to fully develop the subject;

____ closes with a smooth, satisfying conclusion;

____ speaks in a firm, clear, expressive voice;

____ makes frequent eye contact with the audience;

____ appears physically relaxed and composed, with no distracting mannerisms;

____ maintains an appropriate level of formality—neither too casual nor too solemn;

____ delivers in an alert, engaging manner;

____ satisfies but does not exceed the appropriate length for the presentation.

EXERCISES

EXERCISE 9.1

Prepare and deliver a five- to ten-minute oral presentation on one of the following autobiographical topics:

- A Childhood Memory
- My Brush with Danger
- An Angry Moment
- A Very Satisfying Accomplishment
- My Career Goals
- What I Expect My Life to Be Like in Ten Years

EXERCISE 9.2

Prepare and deliver a five- to ten-minute oral presentation that summarizes a book, article, lecture, film, or television broadcast related to your field of study or employment (see Chapter 5).

EXERCISE 9.3

Prepare and deliver a five- to ten-minute oral presentation in which you explain how to use a specific mechanical device related to your field of study or employment.

Present an actual example of such a mechanism along with any audiovisual aids that may be helpful to your audience. (See Chapter 7.)

EXERCISE 9.4

Prepare and deliver a five- to ten-minute oral presentation describing a procedure related to one of your hobbies or pastimes (see Chapter 7). Present any audiovisual aids that may be helpful to your audience.

EXERCISE 9.5

Prepare and deliver a five- to ten-minute oral presentation describing a procedure related to your field of study or employment (see Chapter 7). Present any audiovisual aids that may be helpful to your audience.

EXERCISE 9.6

Prepare and deliver a five- to ten-minute oral presentation in which you evaluate three nearby restaurants featuring specific cuisines (for example, Chinese, Italian, or Middle Eastern) or three nearby stores that sell essentially the same product (for example, athletic shoes, books & music, or clothing). Present any audiovisual aids that may be helpful to your audience.

EXERCISE 9.7

Prepare and deliver a five- to ten-minute oral presentation explaining how to perform a specific mathematical procedure (for example, solving a quadratic equation). Use the blackboard.

EXERCISE 9.8

Prepare and deliver a five- to ten-minute oral presentation in which you inform your audience about some significant event in world, national, or local history. Present any audiovisual aids that may be helpful to your audience.

EXERCISE 9.9

Using the Internet along with print sources, prepare and deliver a five- to ten-minute oral presentation in which you discuss employment requirements and opportunities in your field of study. Present any audiovisual aids that may be helpful to your audience.

EXERCISE 9.10

Access the Web site entitled "50 Incredible, Historical Speeches You Should Watch Online." Here's the link: www.onlineuniversities.com/blog/...50-incredible-historical-speeches.

   View three of these speeches and write a short report in which you evaluate them, using the criteria identified in the Checklist on pg. 164. Your report should rank-order the speeches, providing concrete reasons for your rankings.

Proposals

LEARNING OBJECTIVES

When you complete this chapter you'll be able to:

- follow directions when creating a solicited proposal in response to a Request for Proposal (RFP).
- craft a targeted unsolicited proposal in response to a perceived problem or need.
- adapt to the differing natures of internal and external proposals.
- create proposals in a variety of formats: memo, e-mail, memo report, long report.
- apply the proven principles of persuasive writing, maintaining a positive, reader-centered tone.

Like the various other kinds of workplace writing, proposals are a major example of business communication. Simply put, a *proposal* is a persuasive offer intended to secure authorization to perform a task or provide products or services that will benefit the reader. There are basically two kinds of proposals: solicited and unsolicited (that is, requested and unrequested). But there are subcategories within those broad divisions, including internal and external proposals. This is not really as complicated as it seems because the conventions governing proposal writing are well-established and quite logical. This chapter explores these issues and provides examples of solicited and unsolicited proposals.

Solicited Proposals

In this case, the business, agency, or organization seeking proposals has already identified a situation or problem it wants to address. Accordingly, it issues a request for proposal (RFP) that spells out the details of the project and provides instructions to outsiders for submitting bids. Many RFPs are quite lengthy and complex. They appear in trade publications, as government releases, and on the Internet. An individual or organization wishing to compete for a particular contract must craft a proposal that convincingly demonstrates its superiority to the many others received.

In one sense, however, responding to an RFP is easier than writing an unsolicited proposal because the problem or goal has already been established and there is no need to convince anyone of its existence or importance. In addition, the RFP usually provides explicit instructions regarding the format, design, and content of the proposal, so those requirements—which must be followed exactly—are already in place.

Unsolicited Proposals

In this case, the proposal originates with the writer, who has perceived a problem or need that the writer's expertise might be able to remedy. Although an unsolicited proposal may face no direct competition, it's more challenging to compose because it must convince the reader of the potential benefits. In short, it must be more strategically persuasive than a solicited proposal, whose acceptance or rejection is often based largely on cost and time projections as well as the writer's credentials and experience on similar projects—all of which is fairly objective information.

Internal and External Proposals

As with most other kinds of business writing, a proposal—solicited or not—may be either an in-house document or an external one.

Internal proposals: These are often rather short because the writers and readers are already known to each other and the context is mutually understood. Solicited in-house proposals are not usually written in response to a formal RFP but rather to a direct assignment from a manager, supervisor, or other administrator. Unsolicited in-house proposals are motivated by an employee's own perception of need—for example, the belief that a particular policy or procedure should be adopted, modified, or abandoned.

External proposals: As mentioned previously, solicited external proposals are nearly always in response to formal RFPs, but unsolicited external proposals—which are more difficult to create—obviously are not. External proposals are motivated primarily by the desire for financial reimbursement. In effect, they might almost be considered as a form of employment application.

Formats of Proposals

If in-house, short proposals usually take the form of a memo, e-mail, or memo report; if external, they are typically sent as a letter. Longer, more fully developed proposals can include many sections (they closely resemble long reports) and are sometimes written collaboratively (see Chapter 11).

Objectives of Proposals

Regardless of whether a proposal is solicited or unsolicited, internal or external, short or long, it should accomplish several objectives, some of which may overlap:

- Clearly summarize the situation or problem that the proposal is addressing. If unsolicited, the proposal must convince the reader that there is in fact an important unmet need.

- Provide a detailed explanation of how the proposal will correct the situation or problem. This is sometimes called the *project description,* and it typically contains several parts.

- Confirm the feasibility of the project and the anticipated benefits of completing it, as well as possible negative consequences of not doing so.

- Convincingly refute any probable objections.

- Establish the writer's credentials and qualifications for the project.

- Identify any necessary resources, equipment, or support.

- Provide a reliable timeline for completion of the project. A Gantt chart (see Chapter 3) is sometimes used for this.

- Provide an honest, itemized estimate of the costs. Deliberately understating the timeline or the budget is not only unethical (see Chapter 1) but also fraudulent. Doing so can incur legal liability.

- Close with a strong conclusion that motivates the reader to accept the proposal. A convincing cost/benefit analysis is helpful here.

As mentioned in earlier chapters, workplace communications must always be sensitive to considerations of audience, purpose, and tone. This is especially important in proposal writing because of its fundamentally persuasive nature. A proposal writer must be alert to the differing requirements of upward, lateral, downward, and outward communication. The phrasing should be reader-centered, using the "you" approach. And because by definition proposals seek to improve conditions by rectifying problems, it's important that they remain positive and upbeat in tone. The writer must refrain from assigning blame for existing difficulties and should instead focus on solutions. This is especially important when writing in-house, where a hostile climate can result if the writer neglects to consider people's needs and feelings, particularly if the proposal's recommendations might alter or otherwise affect the responsibilities of coworkers or departments.

Like any workplace document, a proposal is far more likely to succeed if well-written. Nothing tarnishes credibility more quickly than careless typos and basic errors in spelling, punctuation, or grammar. In addition, workplace writing should always be accurate, clear, and well-organized. The wording should be simple, direct, and concise, using active verbs and everyday vocabulary, with no rambling, wordy expressions. The crucial point to remember is that no amount of study from a textbook will enable you to compose your best writing on the first try. Any professional writer will tell you that the key is to revise, revise, and revise. Finally, proofread carefully.

In addition, a proposal should look inviting. As explained in Chapter 4, our ability to comprehend what we read is greatly influenced by its physical arrangement on the page or screen. When we see a document we form an involuntary subconscious opinion of it before we begin to actually read. Obviously, a positive initial impression goes a long way toward fostering a more receptive attitude in a reader. Therefore, strive for a visually appealing page design by applying the principles outlined in Chapter 4.

Figures 10.1–10.20 present several sample proposals:

- From a student to her instructor regarding a topic for her long report assignment
- From an employee to her supervisor regarding improvements to the company's day care facilities
- From a landscaping company to a real estate agency regarding improvements to the agency's grounds
- From a community group to a philanthropic agency regarding the restoration of a trail system

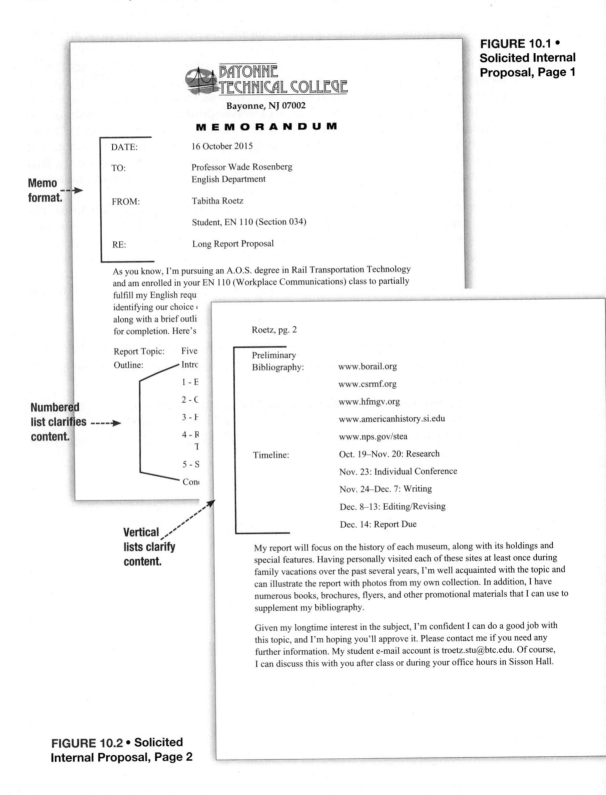

FIGURE 10.1 •
Solicited Internal
Proposal, Page 1

Memo
format.

BAYONNE
TECHNICAL COLLEGE
Bayonne, NJ 07002

M E M O R A N D U M

DATE: 16 October 2015

TO: Professor Wade Rosenberg
               English Department

FROM: Tabitha Roetz

               Student, EN 110 (Section 034)

RE: Long Report Proposal

As you know, I'm pursuing an A.O.S. degree in Rail Transportation Technology
and am enrolled in your EN 110 (Workplace Communications) class to partially
fulfill my English requ
identifying our choice
along with a brief outli
for completion. Here's

Report Topic: Five
Outline: Intro

Numbered
list clarifies
content.

1 - E

2 - C

3 - F

4 - R
   T

5 - S

Con

Roetz, pg. 2

Preliminary
Bibliography: www.borail.org

                     www.csrmf.org

                     www.hfmgv.org

                     www.americanhistory.si.edu

                     www.nps.gov/stea

Timeline: Oct. 19–Nov. 20: Research

                     Nov. 23: Individual Conference

                     Nov. 24–Dec. 7: Writing

                     Dec. 8–13: Editing/Revising

                     Dec. 14: Report Due

Vertical
lists clarify
content.

My report will focus on the history of each museum, along with its holdings and
special features. Having personally visited each of these sites at least once during
family vacations over the past several years, I'm well acquainted with the topic and
can illustrate the report with photos from my own collection. In addition, I have
numerous books, brochures, flyers, and other promotional materials that I can use to
supplement my bibliography.

Given my longtime interest in the subject, I'm confident I can do a good job with
this topic, and I'm hoping you'll approve it. Please contact me if you need any
further information. My student e-mail account is troetz.stu@btc.edu. Of course,
I can discuss this with you after class or during your office hours in Sisson Hall.

FIGURE 10.2 • Solicited
Internal Proposal, Page 2

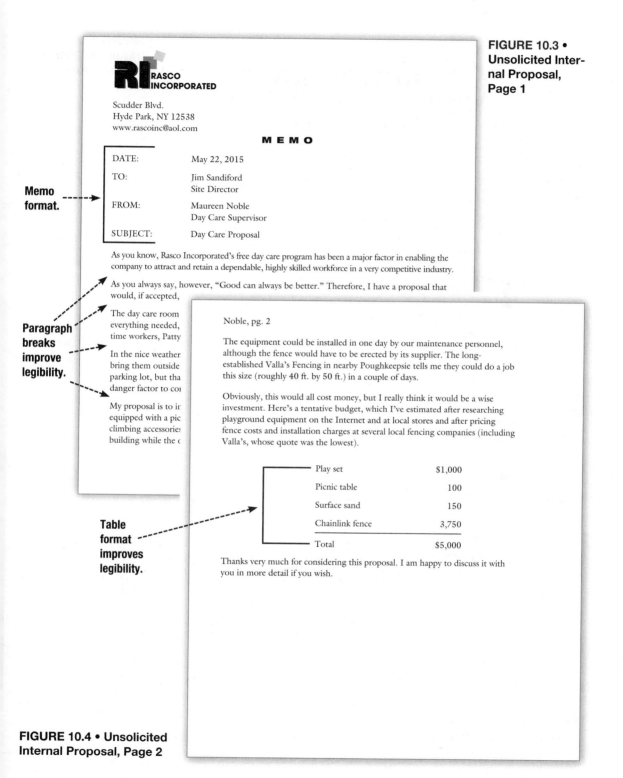

Memo format.

Paragraph breaks improve legibility.

Table format improves legibility.

RASCO INCORPORATED

Scudder Blvd.
Hyde Park, NY 12538
www.rascoinc@aol.com

M E M O

DATE: May 22, 2015

TO: Jim Sandiford
                   Site Director

FROM: Maureen Noble
                   Day Care Supervisor

SUBJECT: Day Care Proposal

As you know, Rasco Incorporated's free day care program has been a major factor in enabling the company to attract and retain a dependable, highly skilled workforce in a very competitive industry.

As you always say, however, "Good can always be better." Therefore, I have a proposal that would, if accepted,

The day care room everything needed, time workers, Patty

In the nice weather bring them outside parking lot, but tha danger factor to co

My proposal is to i equipped with a pic climbing accessorie building while the c

Noble, pg. 2

The equipment could be installed in one day by our maintenance personnel, although the fence would have to be erected by its supplier. The long-established Valla's Fencing in nearby Poughkeepsie tells me they could do a job this size (roughly 40 ft. by 50 ft.) in a couple of days.

Obviously, this would all cost money, but I really think it would be a wise investment. Here's a tentative budget, which I've estimated after researching playground equipment on the Internet and at local stores and after pricing fence costs and installation charges at several local fencing companies (including Valla's, whose quote was the lowest).

Play set	$1,000
Picnic table	100
Surface sand	150
Chainlink fence	3,750
Total	$5,000

Thanks very much for considering this proposal. I am happy to discuss it with you in more detail if you wish.

FIGURE 10.3 • Unsolicited Internal Proposal, Page 1

FIGURE 10.4 • Unsolicited Internal Proposal, Page 2

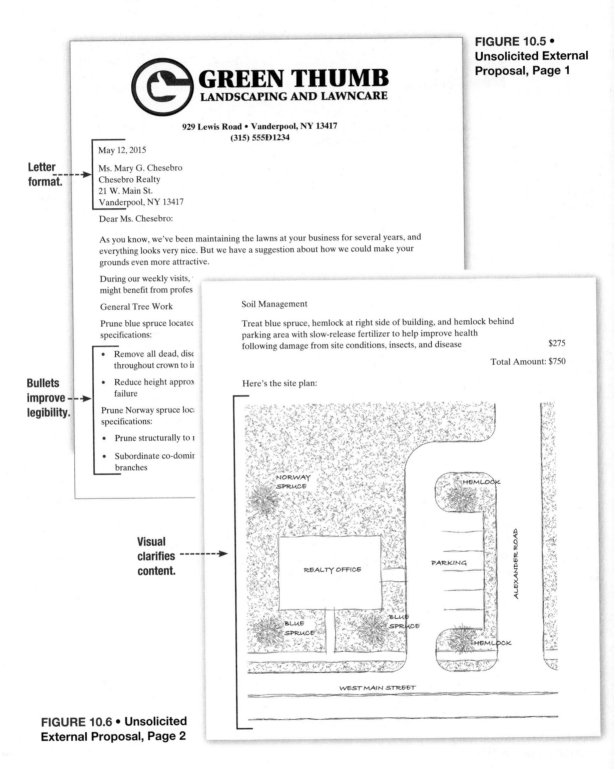

FIGURE 10.5 •
Unsolicited External
Proposal, Page 1

GREEN THUMB
LANDSCAPING AND LAWNCARE

929 Lewis Road • Vanderpool, NY 13417
(315) 555Ð1234

May 12, 2015

Ms. Mary G. Chesebro
Chesebro Realty
21 W. Main St.
Vanderpool, NY 13417

Letter format.

Dear Ms. Chesebro:

As you know, we've been maintaining the lawns at your business for several years, and everything looks very nice. But we have a suggestion about how we could make your grounds even more attractive.

During our weekly visits, ⋯ might benefit from profes⋯

General Tree Work

Prune blue spruce located ⋯ specifications:

- Remove all dead, dise⋯ throughout crown to i⋯

Bullets improve legibility.

- Reduce height approx⋯ failure

Prune Norway spruce loc⋯ specifications:

- Prune structurally to r⋯

- Subordinate co-domin⋯ branches

Soil Management

Treat blue spruce, hemlock at right side of building, and hemlock behind parking area with slow-release fertilizer to help improve health following damage from site conditions, insects, and disease $275

Total Amount: $750

Here's the site plan:

Visual clarifies content.

NORWAY SPRUCE

HEMLOCK

REALTY OFFICE

PARKING

ALEXANDER ROAD

BLUE SPRUCE

BLUE SPRUCE

HEMLOCK

WEST MAIN STREET

FIGURE 10.6 • Unsolicited
External Proposal, Page 2

All Green Thumb Landscaping and Lawncare jobs are performed in a professional manner by highly trained workers using state-of-the-art tools and equipment. In addition, we clean up after every job, removing all wood, brush, and debris. We carry full liability insurance, and all our employees are covered by workers' compensation.

If you wish to discuss this proposal, please contact our office at your convenience. If you accept, we'll send you a contract to sign and return.

Polite closing. → Thank you very much for being a Green Thumb client!

Sincerely,

Elvir Vlasic

Elvir Vlasic
Office Manager
(e-mail: evlasic@greenthumb.com)

FIGURE 10.7 • Unsolicited External Proposal, Page 3

CITY PARK
TRAIL RESTORATION
PROPOSAL

Submitted to

Elizabeth Cortwright, Director
Ethanton Philanthropic Foundation

by

Ethanton Striders
Running Club

March 16, 2015

FIGURE 10.8 • Solicited External Proposal (Title Page)

CONTENTS

FIGURE 10.9 • Solicited External Proposal (Table of Contents)

PROJECT SUMMARY

For several years the Ethanton Striders Running Club has been formulating plans to rehabilitate the deteriorating footpath in the wooded area of Ethanton City Park. The project will involve three phases. At this point we are requesting a matching grant of $20,000 from the Foundation to complete the first part of the project, which includes enhancement of the entrance to the woods, in part by installing gates and repaving the roadway. Funding for the second and third parts of the project will be sought from other nongovernmental sources.

PROJECT DESCRIPTION

Originally a carriage path, the present trail took shape as a Works Progress Administration (WPA) project during the Great Depression and enjoyed considerable popularity until fairly recently. Now, however, natural deterioration has taken its toll and the trail is endangered. Broken culverts and clogged drainage ditches have allowed water runoff to erode the trail, and in many places the road surface is badly damaged. In short, potentially unsafe conditions are inhibiting full use of the trail and may eventually cause it to be closed.

The Striders are committed to preventing this because we see the trail as an important community resource that must be protected. We envsion a return to the trail's former diverse-use status. We want the trail to remain a resource for running and other outdoor sports, but we are hopeful that the proposed improvements will also afford a broad range of other nonmotorized leisure opportunities as well.

As mentioned previously, we envision a three-part plan:

Phase One

- Creating a defining entrance vista and increased visibility; improving security of pavilion area by landscaping, tree and brush removal, and signage
- Installing two locking gates—one near the pavilion and one below—to restrict vehicle access while allowing pedestrian access
- Improving drainage provisions above and near the pavilion
- Upgrading of existing pavilion parking area
- Resurfacing of roadway leading to the entrance

FIGURE 10.10 • Solicited External Proposal, Page 1

Phase Two

- Replacing and backfilling fifteen unsalvageable drainage culverts
- Cleaning out and repairing seven additional salvageable culverts
- Boxing out and grading area around all twenty-two culverts
- Placing 2 inches of Type 3 binder to stabilize area around all twenty-two culverts in preparation for paving trail
- Cleaning out drainage ditches alongside trail

Phase Three

- Installing riprap (filler stone) to inhibit water runoff
- Applying two layers of surfacing—a base and a covering of fine stone mixed with rolled petroleum slurry—all along the trail
- Paving entire 2 miles (10,560 linear feet) of trail, 8 feet across, with 1/2 inch of true and 1 inch of top macadam

RATIONALE

This project is currently the Striders' top priority for several reasons. A not-for-profit citizens' organization, we are dedicated to promoting physical fitness through running, and the trail plays a significant role in that endeavor. It comprises a major part of the annual Autumn Leaves 10k Roadrace course, and of the summer Thursday Training Runs course as well. The Autumn Leaves is a premier competitive running event and was recently featured in an article in *Runner's Times* magazine. Attracting participants from all over the Northeast, the Autumn Leaves pumps many thousands of dollars into the local economy the second weekend of every October. The family-oriented Thursday Training Runs are a long-established, ongoing series of weekly "fun runs" enjoyed by hundreds of local participants on twelve consecutive Thursday evenings during the months of May, June, and July.

But the importance of our project extends far beyond these two events because the City Park trail is used year-round for a wide variety of nonvehicular recreational activities: hiking, bicycling, bird-watching, cross-country skiing, snow-shoeing, and the like. The Striders believe that the project will foster positive and significant changes

FIGURE 10.11 • Solicited External Proposal, Page 2

in the community, ones that identify and enhance local strengths and that focus on identifiable outcomes that will make a difference. Our goals are quite clearly defined and—if achieved—will certainly impact most favorably on the quality of life here in Ethanton. Now that the area is undergoing something of a revitalization, we wish to contribute an additional dimension by championing a renewed commitment to one of our city's most valuable resources—the City Park Trail.

RFP CRITERIA

The Ethanton Philanthropic Foundation's RFP includes specific criteria by which each proposal will be judged. What follows is a point-by-point response to these parameters.

Describe the degree to which the project provides for enhanced public enjoyment of outdoor amenities in the greater Ethanton area.

Despite its deteriorated condition, the City Park Trail is used on a year-round basis. It is used primarily for running, hiking, and bicycling during the nonwinter months of April through October. From November through March, the trail is used by cross-country skiers and snowshoers. The trail is central to the Thursday Training Runs series from May through July, to the annual Autumn Leaves 10k Roadrace every October, and to several other fund-raising running events. Our proposal will ensure that these activities continue without fear of injuries caused by poor footing or surface conditions. In addition, the project will again provide the high school cross-country ski and running teams with a natural training site entirely within city limits. Until recently the school had used the trail in this way, but for the past three years school officials have considered the trail too unsafe. This has forced the ski team to travel to Little Davos Mountain (some 15 miles away) to practice, creating added expense.

Describe the degree to which the project furthers a specific goal of state, regional, or local planning bodies.

The Ethanton City Council has officially identified the City Park Trail problem as a high-priority issue. The Striders Board of Directors has been working closely with the Mayor's office about this, and we have received assurances of full cooperation.

FIGURE 10.12 • Solicited External Proposal, Page 3

(See Appendix.) Indeed, at least some of the work involved will almost certainly be performed pro bono by Ethanton Parks Department personnel.

Specify the project's Index of Need (statistically driven rating assigned by Regional Grants Office).

The Regional Grants Office has assigned a preliminary rating of 78.

Describe the degree of citizen involvement in project conception and implementation.

The project is under the direction of the Ethanton Striders Running Club, a 200+ member not-for-profit citizens' organization whose mission is to promote health and fitness through running. Other citizens' groups from the greater Ethanton area have committed resources toward the completion of the project. Members of the Striders will provide project administration and supervision. In addition, a volunteer group consisting of employees of a large local business will provide equipment and operators for much of the tree removal, drainage ditch clearing, and drainage restoration. As mentioned previously, it is expected that additional assistance (engineering and oversight) will be provided by the City Parks Department.

Describe the degree to which the project relates to other Ethanton-area initiatives (natural, cultural, historical, or recreational).

City Park, located entirely within Ethanton city limits, is a large recreation area comprising a pavilion, a nine-hole municipal golf course, tennis courts, and playing fields. Until its deterioration, the trail through the wooded area was an integral part of this multi-use park. It is our intention to restore the trail to provide a safe environment for runners, hikers, bicyclists, cross-country skiers, and snowshoers, thereby promoting greater citizen enjoyment of the natural world. The trail in question connects to other park roads, which are currently shared-use roadways for nonmotorized and motorized access to park facilities.

Describe the degree to which volunteer labor, nontraditional labor, and other certified donations will be used to accomplish the project's goals.

FIGURE 10.13 • Solicited External Proposal, Page 4

At least three area citizens' organizations, the Striders included, have committed resources to the completion of the trail restoration project. Two of the three will provide a considerable amount of volunteer labor and equipment. The third organization has committed up to $20,000 in financial support, pending approval of this proposal by the Ethanton Philanthropic Foundation. In addition, the Striders are able to call upon an extensive list of volunteers who have signed up to help during other club-sponsored initiatives. A community service group affiliated with a large local corporation will supply heavy equipment and operators for much of the work.

Describe the impact the proposal will have on the cultural, social, and recreational needs of the region.

As mentioned in several other parts of this proposal, the trail restoration project is specifically designed to serve the recreational needs of the region by ensuring the continuation of the Thursday Training Runs, the Autumn Leaves Roadrace, and other community-oriented running events. In addition, successful completion of the project will greatly enhance the opportunities for recreational running, hiking, cross-country skiing, bicycling, and snow-shoeing. And restoration of the trail will permit its use by the Ethanton High School cross-country ski and running teams. In addition, we expect that the refurbished trail will invite use by bird-watchers and other nature lovers as part of the existing system of interlocking trails within the park.

TIMELINE

Obviously, any scheduling projections for a project of this scope must be tentative at best because the project depends on several variables including funding and weather. The Striders are hoping to secure adequate financing through a variety of means (see Budget section of this proposal), but this may take longer than expected. In addition, the Vermont winters certainly preclude any progress during that season, leaving only the spring and fall seasons to complete work (we hope to keep the trail open for use during the summer). What follows, then, is a very optimistic timeline. We will make every effort to stay on schedule, but we realize that full completion of the project may take somewhat longer than planned.

FIGURE 10.14 • Solicited External Proposal, Page 5

Phase One: Fall 2015

Phase Two: Spring 2016

Phase Three: Fall 2016

BUDGET

PHASE ONE

<u>Expenses</u>

Architectural fees	$ 1,000
Replacement of culvert at entrance	2,000
Purchase and install main gate	6,500
Erect main gate brick pillars	2,200
Clear and pave two parking areas	5,000
Clean out, repair, and reline two culverts	3,000
Repave road from main gate to Gate #2	9,500
Clear trees and landscape east area	6,000
Clean drainage trenches	3,500
Purchase and install Gate #2	800
Purchase and install signage at both gates	500
	$ 40,000

<u>Funding Sources</u>

Donated labor for landscaping	$ 4,000
Donated labor and equipment for ditching	3,500
Donated wrought iron for main gate	1,000
Donated materials and installation of signage	500
Partial contribution of architectural fees	700
Cash contributions from Ethanton Striders	10,300
Ethanton Philanthropic Foundation Contribution	20,000
	$ 40,000

FIGURE 10.15 • Solicited External Proposal, Page 6

PHASE TWO

<u>Expenses</u>

Replace and backfill fifteen drainage culverts	$ 30,000
Clean out, repair, and reline seven drainage culverts	7,500
Box out and grade for blacktop at replaced culverts	5,500
Place 2" of Type 3 binder at replaced culverts	4,500
Clean out 1 mile of drainage ditches	11,700
	$ 59,200

PHASE THREE

<u>Expenses</u>

Pave 2 miles of road 8 feet wide, 1/2" true + 1" top	$ 42,500
	$ 42,500
Total Phase Two & Phase Three Expenses	$ 101,700

<u>Funding Sources (Phase Two & Phase Three)</u>

Cash contributions from Ethanton Striders	$ 10,000
Donated labor and equipment for ditching	11,700
Monies from additional grant funding	80,000
	$ 101,700

ETHANTON STRIDERS BOARD OF DIRECTORS

President: Frank Rodgers (CEO, Rodgers Industries)

Vice President for Activities & Events: Joseph Carr (CPA, Donnelly & Co.)

Vice President for Administration & Finance: Rev. Thomas J. Moran (Clergy)

Secretary: Position currently vacant

Treasurer: Eugene Torpey (President, Glenwood, Inc.)

Member: Robert Catanzaro, Ph.D. (Professor, Ethanton Community College)

Member: Thomas Gibbons (Athletic Director, Ethanton High School)

Member: Cathleen McGovern, M.D. (Physician, Meyers Medical Group)

Member: Charles McCabe (Owner, McCabe's Clothiers)

Member: Jane Scerbo (Owner, Ethanton Dry Cleaning)

Member: Robert F. Veale (Comptroller, Lincoln Co.)

Member: Grace Walsh (Principal, St. Aedan's Elementary School)

FIGURE 10.16 • Solicited External Proposal, Page 7

CONCLUSION

A recognized, long-established, high-profile local organization with a large, active membership, the Ethanton Striders Running Club has been successful in eliciting project endorsements from the Mayor's office and several major local businesses. We have also secured pledges of assistance from such groups as the Ethanton Mountain Climbing Club, the Valley Bicycle Club, and the Phi Theta Delta service fraternity at Ethanton Community College. Given the range of expertise and the many professional affiliations represented on the club's Board of Directors, we are confident that we will be able to secure needed materials, services, and cash donations as the project moves forward. At present we are preparing a sizable grant application to be submitted to the Federal Recreational Trails Program, we are planning a new 5k race specifically to benefit the trail project, and we intend to conduct raffles and other fund-raising activities at the Thursday Training Runs and other area events. In short, we know we can succeed in this important endeavor, and we urge the Ethanton Philanthropic Foundation to assist us by approving our grant proposal.

APPENDIX

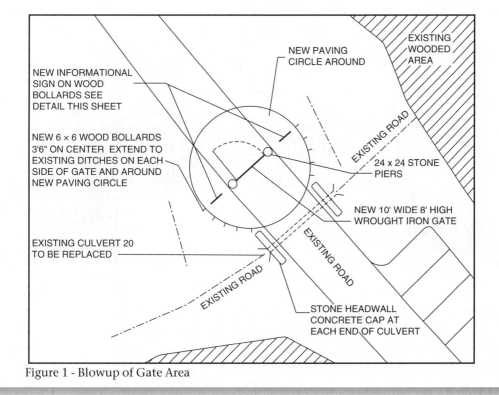

Figure 1 - Blowup of Gate Area

FIGURE 10.17 • Solicited External Proposal, Page 8

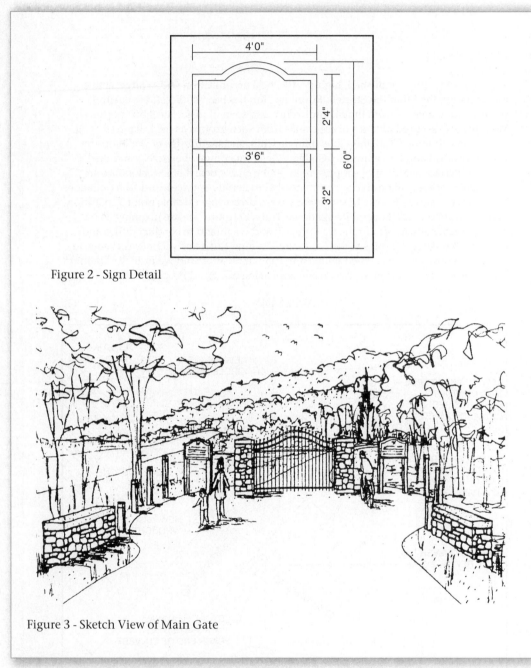

Figure 2 - Sign Detail

Figure 3 - Sketch View of Main Gate

FIGURE 10.18 • Solicited External Proposal, Page 9

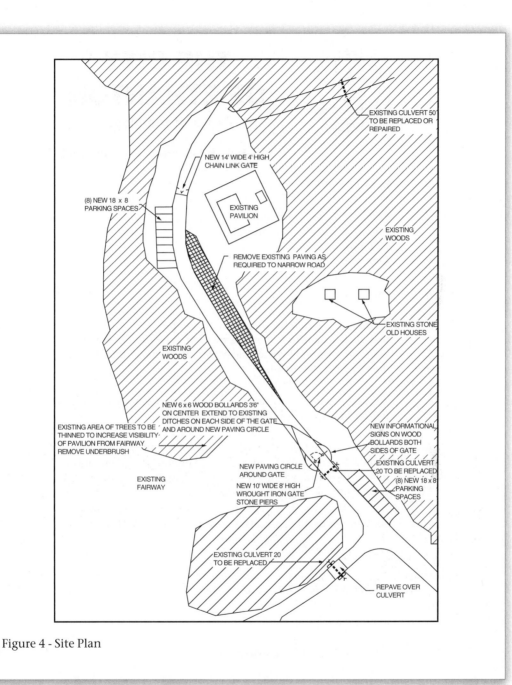

Figure 4 - Site Plan

FIGURE 10.19 • Solicited External Proposal, Page 10

THE CITY
OF ETHANTON
Office of the Mayor

City Hall • Ethanton, Vermont 05201

January 5, 2015

Frank Rodgers, President
Ethanton Striders Running Club
P.O. Box 4141
Ethanton, VT 05201

Dear Frank,

Thanks very much for sharing with me the Ethanton Striders' wonderful plans to restore the trail in City Park. I'm sure you know of my great love for the park and my belief that it's one of the city's greatest assets.

For that reason, your trail restoration project greatly appeals to me, and I fully support your efforts.

I'm pleased that the Striders are willing to undertake this project, and I ask that you keep me informed of your progress. I look forward to the day when the entire community will be able to once again enjoy full use of the trail.

Thanks again! If I can assist in any way, please contact me.

Sincerely,

Hanna Julian

Mayor Hanna Julian

Figure 5 - Mayor's Endorsement

FIGURE 10.20 • Solicited External Proposal, Page 11

Checklist
Evaluating a Proposal

An effective proposal

____ is prepared in a format (e-mail, memo, memo report, letter, or booklet) appropriate to its nature;

____ clearly identifies the situation or problem and fully explains how the proposal addresses it;

____ confirms the feasibility of the proposal, refuting any probable objections and establishing the writer's credentials and qualifications for the project;

____ provides a reliable timeline for completion of the project; identifies any necessary resources, equipment, or support; and includes an itemized budget;

____ closes with a strong, persuasive conclusion that motivates the reader to accept the proposal;

____ uses plain, simple language;

____ maintains an appropriate tone—neither too formal nor too conversational;

____ is well-designed and uses effective visuals—tables, graphs, charts, and the like;

____ contains no typos or mechanical errors in spelling, capitalization, punctuation, or grammar.

EXERCISES

EXERCISE 10.1
Teaming up with one or more classmates, write a proposal seeking approval from your college's student activities director to create a new campus club or organization.

EXERCISE 10.2
Write a proposal seeking approval from your college's athletic director to implement an improvement to the intramural sports program.

EXERCISE 10.3
Write a proposal seeking approval from the department head in your major field of study to take an elective course not among the program's recommended electives.

EXERCISE 10.4

Write a proposal seeking approval from your workplace supervisor to implement a change in a particular policy or procedure.

EXERCISE 10.5

Write a proposal seeking approval from one of your instructors to create a peer tutoring arrangement or study group designed to enhance students' performance in the course.

EXERCISE 10.6

Write a proposal seeking approval from your clergyperson to create a religion-based club or interest group.

EXERCISE 10.7

Write a proposal seeking approval from your local library director to present a public lecture at the library on a topic you're knowledgeable about.

EXERCISE 10.8

Write a proposal in response to an RFP found on the Internet or in a trade journal or magazine.

EXERCISE 10.9

Create a list identifying each of the proposals in Exercises 10.1–10.8 as solicited or unsolicited and internal or external.

EXERCISE 10.10

Nearly all college-level workplace communications courses include an assignment requiring the completion of a long report. Using Figures 10.1 and 10.2 as a model, write a proposal seeking your instructor's approval of your chosen topic. If the topic has been assigned by the instructor, write a proposal seeking approval of your plan of approach.

Long Reports: Format, Collaboration, and Documentation

11

LEARNING OBJECTIVE

When you complete this chapter you'll be able to:

- identify and evaluate reputable sources of information.
- incorporate information by correct use of summary, paraphrase, and quotation.
- create long reports in accordance with format conventions.
- work collaboratively to produce reports.
- document your sources using both MLA and APA style.

In business, industry, and professions such as medicine and law, important decisions are made every day. Some concern routine matters, but others are more complicated, involving considerable risk and expense. For example, suppose that a hospital administration is debating whether to add a new wing to the main building. Perhaps a police department wants to switch to a different kind of patrol car, or a successful but relatively new business must decide whether to expand now or wait a few years. Each situation requires in-depth study before a responsible decision can be reached. The potential advantages and drawbacks of each alternative as well as the long-range effects must be identified and examined. This is where the long report comes into play.

To prepare you for the challenges involved in writing workplace reports, most college courses (and many high school classes as well) require you to complete one or more research-based assignments. Sometimes the topic is given by the instructor, but at the college level, you are often permitted to choose. In either case, you have to gather information by consulting reliable sources. But you can't simply copy other writers' ideas word for word and present them as if they were your own. That's *plagiarism*. Instead, you're required to use summary, paraphrase, and quotation correctly and provide documentation to identify your sources and indicate where you've used them. This chapter shows you how to complete a long report by finding, evaluating, and properly using appropriate sources of information.

Identification and Evaluation of Sources

Whether your professor assigns the topic of your report or allows you to select your own, you have to conduct research that enables you to gather enough information to cover the topic in depth, going beyond what you already know about it. The basic sources of such information are books, magazines, newspapers, academic journals, and Web sites.

Books

The most traditional source of in-depth information, books are published on an enormous range of topics. Whatever you're writing about, countless books can provide you with abundant material that can help you develop your report. But always look for books that have been published fairly recently. This helps you narrow your focus when searching your college library's holdings. More importantly, the recent titles are the most up to date and reflect current thinking on the topic. In addition, it makes sense to choose books released by major university presses and long-established commercial publishers because they are more selective in choosing what to print. As a result, these publishers' books tend to be more accurate and reliable than those produced by lesser-known publishers. Here are six of the most highly regarded commercial publishing houses, all based in New York:

- Farrar, Straus, and Giroux
- Harper Collins
- Houghton Mifflin
- Alfred A. Knopf
- W.W. Norton & Company
- Random House

Magazines

Even a brief glance at the magazine display rack in any store reveals that countless periodicals are published on a weekly or monthly basis. Some are quite well-known, others less so. But the mere fact that a magazine enjoys high visibility does not necessarily mean it's a good source. Many popular magazines are quite superficial, devoted to coverage of celebrity gossip and other trivial concerns. There are also many good but highly specialized magazines (such as *Car & Driver*, *Psychology Today*, and *Wired*) that focus exclusively on one area of interest. Others, however, have a broader appeal. Here's a short list of some of the best general audience magazines:

- *The Atlantic*
- *The Economist*
- *Harper's*
- *The Nation*
- *The New Republic*
- *The New Yorker*
- *Time*

The Economist, The Nation, The New Yorker, and *Time* are published weekly, while *The Atlantic, Harper's,* and *The New Republic* appear monthly. Most college and university libraries subscribe to these magazines along with many others. It's a good idea to check with your instructor before using magazines as sources because some instructors consider them too lightweight and will not accept them.

Newspapers

Although several major U.S. newspapers have gone out of business or been replaced by online versions in recent years, hundreds are still being published. But only a few are typically cited as sources in academic writing:

- *The Los Angeles Times*
- *The New York Times*
- *The Wall Street Journal*
- *The Washington Post*

The New York Times and *The Washington Post* (*not* to be confused with the tabloid-format *New York Post*) are considered the most reputable. Indeed, *The New York Times* is one of the most respected newspapers not just in this country but also in the world. Virtually all college and university libraries subscribe to *The New York Times* and *The Wall Street Journal* along with local papers and may maintain microfilm files going back many years. In addition, numerous Web site and database archives provide access to past issues.

Academic Journals

Every area of academic study supports scholarly journals that publish highly specialized articles, almost always written by professors and researchers in that field. Accordingly, these essays often discuss recent research or newly emerging theories. Given their familiarity with the journals, many professors require their students to consult such sources when completing research-based assignments. To find journal articles (or, for that matter, articles in magazines and newspapers as well), it's easiest to consult computerized databases that allow you to locate material related to your topic. Here are several very useful such resources, all available online from EBSCOhost, a service subscribed to by college and university libraries:

- **Academic Search Complete** is the most comprehensive database, covering articles in thousands of publications in all disciplines.

- **Associates Program Source** is geared to the needs of community college students, focusing on nearly 1,000 journals aligned with programs of study typical of the two-year schools.

- **Business Source Complete** is devoted exclusively to indexing abstracts of business articles as far back as the 1880s.

- **CINAHL Plus with Full Text** is a database for articles about nursing and allied health services, covering more than 750 scholarly journals in those fields.

- **Computer Source** provides up-to-date information on articles about trends and developments in the field of technology.

- **ERIC** is the Education Resource Information Center database, containing links to more than 300,000 articles dating back to the 1960s.

- **GreenFILE** covers the environment, with information on nearly 5,000 articles about global warming, green building, pollution, sustainable agriculture, renewable energy, recycling, and related concerns.

- **Humanities International Complete** includes data on more than 2,000 journals devoted to the humanities (art, music, literature, film, etc.)

- **Newspaper Source Plus** covers more than 700 newspapers along with more than half a million television and radio news transcripts.

- **Vocational and Career Collection** serves community colleges and trade schools by providing information on articles in more than 300 trade- and industry-related periodicals.

Web Sites

As anyone who has ever clicked a mouse has immediately discovered, the amount of information available on the Web is seemingly unlimited. A Google search for virtually any topic may result in hundreds of results. But the quality of this material varies greatly. For example, despite its wide range and resulting popularity among Internet users, Wikipedia, the free encyclopedia, is not considered an acceptable source for academic research. For that matter, most professors will not accept print encyclopedias either. But encyclopedias—Wikipedia included—can lead you to more highly regarded sources because encyclopedia entries commonly include a bibliography of related works. For detailed advice on how to evaluate Web sites, see the "Tech Tips" on page 206.

Integration of Sources

When developing your paper by inserting information you've gathered from your research, there are basically three approaches you can use: summary, paraphrase, and quotation. Most research-based writing relies on all three, but they are quite different from one another.

Summary

As explained in Chapter 5, "the term *summary* refers to a brief statement of the essential content of something heard, seen, or read. For any kind of summary, the writer reduces a body of material to its bare essentials. . . . Summary writing . . . demands an especially keen sense of not only what to include but also of what to *leave out*. The goal is to highlight key points and not burden the reader with unnecessary details." Not surprisingly, a summary is always much shorter than the original.

Paraphrase

Paraphrase, on the other hand, is often *longer* than the original. That's because its purpose is not only to present the original information but also to clarify it. Sometimes this is accomplished by choosing more familiar words. Often it involves providing explanations or resequencing the original information to make it easier to understand. Paraphrase is especially useful when you're attempting to deal with technical or otherwise specialized subject matter.

Quotation

Sometimes called *direct quotation,* this involves using exactly the same phrasing that appears in the original, repeating it *verbatim* (word for word), and enclosing it within quotation marks. Indeed, that's the main purpose of quotation marks—to indicate that what appears between them is an exact copy. For example, direct quotation was used in the preceding explanation of summary. Notice the four periods that appear after the second sentence there. The first is the period ending the sentence after "essentials." The subsequent periods are the *ellipsis*. An ellipsis indicates that something from the original—two entire sentences, in this case—has been removed at that point. When something is removed *within* a sentence, only three periods are used (no sentence-ending punctuation is included). Although quotation certainly has value, not the least because it exactly captures the content and tone of the source, do not depend on it too heavily. Good research-based writing is never simply an exercise in stringing quotes together. No more than 20 percent of your paper should consist of quotation.

Report Format

Obviously, both the subject matter and the formatting of long reports will vary from one workplace to another and, in the academic context, from one discipline to another and even from one instructor to another. Nevertheless, most long reports share the components described in the following paragraphs.

Transmittal Document

Prepared according to standard memo or business letter format (see Chapter 2), the transmittal document accompanies a long report, conveying it from whoever wrote it to whoever requested it. The transmittal document says, in effect, "Here's the report you wanted" and briefly summarizes its content. The memo or e-mail format is used for transmitting in-house reports, whereas the letter format is used for transmitting reports to outside readers. Often, the transmittal document serves as a cover sheet, although it's sometimes positioned immediately after the title page of the report. Figure 11.1 is a sample transmittal e-mail.

Title Page

In addition to the title itself, this page includes the name(s) of whoever prepared the report, the name(s) of whoever requested it, the names of the companies or organizations involved, and the date. In an academic context, the title page includes the title, the name(s) of the student author(s) and the instructor who assigned the report, the course name (along with the course number and section number), the college, and the date. Figure 11.2 is a sample title page prepared for a workplace context.

Abstract

Sometimes called an *executive summary,* this is simply a brief synopsis—a greatly abbreviated version of the report (see Chapter 5). An effective abstract captures the essence of the report, including its major findings and recommendations. In the workplace, the abstract assists those who may not have time to read the entire report but need to know what it says. Sometimes the abstract is positioned near the front of the report; at other times, it appears at the end. For a ten- to twenty-page report, the abstract should not be longer than one page and can be formatted as one long paragraph. Figure 11.3 is an example of a concise abstract.

Table of Contents

As in a book, the table of contents for a long report clearly identifies each section of the report, with its title and the page on which it appears. Many also show subdivisions within sections. When fine-tuning a report before submitting it, ensure that the section titles and page numbers used in the table of contents are consistent with those in the report itself (see Figure 11.4).

List of Illustrations

This list resembles the table of contents, but rather than referring to text sections, it lists tables, graphs, charts, and all other visuals appearing in the report—each numbered and titled—and their page numbers. As with the table of contents, always ensure that your illustrations list accurately reflects the visual contents of the report and the corresponding labeling/captions (see Figure 11.5).

Glossary

A "mini-dictionary," the glossary defines all potentially unfamiliar words, expressions, or symbols in your report. Not all reports need a glossary; it depends on the topic and the intended audience. But if you're using specialized vocabulary or symbols that may not be well-known, it's best to include a glossary page with terms alphabetized for easy reference and symbols listed in the order in which they appear in the text (see Figure 11.6).

Text

One major difference between a long report and an academic term paper is that a report is divided into sections, each with its own title. As mentioned previously, it's important that these divisions within the text be accurately reflected in the table of contents.

Every long report also includes an introduction and a conclusion. The introduction provides an overview of the report, identifying its purpose and scope and explaining the procedures used and the context in which it was written. The conclusion summarizes the main points in the report and lists recommendations, if any.

Visuals

A major feature of many reports, visuals (see Chapter 3) sometimes appear in a separate section—an appendix—at the end of a report. However, a better approach is to integrate them into the text because this is more convenient for the reader. Either way, you should draw the reader's attention to pertinent visuals (stating, for example, "See Figure 5"), and every visual must be properly numbered and titled, with its source identified. The numbering/titling must be the same as in the list of illustrations.

Pagination

Number your report pages correctly. There are several pagination systems in use. Generally, page numbers (1, 2, 3, and so on) begin on the first page of the introduction and continue until the last page of the report. Frontmatter pages (abstract, table of contents, list of illustrations, glossary, and anything else that precedes the introduction) are numbered with lowercase Roman numerals (i, ii, iii, iv, and so on). There is no page number on the transmittal document or the title page, although the latter "counts" as a front-matter page, so the page immediately following the title page is numbered as ii. The best position for page numbers is in the upper-right corner because that location enables the reader to find a particular page simply by thumbing through the report. Notice the page numbering throughout the sample report in this chapter (Figures 11.1–11.13).

Collaboration

A memo, letter, or short report is nearly always composed by one person working individually. This is sometimes true for long reports. However, because the subject matter of long reports is usually complex and multifaceted, they are often written collaboratively. Indeed, nearly all workplace writers are called on to collaborate at least occasionally. Teamwork is so common in the workplace because it provides certain obvious advantages. For example, a group that works well together can produce a long report *faster* than one person working alone. In addition, the team possesses a broader perspective and a wider range of knowledge and expertise than an individual. To slightly amend the old saying, two heads—or more—are better than one. In addition, with the increasing sophistication of *groupware* (word-processing and document design programs created specifically for collaborative use), teamworking has become easier and faster than ever.

Nevertheless, collaboration can pose problems if the members of a group have difficulty interacting smoothly. Real teamwork requires everyone involved to exercise tact, courtesy, and responsibility. The following factors are essential to successful collaboration:

1. Everyone on the team must fully understand the purpose, goals, and intended audience of the document.
2. There must be uniform awareness of the project's confidentiality level, especially if individual team members must consult outside sources for data, background information, or other material.
3. Team members must agree to set aside individual preferences in favor of the group's collective judgment.
4. A team leader must be in charge of the project—someone whom the other members are willing to recognize as the coordinator. Ideally, the leader is elected from within the group (although the leader is sometimes appointed by someone at a higher level of authority). The leader must be not only knowledgeable and competent but also a "people person" with excellent interpersonal skills. The leader has many responsibilities:

   - Schedules, announces, and conducts meetings

   - Helps establish procedural guidelines, especially regarding progress assessment

   - Monitors team members' involvement, providing encouragement and assistance

- Promotes consensus and mediates disagreements
- Maintains an accurate master file copy of the evolving document

    In short, the leader operates in a managerial capacity (much like a professor in a college class), ensuring a successful outcome by keeping everyone on task and holding the whole effort together.

5. The team must assign clearly defined roles to the other members, designating responsibilities according to everyone's talents and strengths. For example, the group's most competent researcher takes charge of information retrieval. Someone trained in drafting or computer-assisted design agrees to format the report and create visuals. The member with the best keyboarding skills (or clerical support) actually produces the document. The best writer is the overall editor, making final judgments on matters of organization, style, mechanics, and the like. If an oral presentation is required, the group's most confident public speaker assumes that responsibility. A given individual might assume more than one role, but everyone must feel satisfied that the work has been fairly distributed.

6. Once the project begins, the team meets regularly to assess its progress, prevent duplication of effort, and resolve any problems that arise. All disagreements or differences of opinion are reconciled in a productive manner. In any group undertaking, a certain amount of conflict is inevitable and indeed necessary to achieve consensus. But this interplay should be a source of creative energy, not antagonism. Issues must be dealt with on an objectively intellectual level, not in a personal or emotional manner. To this end, the group should adopt a code of interaction designed to minimize conflict and maximize the benefits of collaboration. Here are some guidelines:

- Make a real effort to be calm, patient, reasonable, and flexible—in short, *helpful*.

- Voice all reservations, misgivings, and resentments rather than letting them smolder.

- Direct criticism at the issue, not the person ("There's another way of looking at this" rather than "You're looking at this only one way"), and try not to *interpret* criticism personally.

- Make an effort to really *listen* to others' remarks and not interrupt.

- Paraphrase others' statements to be sure of their meaning ("What you're saying, then, is . . .").

- Identify strengths in other people's work before mentioning weaknesses ("This first section is very well-written, but I have a suggestion for revising the second section").

- Avoid vague, unhelpful criticism by addressing specifics ("In paragraph 3, it's unclear whether Dept. A or Dept. B will be in charge" rather than "Paragraph 3 is unclear"). This is especially important when providing *written* feedback.

- Try not to concentrate on picky, inconsequential fine points. Although glaring errors in spelling, grammar, and the like should certainly be corrected, the focus should be on the "big picture."

- Accentuate the positive rather than the negative ("Now that we've agreed on the visuals, we can move on" instead of "We can't seem to agree on anything but the visuals").

- Suggest rather than command ("Maybe we should try it this way" instead of "Do it this way!") and offer rather than demand ("If you'd like, I'll . . ." instead of "I'm going to . . .").

- Be aware of your body language, which can send negative signals that impede progress by creating resistance on the part of your teammates.

- In cases of major conflict, the leader must mediate to prevent the group from bogging down. One solution is to table the problematic issue and move on, addressing it at a later meeting after everyone has been able to consider it in greater depth. If there's a severe clash between two group members, it's usually best for the leader to meet privately with them to reach compromise.

7. All members of the group must complete their fair share of the work in a conscientious fashion and observe all deadlines. Nothing is more disruptive to a team's progress than an irresponsible member who fails to complete work punctually or "vanishes" for long periods of time. To maintain contact between regularly scheduled meetings of the group, members should exchange phone numbers and/or e-mail addresses. If all team members are sufficiently tech-savvy, they can maintain contact through synchronous electronic discussion in real time using a virtual conference room or multiuser domain (MUD) accessible via the Internet. But exchanges in such settings should be brief and to the point because lengthy comments take too long to write and read, thus inhibiting the free and spontaneous flow of ideas so necessary to productive collaboration. Another option is to use file transfer protocol (FTP) to create a common Web site to which group members can post drafts for review by their teammates. In any case, electronic communication should be seen simply as a way to keep in touch between meetings and should not become a substitute for frequent face-to-face interaction.

Regardless of how the team goes about its work, it's extremely helpful to the eventual editor if all sections of the document have been prepared according to uniform procedures. Therefore, unless the workplace has adopted an organization-wide style manual that governs such matters, the team should formulate its own guidelines. The editor then doesn't have to waste valuable time imposing conformity on various members' work but can concentrate instead on more important matters such as organization and content. To be useful, however, the guidelines shouldn't be too extensive. Their purpose is simply to ensure that all members are preparing their drafts in a consistent way. Here are ten areas to consider:

- Margins: Usually, 1" or 1 1/2" margins are used.

- Fonts: Simple fonts are the most legible; the standard Microsoft Word font for documents is Times New Roman.

- Type size: 12-point type is the norm, although headings can be larger.

- Spacing: Double-spacing is best for drafts (to facilitate editing), but final versions of documents are often single-spaced with double-spacing between sections.

- CAPITALS, **boldface**, *italics*, and <u>underlining</u>: There must be agreement on when and how to use these options.

- Abbreviations, acronyms, and numbers: Again, the team must agree on their use.

- Page numbers: Position them in the upper-right corners of all draft pages.

- Placement and labeling of visuals: For recommendations, see Chapter 3.

- Headings: Depending on the nature of the document, headings can take many forms, including single words, phrases, statements, questions, and commands. They should be parallel in construction. As with all other format features, however, there should be uniformity in all sections.

- Documentation: If documentation is required, the same system (usually MLA or APA) should be used throughout.

Theoretically, a group can handle the writing of a report or other document in one of three ways:

- The whole team writes the report collectively and then the editor revises the draft and submits it to the group for final approval or additional revisions.

- One person writes the entire report and then the group, led by the editor, revises it collectively.

- Each team member writes one part of the report individually and then the editor revises each part and submits the complete draft to the whole group for final approval or additional revisions.

Of these alternatives, the first is the most truly collaborative but is also extremely difficult and time-consuming, requiring uncommon harmony within the group. The second method is preferable but places too great a burden on one writer. The third approach is the most common and is certainly the best provided the editor seeks clarification from individuals whenever necessary during the editing process. For this reason, the third approach is the one that underlies most of what's been said here. However, note that in all three approaches, the whole group gets to see and comment on the report in its final form. Because everyone's name will be on it, no one should be dissatisfied with the finished product. After all, collaboration is a team effort with the goal of producing a polished document approved by all members of the team.

Documentation

Whatever sources you finally use in a research assignment, you must provide documentation. That is, you must identify those sources and indicate where you have used them. In everyday writing, this is often accomplished by inserting the relevant information directly into the text, as in this example:

In "Fancy Footwork," her February 2015 *Wired* article about the role of computers in typeface design, journalist Margaret Rhodes points out that "to be sold globally, modern fonts can require more than 600 characters to cover every major language."

This straightforward approach eliminates the need for a bibliography (list of sources) at the end of the piece. In academic writing, however, documentation nearly always includes both a bibliography and parenthetical citations identifying the origin of each quotation, statistic, paraphrase, or visual when it appears within the text.

Documentation is necessary to avoid plagiarism—the use of someone else's work without proper acknowledgement. As the eighth edition of the *MLA Handbook* explains, it's considered a serious offense: "literary theft. . . . passing off another person's ideas, information, expressions as one's own" (6). The former (7th) edition of the Handbook provided guidelines for recognizing and avoiding plagiarism:

You have plagiarized if:

- you took notes that did not distinguish summary and paraphrase from quotation and then you presented wording from the notes as if it were all your own.
- while browsing the Web, you copied text and pasted it into your paper without quotation marks or without citing the source.
- you repeated or paraphrased someone's wording without acknowledgment.
- you took someone's unique or particularly apt phrase without acknowledgment.
- you paraphrased someone's argument or presented someone's line of thought without acknowledgment.
- you bought or otherwise acquired a research paper and handed in part or all of it as your own.

You can avoid plagiarism by:

- making a list of the writers and viewpoints you discovered in your research and using this list to double-check the presentation of material in your paper.
- keeping the following three categories distinct in your notes: your ideas, your summaries of others' material, and exact wording you copy.
- identifying the sources of all material you borrow—exact wording, paraphrases, ideas, arguments, and facts.
- checking with your instructor when you are uncertain about your use of sources (pp. 60–61).

Bibliography

When creating the list of sources that must appear at the end of your report, you will be expected to use one of the established formats. The MLA format, which titles the list "Works Cited," and the American Psychological Association (APA) format, which titles the list "References," are most commonly taught in college courses, although a great many others do exist, including those of the American Chemical Society (ACS), American Institute of Physics (AIP), American Mathematical Society (AMS), American Medical Association (AMA), the Council of Biology Editors (CBE), and the format described in *The Chicago Manual of Style* (sometimes referred to as "Turabian," after Kate L. Turabian, the University of Chicago secretary who wrote the first version of the manual in the 1930s), to name just a few. Here is a typical bibliography entry formatted according to MLA and APA guidelines:

> **MLA** Baron, Naomi S. *Alphabet to Email: How Written English Evolved and Where It's Heading.* Routledge, 2000.

> **APA** Baron, N. S. (2000). *Alphabet to email: How written English evolved and where it's heading.* London, England: Routledge.

Notice the differences between the two formats. Perhaps the most obvious is the placement of the publication date. But variations also exist with respect to capitalization, punctuation, and abbreviation. In both systems, however, double-spacing is used throughout, and titles—like those of books, newspapers, magazines, journals, and other periodicals—are italicized. In both formats, entries appear in alphabetical order by authors' last names or, for anonymous works, by the first significant word in the title.

There are many other kinds of sources besides single-author books, however, and each requires a slightly different handling. Here are some of the most common citations:

Book by Two Authors

> **MLA** Moniz, B.J., and R.T. Miller. *Welding Skills.* 4th ed. American Technical, 2010.

> **APA** Moniz, B. J., & Miller, R. T. (2010). *Welding skills* (4th ed.). Orland Park, IL: American Technical.

Book by Three Authors

> **MLA** Lawson, Judy, Joanna Kroll, and Kelly Kowatch. *The New Information Professional: Your Guide to Careers in the Digital Age.* Neal, 2010.

> **APA** Lawson, J., Kroll, J., & Kowatch, K. (2010). *The new information professional: Your guide to careers in the digital age.* New York: Neal-Schuman.

Book by a Corporate Author

> **MLA** American Welding Society. *Welding Inspection Handbook.* 3rd ed. AWS, 2000.

> **APA** American Welding Society (2000). *Welding inspection handbook* (3rd ed.). Miami, FL: Author.

Edited Book of Articles

MLA Gerdes, Louise I., editor. *Cyberbullying.* Greenhaven, 2012.

APA Gerdes, L. I. (Ed.). (2012). *Cyberbullying.* Farmington Hills, MI: Greenhaven.

Chapter in an Edited Book

MLA Willard, Nancy. "Schools Have the Right to Punish Cyberbullies." *Cyberbullying.* Edited by Louise I. Gerdes, Greenhaven, 2012.

APA Willard, N. (2012). Schools have the right to punish cyberbullies. In L. I. Gerdes (Ed.), *Cyberbullying* (pp. 71–78). Farmington Hills, MI: Greenhaven.

Article in a Newspaper

MLA Markoff, John. "Scientists Find Cheaper Way to Ensure Internet Security." *The New York Times*, 20 Nov. 2012, p. B5.

APA Markoff, J. (2012, November 20). Scientists find cheaper way to ensure Internet security. *The New York Times*, p. B5.

Anonymous Article in a Newspaper

MLA "Scientists Confirm Ice Present on Mars." *The Wall Street Journal*, 30 Nov. 2012, p. A6.

APA Scientists confirm ice present on mars. (2012, November 30). *The Wall Street Journal*, p. A6.

Article in a Weekly or Biweekly Magazine

MLA Park, Alice. "Field Goal: How Scientists Are Making Football Safer." *Time*, 1 Oct. 2012, p. 14.

APA Park, A. (2012, October 1). How scientists are making football safer. *Time, 180,* 14.

Article in a Monthly or Bimonthly Magazine

MLA Broida, Rick. "What Features Will the Next Generation of Smartphones Have?" *Popular Science*, Nov. 2011, p. 88.

APA Broida, R. (2011, November). What features will the next generation of smartphones have? *Popular Science, 279,* 88.

Anonymous Article in a Magazine

MLA "Galvanizer Eliminates Hazardous Waste." *MSC: Modern Steel Construction*, Jan. 2010, p. 17.

APA Galvanizer eliminates hazardous waste. (2010, January). *MSC: Modern Steel Construction, 50*, 17.

Article in a Trade Journal or Academic Journal

MLA Galvin, Robert. "Aerial Imaging Aids Forensics." *Professional Surveyor Magazine*, vol. 32, no. 7 (2012), pp. 42–44.

APA Galvin, R. (2012). Aerial imaging aids forensics. *Professional Surveyer Magazine, 32* (7), 42–44.

Entry in an Encyclopedia or Other Reference Work

MLA Gran, Richard J. "Magnetic Levitation Train." *The World Book Encyclopedia*, 2000.

APA Gran, R. J. (2000). Magnetic levitation train. In *The World Book Encyclopedia* (Vol. 13, pp. 55–56). Chicago: World Book.

Personal Interview

MLA Britton, William. Personal interview. 10 Nov. 2013.

APA In APA style, all personal communications (conversations, interviews, e-mails, and the like) are excluded from the list of references. Such sources are documented only within the body of the text, like this:

> Financial officer William Britton (personal communication, November 12, 2013) stated that the "total cost of the project may be well over a million dollars."

Link Within an Internet Site

MLA "How to File a Complaint with OSHA." Occupational Health & Safety Administration, United States Department of Labor, 17 Apr. 2013, www.osha.gov/as/opa/worker/complain.html.

APA How to file a complaint with OSHA. Occupational Health & Safety Administration, Department of Labor. Retrieved April 17, 2013, from http://www.osha.gov/as/opa/worker/complain.html

Online Newspaper Article

MLA Firestone, David. "Republicans Would Rather Laugh Than Bargain." *The New York Times*, 30 Nov. 2012, takingnote.blogs.nytimes.com/ 2012/11/30/republicans-would-rather-laugh-than-bargain/?_r=0.

APA Firestone, D. (2012, November 30). Republicans would rather laugh than bargain. *The New York Times*. Retrieved from http://www.nytimes.com

Online Magazine Article

MLA Paul, Ann Murphy. "How to Use Technology to Make You Smarter." *Time*, 29 Nov. 2012, ideas.time.com/2012/11/29/how-to-use-technology-to-make-you-smarter/?iid=sr-link1.

APA Paul, A. M. (2012, November 29). How to use technology to make you smarter. *Time*. Retrieved from http://time.com

Article in a Database

MLA Ashby, Mike. "Designing Architectured Materials." *Scripta Materialia*, vol. 68, no. 1, pp. 4–7. *Academic Search Complete*, 4 Dec. 2012, doi: 10.1016/j.scriptamat.2012.04.033.

APA Ashby, M. (2013). Designing architectured materials. *Scripta Materialia*, *68*(1), 4–7. doi: 10.1016/j.scriptamat.2012.04.033

E-Mail Message

MLA Powers, Bill. "Re: Monday's Meeting." Received by Edward Ahern, 12 Mar. 2013.

APA In APA style, all personal communications (e-mail, conversations, interviews, and the like) are excluded from the list of references. Such sources are documented only within the text, like this:

> Human Resources director Bill Powers (personal communication, March 12, 2013) agrees that Monday's meeting "did not fully accomplish its objectives."

The last several examples illustrate the basic formats recommended by the MLA and the APA for documenting electronic sources. As you can see, both styles provide essentially the same information to identify print sources: the author's name (if known), the title of the work, and so on. But electronic sources are of many different kinds, not all of which can be covered here. For a more complete explanation of how electronic (and print) sources are handled, you should consult the two organizations' Web sites or the most recent editions of their handbooks, readily available in virtually all academic libraries:

MLA Handbook, 8th ed. MLA, 2016.
Publication Manual of the American Psychological Association (6th ed.). Washington, DC: APA, 2010.

In addition, numerous Web sites actually provide you with correctly formatted bibliography entries in various styles, including MLA and APA. Typically, these sites use a "fill-in-the-blanks" approach. You type in the information and the computer does the rest. Of course, you must be very careful to enter the data correctly. The best of these can be found at www.easybib.com, although it charges a fee for styles other than MLA. In addition, Microsoft Word includes a documentation feature that operates in much the same way and comprises MLA, APA, and other styles.

Parenthetical Citations

Every time you use a source within the body of a paper—whether summarizing, paraphrasing, or directly quoting—you must identify the source by inserting parentheses. The contents and positioning of these parentheses vary somewhat depending on whether you're using MLA or APA style. Here are examples of how to cite quotations:

> **MLA** "E-mail has emerged as a medium that allows communication in situations where neither speech nor writing can easily substitute" (Baron 259).

> **APA** "E-mail has emerged as a medium that allows communication in situations where neither speech nor writing can easily substitute" (Baron, 2000, p. 259).

If you mention the author's name in your own text, neither MLA nor APA requires that the name appear in the parentheses, although the APA system then requires *two* parenthetical insertions. The first provides the date of publication and the second the page number.

> **MLA** As Baron observes, "E-mail has emerged as a medium that allows communication in situations where neither speech nor writing can easily substitute" (259).

> **APA** As Baron (2000) observes, "E-mail has emerged as a medium that allows communication in situations where neither speech nor writing can easily substitute" (p. 259).

When you're summarizing or paraphrasing, and whether mentioning the author's name or not, the differences between the two styles are as follows:

> **MLA** As Baron observes, e-mail is sometimes more practical than speech or writing (259).

> **APA** As Baron (2000) observes, e-mail is sometimes more practical than speech or writing (p. 259).

> **MLA** E-mail is sometimes more practical than speech or writing (Baron 259).

> **APA** E-mail is sometimes more practical than speech or writing (Baron, 2000, p. 259).

Credit a quote from an unsigned source (such as the "Anonymous Article in a Magazine" example shown earlier) as follows:

MLA "A patent was not secured on this machine because the company wants to help other companies achieve the same success in hazardous waste reduction" ("Galvanizer" 17).

APA "A patent was not secured on this machine because the company wants to help other companies achieve the same success in hazardous waste reduction" ("Galvanizer eliminates," 2010, p. 17).

To credit a paraphrase from an unsigned source, follow the same pattern:

MLA The company did not secure a patent so other companies could also reduce hazardous waste by creating such machines ("Galvanizer" 17).

APA The company did not secure a patent so other companies could also reduce hazardous waste by creating such machines ("Galvanizer eliminates," 2010, p. 17).

The purpose of parenthetical citations is to enable readers to find your sources on the Works Cited or References page in case they want to consult those sources in their entirety. Obviously, proper documentation is an important part of any report that has drawn on sources beyond the writer's own prior knowledge. What follows is a research-based report prepared according to MLA guidelines (Figures 11.1 through 11.13).

Tech**Tips**

The *MLA Handbook* says it quite well:

Today, the Internet, with its many publications, databases, archives, and search engines, has accelerated the process of finding and retrieving sources— but at the same time it has complicated the researcher's assessment of their reliability. The amount and variety of information available have grown exponentially, but the origins of that information are too often unclear (11).

Consequently, you must exercise great selectivity when gathering information online. Here are some questions to ask when evaluating electronic sources:

- Who has posted or sponsored the site? An individual? An organization? A special interest or advocacy group? What are their credentials or qualifications? The final suffix in the URL indicates a site's origins:

.com	Commercial enterprise
.org	Nonprofit organization
.edu	College, university, or other educational institution
.gov	Government agency
.mil	Military group
.net	Network

- Sometimes, it's helpful to enter the individual's or group's name in a search engine to see what related sites emerge. This often reveals affiliations and biases that have an impact on credibility.

- Does the site provide links to related sites? Does it credit its own sources?

- Is the information presented in a reasonably objective fashion or does the site seem to favor or promote a particular viewpoint or perspective?

- Does the site provide an e-mail address or other contact information that you can use to seek more information?

- What is the date of the posting? Is the information current?

- How well-written is the site? How well-designed? In short, does it seem to be the work of professionals or amateurs?

| File | Edit | View | Tools | Message | Help |

| Reply | Reply All | Forward | Print | Delete | Previous | Next | Addresses |

From: William Congreve, Administrative Assistant
Date: 7/10/2015
To: Rosa Sheridan, Director, Human Resources
Subject: Drug-Testing Report

As you may recall, we recently decided that I should prepare a report about the various methods and procedures that we must consider now that we've decided to introduce a drug-testing program at Paramount. Here's the report. If you have any questions, I'd be happy to provide further details.

FIGURE 11.1 • Drug-Testing Report, Transmittal E-mail

DRUG TESTING
IN THE WORKPLACE:
METHODS & PROCEDURES

by

William Congreve
Administrative Assistant

Submitted to

Rosa Sheridan
Director of Human Resources

Paramount Construction, Inc.
Mission Viejo, California

July 10, 2015

FIGURE 11.2 • Drug-Testing Report, Title Page

ii

ABSTRACT

Paramount Construction has decided to introduce a mandatory drug-testing program based on EMIT testing of urine samples. To avoid costly lawsuits and other setbacks, we'll observe several key features of successful drug-testing protocol: a clear policy statement, strict guidelines for specimen collection, use of NIDA-certified laboratories, confirmation of all positive test results, and employee assistance services. Paramount will begin by testing job applicants only rather than the existing workforce, but we will first establish an EAP. In addition, we'll seek assistance from an outside (NIDA) consultant.

FIGURE 11.3 • Drug-Testing Report, Abstract

iii

TABLE OF CONTENTS

FIGURE 11.4 • Drug-Testing Report, Table of Contents

iv

LIST OF ILLUSTRATIONS

FIGURE 11.5 • Drug-Testing Report, List of Illustrations

v

GLOSSARY

CDC	Centers for Disease Control and Prevention
EAP	Employee Assistance Program
EMIT	Enzyme Multiplied Immunoassay Technique
false negative	Test result that incorrectly indicates the absence of the substance(s) tested for
false positive	Test result that incorrectly indicates the presence of the substance(s) tested for
GC/MS	Gas Chromatography/Mass Spectrometry
immunoassay	Analysis of a substance to determine its constituents and the relative proportions of each
metabolites	Drug byproducts that remain in the body after the effects of the drug have worn
MRO	Medical R~~e~~ substance ~~a~~
NIDA	National I~~n~~

FIGURE 11.6 • Drug-Testing Report, Glossary

INTRODUCTION

1

Since the founding of the company in 1952, Paramount Construction has always sought to achieve maximum productivity while providing safe, secure, and conducive work conditions for our employees. In keeping with these goals and in view of the fact that 7 million people are estimated to be drug—dependent or abusers (see Figure 1), management has determined that it is now time for Paramount to take a more active role in the war against drugs by adopting measures to ensure a substance-free workplace. Accordingly, we'll create a mandatory drug-testing policy for all new employees.

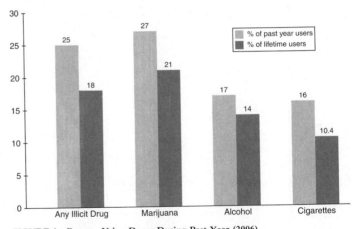

FIGURE 1 • Persons Using Drugs During Past Year (2006)
(Source: "The President's National Drug Control Strategy, February 2007")

KINDS OF TESTING

Among companies that test, several approaches are used: pre-employment, routine, reasonable suspicion/post-accident, return to work, and random (Brunet 6–7).

Pre-Employment: Required of successful job applicants about to be hired, as a condition of employment. Indeed, some employers don't even bother

FIGURE 11.7 • Drug-Testing Report, Page 1

2

to confirm a positive pre-employment test result, even though most guidelines strongly recommend such confirmation of all positive results (Hawkins 44). Sometimes, a follow-up test is required after the new worker's probationary period or when the worker is being transferred or promoted. Pre-employment testing is the most common kind (White 1895).

Routine: Required of all employees at regular intervals, sometimes as part of an annual physical exam or performance review and sometimes more often.

Reasonable Suspicion/Post-Accident: Required of all employees whose supervisors have observed behaviors that seem to indicate substance abuse. Similarly, required of employees who have been involved in a workplace accident, on the assumption that controlled substances may have been a cause.

Return to Work: Required of all returning employees who have been off the job because of a prior violation and have completed a treatment program. This assumes, of course, that the company offers such a program as part of its EAP. Many companies do not, opting instead for immediate termination of anyone who fails a drug test, even if it's a first offense.

Random: Required of some employees without prior notification. "Computer-based, random-name generated software keeps the process completely objective. Consequently, some employees might be tested several times in a row, or they may not be tested for a long period of time—it's the nature of random testing. It is for this reason, however, that random testing both decreases and deters drug usage—employees don't know when they'll be tested" (Swartley 25). Because of its haphazard nature, this approach is the most effective. But it's also the most controversial, drawing fire from civil libertarians, labor unions, and workers themselves. As a result, it's the least common kind of testing (White 1895).

METHODS OF TESTING

Simply put, drug testing is done by analyzing biological specimens for drugs or drug metabolites in the body of the test subject. Typically, an initial immunoassay test such as an EMIT is used, followed by a confirmatory GC/MS test if the first test is positive. Several different kinds of specimens can be analyzed: sweat, saliva, blood, hair, and urine (Brunet 4–5).

Sweat: A sweat specimen can be obtained by having the test subject wear an adhesive patch that in effect soaks up the person's perspiration, which can then be tested for drug residue. This test is almost impossible to falsify, but its

FIGURE 11.8 • Drug-Testing Report, Page 2

3

critics contend that the patch is susceptible to outside contamination that can produce false positives as well as false negatives. In any case, it's not widely used (Hawkins 45).

Saliva: A saliva specimen can be obtained by placing in the subject's mouth a small, specially designed sponge that soaks up oral fluids, which can then be tested for drugs or drug residue. Like the sweat test, this procedure is fairly reliable and quite noninvasive, but it has not yet gained wide acceptance.

Blood: A blood specimen can be obtained through the usual clinical procedure and is quite reliable but has the disadvantage of being highly invasive. In addition, it requires "stringent medical conditions, because of the risk of blood-borne infectious diseases" (White 1893). For these reasons, it's not widely used.

Hair: A hair specimen can be easily obtained by simply cutting some off the subject's head, starting near the scalp. Analysis of such a 1.5-inch specimen will provide an accurate 90-day drug history. Thousands of employers are using this kind of test, but it's controversial because results can be skewed by certain shampoos, airborne contaminants, and the like. In addition, NIDA research has revealed that certain drug molecules bind more readily to darker hair, thus putting some racial and ethnic groups at a disadvantage. As one Substance Abuse and Mental Health Services Administration official put it, "If two employees use cocaine, the blond may barely test negative, and the other will get caught" (Hawkins 46).

Urine: A urine specimen is readily obtainable, and an uncontaminated sample is generally reliable, although the time-frame governing detectability varies according to the drug (see Table 1). And the urine test is easiest to falsify because the subject is usually afforded privacy while producing the sample. Obviously, then, this allows for various ways to alter, dilute, or even substitute the sample. Nevertheless, the urine test remains by far the most popular method of testing. Despite its relative unreliability, urine is "preferred over blood samples because it requires a less invasive procedure, contains the metabolite . . . and is available in greater quantities" (Brunet 4).

CHARACTERISTICS OF AN EFFECTIVE PROGRAM

Employers agree that for any drug-testing program to succeed, every effort must be made to safeguard against error (and attendant liability) and to minimize any potentially negative impact on employee morale. To this end, most progressive companies design their programs according to the NIDA guidelines. Some key features are as follows:

Clear policy statement: Using input from Human Resources, employee relations, union and legal department representatives, and employees themselves, a clear, comprehensive policy statement must be written. The statement should

FIGURE 11.9 • Drug-Testing Report, Page 3

4

spell out the company's standards of employee conduct, details of how and under what circumstances testing will occur, and what steps will be taken in response to a positive test result.

Strict guidelines for specimen collection: A company may choose to collect specimens in house (usually at the company's health or medical facility) or offsite, at a hospital or clinic or at a facility specializing in such procedures. In any case, it is absolutely crucial that collection be conducted according to the strictest NIDA standards. "Because the first few links in the chain of custody are forged here . . . many experts feel that choosing your collection site merits greater attention than choosing your lab" (Brookler 130).

NIDA-certified laboratory: To become NIDA-certified, a lab must meet the most stringent standards of accuracy and protocol, especially regarding the chain of custody governing the handling of specimens. In short, NIDA-certified laboratories are the most reliable and certainly the most credible in court.

Confirmation of positive results: Positive test results should be confirmed by means of a GC/MS follow-up test. "Without the GC/MS confirmation, you aren't legally defensible" (Brookler 129). In the event of a positive confirmation, the case must then be referred to the company's MRO, who searches for alternative medical explanations for the positive test result before providing final confirmation. The MRO may refer the case back to management only after the employee has been given the opportunity to meet with the MRO. At most companies, the MRO is a contract employee. When enlisting an MRO, it's important to ensure that the person is certified by the AAMRO, the American Association of Medical Review Officers (Kerns and Stopperan 232).

Employee assistance program: Because substance abuse is recognized as a disease, many employers now provide EAPs. Rather than being terminated, employees who test positive may instead be referred for counseling. In such instances, the rehabilitation option is usually presented as a condition of continued employment. This approach, which stresses rehabilitation rather than punishment, is consistent with nationwide trends. Currently, for example, there are nearly 2,000 "drug courts" throughout the country (see Figure 2). "Using the coercive power of the court system coupled with the support of family, friends, counselors, and treatment providers, drug courts bring a unique mix of sanctions and incentives to help people achieve abstinence from drug use" ("The President's").

FIGURE 11.10 • Drug-Testing Report, Page 4

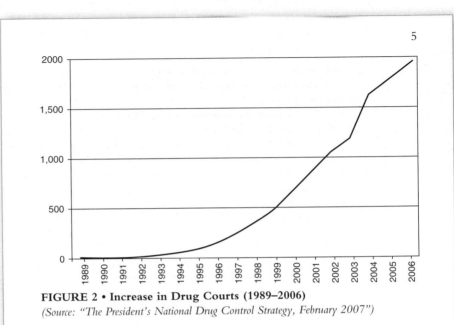

5

FIGURE 2 • Increase in Drug Courts (1989–2006)
(Source: "The President's National Drug Control Strategy, February 2007")

CONCLUSION

Certainly, the whole subject of drug testing in the workplace is controversial, but several things do seem clear:

> Substance abuse costs employers, both directly and indirectly. Substance abuse in employees leads to reduced productivity, additional costs of hiring and training workers, and administrative costs of absenteeism and worker's compensation claims. It can also result in loss of customers and sales, and damage your organization's reputation. . . . The right drug and alcohol testing program protects employees, customers, and your bottom line. It can increase employee productivity and retention, decrease absenteeism, and save you money. (Current 34)

Paramount Construction will introduce a program based on EMIT testing of urine samples. But we'll begin by testing job *applicants* only—at least at first. This will enable us to become gradually acquainted with the procedures and problems involved, without the risk of alienating employees already on board. We might

FIGURE 11.11 • Drug-Testing Report, Page 5

6

Drugs	Approximate Duration of Detectability
Amphetamines	2 days
Barbiturates	1–7 days
Benzodiazepines	3 days
Cocaine metabolites	2–3 days
Methadone	3 days
Codeine	2 days
PCP	8 days
Cannabinoids	
Single use	3 days
Moderate smoker (4 times/week)	5 days
Heavy smoker (daily)	10 days
Chronic heavy smoker	21 days

Table 1 • Approximate Duration of Detectability of Selected Drugs in Urine (Source: Rothstein. Used with permission from the publisher.)

expand the program at a later date but not in the form of random testing, which has been shown to engender resentment and legal challenges. Any future testing of the established workforce should be done only on a for-cause basis—in response to habitual absenteeism, erratic behavior, on-the-job accidents, and the like. And we definitely should establish provisions for an EAP before any testing occurs. The next step should be to call in an outside consultant, preferably from NIDA, to provide guidance.

FIGURE 11.12 • Drug-Testing Report, Page 6

7

Works Cited

Brookler, Rob. "Industry Standards in Workplace Drug Testing." *Personnel Journal*, Apr. 1992, pp. 128-132.

Brunet, James R. *Drug Testing in Law Enforcement Agencies: Social Control in the Public Sector.* LFB Scholarly Pub., 2005.

Current, Bill. "New Solutions for Ensuring a Drug-Free Workplace." *Occupational Health & Safety*, vol. 71, no. 4 (2002), pp. 34-35.

Hawkins, Dana. "Drug Tests are Unreliable." *Drug Testing.* Edited by Cindy Muir, Greenhaven, 2006, pp. 41-46.

Kerns, Dennis L., and William I. Stopperan. "Keys to a Successful Program." *Occupational Health & Safety*, vol. 69, no. 10 (2000), pp. 230-33.

Rothstein, Mark A. "Drug Testing in the Workplace: The Challenge to Employment Relations and Employment Law." *Chicago-Kent Law Review*, vol. 63, no. 3 (1987).

Swartley, Judith A. "Workplace Drug Testing is Cost Effective." *Drug Testing.* Edited by Cindy Muir, Greenhaven, 2006, pp. 23-28.

United States Office of National Drug Control Policy. "The President's National Drug Control Strategy, February, 2007, www.whitehouse.gov/ondcp/drugpolicyreform.

White, Tony. "Drug Testing at Work: Issues and Perspectives." *Substance Use & Abuse*, vol. 38, no. 11-13 (2003), pp. 1891-1902.

FIGURE 11.13 • Drug-Testing Report, Page 7

Checklist
Evaluating a Long Report

An effective long report

____ is accompanied by a transmittal document (memo or letter);

____ includes certain components:

☐ Title page that includes the title of the report, name(s) of author(s), name of company or organization, name(s) of person(s) receiving the report, and the date

☐ Abstract that briefly summarizes the report

☐ Table of contents, with sections titled and page numbers provided

☐ List of illustrations, each numbered and titled, with page numbers provided

☐ Glossary, if necessary

____ is organized into sections titled in conformity with the table of contents, covering the subject fully in an orderly way;

____ is clear, accurate, and sufficiently detailed to satisfy the needs of the intended audience;

____ uses plain, simple language;

____ maintains an appropriate tone—neither too formal nor too conversational;

____ integrates effective visuals—tables, graphs, charts, and the like—each numbered and titled in conformity with the list of illustrations;

____ includes full documentation (bibliography and parenthetical citations) prepared according to MLA or APA format;

____ contains no typos or mechanical errors in spelling, capitalization, punctuation, or grammar.

EXERCISES

EXERCISE 11.1

Rewrite the transmittal e-mail (Figure 11.1) and the title page (Figure 11.2) as if the report were your own work submitted as an assignment in your workplace communications course.

EXERCISE 11.2

Create a table of contents for a report on one of these aspects of your college:

- Degree or certificate program in your field of study
- Student Services provisions
- Athletic program
- Affirmative Action guidelines
- Physical plant

EXERCISE 11.3

Rewrite the "Works Cited" in Figure 11.13 using APA format.

EXERCISE 11.4

Practically all workplace communications courses include a long report assignment at some point during the semester, usually near the end. However, specific features of the project vary greatly from instructor to instructor. Write a long report designed to satisfy your instructor's course requirements.

EXERCISE 11.5

Team up with two classmates, conduct Internet research, and write a detailed report about the three largest employers within a fifty-mile radius of your campus. Each of you will focus on one employer, but the three main sections of the report must then be integrated into a consistent format that discusses the employers in a coherent, uniform way, covering the same basic topics in each section (for example, company history, product line, revenue, management team, employee qualifications and hiring forecast, future projections).

EXERCISE 11.6

Guided by the table of contents on the following page, team up with two or three other students to write a collaborative report entitled "Radar: History, Principles, Applications."

TABLE OF CONTENTS

Appendix A — Ten Strategies to Improve Your Style

1. Create Active Sentences

In an active sentence, the subject is the actor, performing the action of the verb. In a passive sentence, the subject is not the actor and in fact *receives* the action of the verb.

(Subject/Actor) (Verb/Action)

ACTIVE Dr. Polanski interviewed the patient.

(Subject/Receiver) (Verb/Action)

PASSIVE The patient was interviewed by Dr. Polanski.

Because the active approach requires fewer words, it is usually preferable. Of course, there are situations in which you may choose to use the passive approach—for emphasis or variety, perhaps. Or you may want to "hide" the actor, such as in writing about a situation in which some mistake or controversial decision has been made. Here's an example:

(Subject/Actor) (Verb/Action)

ACTIVE Ken Park decided that we should go on strike.

(Subject/Receiver) (Verb/Action)

PASSIVE A decision was made that we should go on strike.

Obviously, the passive voice would probably be better in such a case. There is no reason to bring Ken Park's identity to the attention of anyone who may later wish to retaliate against strike organizers. But use the passive voice only with good cause; every use should be deliberate rather than accidental.

EXERCISE A.1

Revise these sentences by making them active rather than passive, but do not change the meaning.

1. Electrical shock can be avoided if certain basic rules are followed by the worker.
2. When the patient's parents were interviewed by Ms. Rodriguez, their responses were thought to be hostile.
3. When drilling holes for running cable through masonry, a ½-inch, carbide-tipped masonry bit should be used by the contractor.
4. Compact fluorescent light bulbs should be purchased by the energy-conscious consumer.
5. All the necessary forms have been received by the social worker.
6. Preparation times for each dish should be known by the server.
7. When the patient's jacket was examined by the ward nurse, the buttons were seen to be missing.
8. If a lamp or ceiling fixture cannot be turned on using the switch, first the light bulb should be checked by the homeowner.
9. A dose of 150 mg of imipramine is taken by this patient daily.
10. The knife blade is held flat against the sharpening stone, with the sharp edge facing right, and the blade is drawn across the stone from right to left. Then the blade is turned so that the sharp edge faces left, and the blade is drawn across from left to right. This procedure is repeated several times in rapid succession.

2. Keep Subjects and Verbs Close Together

The heart of any sentence is the subject and its verb. Whether active or passive, English sentences are easiest to understand when subjects and verbs are as close together as possible. For example, both of the following sentences are grammatical, but the second is smoother because the first creates an interruption between the subject and the verb.

(Subject)

<u>Dr. Simmons</u>, because she was concerned about safety,

(Verb)

<u>recommended</u> additional supervision of the pediatric ward.

(Subject)   (Verb)

<u>Dr. Simmons</u> <u>recommended</u> additional supervision of the pediatric ward because she was concerned about safety.

Whenever possible, try to keep subjects and verbs side by side. This not only ensures maximum clarity but also helps you avoid grammatical errors involving subject–verb agreement (see Appendix B, pages 251–252).

EXERCISE A.2

Rewrite these sentences, putting subjects and verbs closer together.

1. Because outdoor electrical conductors usually run underground, you must, if they are to endure years of burial in damp earth, enclose them in conduit.
2. Wood doors, unlike steel, hollow aluminum, or hollow vinyl doors, react very little to heat and cold.
3. The construction of the new annex on Building 7, because inflation had not been taken into consideration when the project was given approval, is costing far more than originally anticipated.
4. In the case file, a complete report on the patient's past history of hospitalization is included.
5. The continuing deterioration of Willard's peer-group relationships, unless some form of alternative school placement is implemented, may eventually cause lasting psychological problems for him.
6. Welding, which requires manual dexterity, good hand-eye coordination, and a great deal of technical expertise, can be an art as well as a trade.
7. A transformer, by reducing the voltage and increasing the current, allows us to operate model trains using ordinary house current.
8. Silk-screen printing, as we know it today, is simply a more sophisticated version of the stencil printing techniques used in ancient times.
9. Food servers, because kitchen doors always open to the right, must learn to carry trays left-handed.
10. Hans Christian Oersted, nearly 200 years ago at Copenhagen University in Denmark, discovered that a current flowing steadily through a wire sets up a magnetic field around the wire.

3. Put Modifiers Next to What They Modify

A modifier is a word or a phrase that makes another word or phrase more specific by limiting or qualifying its sense. For example, in the phrase *the red car,* the word *red* modifies the word *car.* In the sentence *Exhausted, he fell asleep at the wheel,* the word *Exhausted* modifies *he* and the phrase *at the wheel* modifies the word *asleep.* In the sentence *The social worker noticed marijuana growing in the closet,* the word *growing* modifies the word *marijuana* and the phrase *in the closet* modifies the word *growing.*

Obviously, then, it makes sense to put modifiers alongside what they modify to avoid confusion or unintentionally comical effects. Notice what happens if the *social worker* sentence is misarranged:

> Growing in the closet, the social worker noticed marijuana.

Certainly the social worker was not *growing in the closet,* yet that is what the sentence now says because the modifiers are in the wrong place, "dangling" off the front of the sentence.

Of course, nobody would be likely to misinterpret the sentence that way, but misplaced modifiers can indeed create misunderstanding when more than one interpretation is possible. Avoid problems by always putting modifiers next to what they modify.

EXERCISE A.3

Revise these sentences, putting the modifiers where they belong.

1. Sometimes it is profitable to buy an older home in a nice neighborhood that needs a lot of repairs.
2. Hector wrote his report at the last minute, while riding the bus to campus in the back of his notebook.
3. The word processor is now standard equipment in the office instead of the typewriter.
4. While welding a butt joint, several rules must be remembered.
5. Other matters were discussed in the closing moments of the meeting of lesser importance.
6. If the large geriatric population of the state hospital, with its inevitably high death rate, were not present, the overall hospital population would be growing rapidly.
7. In real French restaurants, all food is served from a cart that is kept close to the guests' table on wheels.
8. Inexpensive prints are available to art lovers in all sizes.
9. Placed in a window opening, office workers can be kept comfortable by an air conditioning unit of even moderate size.
10. The unopened wine bottle is presented to the guest, brought from the cellar, for approval before being placed in the cooler.

4. Adjust Long Sentences

A sentence can be very long and still be grammatical. Many highly regarded authors (the American novelist William Faulkner, for example) have favored elaborate sentence structure. But most of us are not literary artists. We write for a different purpose—to convey information, not to entertain, dazzle, or impress.

The more information you pack into a sentence, the harder it is for the reader to process. If a sentence goes much beyond twenty-five or thirty words, the reader's comprehension decreases.

To ensure maximum readability, therefore, limit your sentence length. Try for an *average* of no more than twenty words per sentence. This can be inhibiting during the actual composing process, so make such adjustments when revising. Identify overly long sentences and break them down into shorter ones. It's usually fairly easy to see where the breaks should be, as in these examples:

ORIGINAL

Welding is a method of permanently joining two pieces of metal, usually by means of heat, which partially melts the surface and combines the two pieces into a single piece, and after the metal cools and hardens, the welded joint is as strong as any other part of the metal. (fifty words)

REVISION

Welding is a method of permanently joining two pieces of metal, usually by means of heat. The partially melted surfaces are combined into a single piece. After the metal cools and hardens, the welded joint is as strong as any other part of the metal. (sixteen words; ten words; nineteen words)

Another good strategy is to present lengthy information in the form of a list, as in this example:

ORIGINAL

There are four major methods of welding: arc welding, which joins metals by means of heat produced by an electric arc; resistance welding, which joins metals by means of heat generated by resistance to an electric current; gas welding, which joins metals by means of heat from a gas torch; and brazing, which joins metals by means of a melted filler metal such as brass, bronze, or a silver alloy.

REVISION

There are four major methods of welding:

- Arc welding joins metals by means of heat produced by an electric arc.
- Resistance welding joins metals by means of heat produced by resistance to the flow of an electric current.
- Gas welding joins metals by means of heat from a gas torch.
- Brazing joins metals by means of a filler metal such as brass, bronze, or a silver alloy.

However, judging whether a sentence is too long depends on its context: what comes before it and what comes after. An occasional long sentence is acceptable, especially before or after a short one.

EXERCISE A.4

Revise these sentences, breaking them down into shorter ones.

1. Electricians are usually expected to have their own hand tools, such as screwdrivers, pliers, levels, hammers, wrenches, and so forth, and an initial investment of several hundred dollars may be necessary to acquire an adequate supply of such tools, although the electrical contractor usually supplies large tools and pieces of equipment, such as hydraulic benders, power tools, ladders, and such expendable items as hacksaw blades, taps, and twist drills.

2. Used extensively and considered a general-purpose welding rod, RG-65 gas welding rods are of low-alloy composition and may be used to weld pipes for power plants, for process piping, and under severe service conditions, and produce very good welds (50,000 to 65,000 psi) in such materials as carbon steels, low-alloy steels, and wrought iron.

3. Fine silk-screen prints were first brought to public attention by Elizabeth McCausland, an art critic and writer who arranged and sponsored exhibits that astonished critics and laypersons alike, and by Carl Zigrosser, an art critic and writer, who arranged some of the earliest exhibitions of silk-screen prints.

4. Lack of fusion in welding may be caused by an incorrect current adjustment, an improper electrode size or type, dirty plate surfaces, failure to raise to the melting point the temperature of the base metal or the previously deposited weld metal, or improper fluxing, which fails to dissolve the oxide and other foreign material from surfaces to which the deposited metal is intended to fuse.

5. A headwaiter is responsible for the proper setup of tables and chairs before the dining room opens and should therefore make a tour of the room beforehand to check on each setup and on the proper placement of furniture and should also go over the menu with the wait staff, briefing them on the characteristics of menu items and on which items are ready to be served and which require longer preparation time.

6. Migration trends are moving the American population away from the Northeast and Midwest to the South and West, where land is more abundant and less expensive, and even within regions, people and jobs are moving away from the downtown areas to the suburbs and outlying areas, causing a housing market boom on the fringes of metropolitan areas, and a virtual halt to new construction within inner cities.

7. Mobile equipment lasts longer and works better if operated on smooth floors by skilled operators, so floors should be kept clean and (if possible) should be treated with urethane or other coatings to minimize dust, which contributes to wear on many lift truck parts, including the wheels, and operators' skills can be assessed by regularly inspecting the condition of the paint on the vehicles and checking doorways, building columns, and walls for damage indicating careless operation.

8. County jails have been the U.S. penal institutions most resistive to change and reform and even today are often unfit for human habitation because characterized by unsanitary conditions, minimally qualified personnel, intermingling of all types

of prisoners (sick and well, old and young, hardened criminals and petty offenders) in overcrowded cell blocks and "tanks," and the almost complete absence of even the most rudimentary rehabilitative programs, constituting a scandalous state of affairs that will be eliminated only when the public begins to support the many sheriffs and jailers who are trying to correct bad conditions and practices.

9. North American rodents include such native animals as field and wood mice, wood rats, squirrels, rabbits, woodchucks, gophers, muskrats, porcupines, and beavers, along with three more destructive species—the house mouse, the roof rat, and the Norway rat—that reached the United States from other countries and can be found everywhere, inhabiting buildings and eating or damaging stored food.

10. A wholesale travel agent may design tour packages marketed under the agency's name, or may take land packages already assembled by a ground operator and combine them with air or surface transportation to form new packages, an especially common practice in the international tourism field where, for example, rather than negotiating directly with hotels, sightseeing operators, and the like, a German wholesaler wishing to offer a New York City program might contract with a New York ground operator for land arrangements and then add international air transportation between the point of origin and the destination.

5. Use Transitions

Transitional words or phrases can serve as links between sentence parts, whole sentences, or paragraphs, clarifying the direction of your train of thought. In effect, they serve as "bridges" from idea to idea within a piece of writing and are therefore quite helpful to the reader. Usually positioned at the beginning of a sentence and followed by a comma, these devices can be loosely categorized according to the various relationships they signal. Here are some common examples:

- *Additional information:* also, furthermore, in addition, moreover
- *Exemplification:* for example, for instance, in other words, to illustrate, specifically
- *Explanation:* in other words, put another way, simply stated
- *Similarity:* in like manner, likewise, similarly
- *Contrast:* conversely, however, nevertheless, on the contrary, on the other hand, yet
- *Cause and effect:* accordingly, as a result, consequently, hence, therefore, thus
- *Emphasis:* clearly, indeed, in fact
- *Summary:* finally, in conclusion, in short, to sum up

Helpful as they are, transitional devices should not be used excessively. Use them only where they provide needed assistance. If the relationship between the ideas is already clear, no transition is needed.

Always exercise great care in selecting transitions. Because these devices greatly influence how a sentence is interpreted, an incorrect choice can badly obscure your meaning. Consider this example:

> Wilson Brothers Plumbing submitted a bid of $10,000 for the project. Therefore, we hired the company to install new pipes.

In this case, the transition *Therefore* indicates that the bid was quite competitive. But a different transition might indicate just the opposite, as in this example:

> Wilson Brothers Plumbing submitted a bid of $10,000 for the project. Nevertheless, we hired the company to install the pipes.

As a writer, you should always choose your words carefully; developing your skill in selecting appropriate transitional devices is an important application of that principle.

EXERCISE A.5

Improve each of these sentence pairs by starting the second sentence with a transitional device that clarifies or reinforces the meaning.

1. The company's engineering department has proudly announced that the number of new projects has more than doubled during the past year. The accounting department has repeatedly asserted that our main focus should not be on the number of new projects but on their relative cost.
2. Area businesses seeking to attract new employees to the region are disturbed by rising crime rates. Armed robbery has increased 12 percent locally since 2009.
3. As forecast last spring, corporate donations to the foundation now total more than a million dollars. Private donations have also met our expectations.
4. Many factors can lower employee morale. Unsafe working conditions are a major source of discontent.
5. For the company to remain viable, we must generate more revenue than expenditures, realizing enough gain to repay our investors. We must achieve a positive profit margin.
6. The motion sensors had somehow been deactivated. The intruders were able to enter the restricted area undetected.
7. This is a major obstacle to continued growth and product development. It is the single biggest problem facing the company.
8. Within the next six months, we must hire three welders, four electricians, and two carpenters. We will need at least two new clerical workers.
9. We have finished the project within budget, on time, and to everyone's complete satisfaction. We have succeeded.
10. Management has offered the salaried employees a nonretroactive 2 percent raise. The union is demanding a retroactive 3 percent increase.

6. Eliminate Clutter

Practically everyone wastes words—at least in a first draft. However, excess verbiage interferes with communication by inflating sentence length and tiring the reader. Therefore, try not to use any more words than necessary. For example, do not say:

> The attitude of the supervisory individual is a good one at the present time. (fourteen words)

Instead, say:

> The supervisor has a good attitude now. (seven words—**half** as long)

There are many kinds of verbal clutter. This section discusses the five most common.

Unnecessary Introductions

It's perfectly acceptable—and sometimes necessary—to open a sentence with an introductory phrase that leads into the main idea. But this depends on who the reader is, what the circumstances are, and other factors. Check your writing for *needless* introductions—phrases in which you're simply spinning your wheels—as in these examples:

> As I look back on what I have said in this e-mail, it seems that . . .
>
> Although this may not be very important, I think . . .
>
> Because all of us attended last week's meeting, there is no need to summarize that discussion, in which we agreed to . . .

Instead, get right to the point:

> It seems that . . .
>
> I think . . .
>
> At last week's meeting, we agreed to . . .

Submerged Verbs

Too often we use a verb plus another verb (hidden or "submerged" within a noun) when one verb (the submerged one) would do, as in phrases like the following:

<u>conduct</u> an <u>investigation</u> = <u>investigate</u>

(Verb) (Noun) (Verb)

<u>reach</u> a <u>decision</u> = <u>decide</u>

(Verb) (Noun) (Verb)

(Verb)   (Noun)   (Verb)

<u>give</u> a <u>summary</u> = <u>summarize</u>

Instead, simply use the "submerged" verb: *investigate, decide, summarize.* This approach is far better because it's more direct.

Long-Winded Phrases

Submerged verbs are one source of clutter, but any long-winded expression using more words than necessary wastes the reader's time and energy. Here are ten common examples:

Original	Revision
At this point in time	Now
Despite the fact that	Although
Due to the fact that	Because
During the time that	While
In many instances	Often
In order to	To
In the course of	During
In the event that	If
In the near future	Soon
On two occasions	Twice

Obvious Modifiers

Sometimes we use words unnecessarily, expressing already self-evident ideas, as in these modifiers:

(Modifier)

<u>personal</u> opinion   *All* opinions are "personal."

          (Modifier)

visible <u>to the eye</u>   Anything visible *must* be visible "to the eye."

(Modifier)

<u>past</u> history   *All* history is "past."

In each case, it would be better to omit the modifier and use a single word: *opinion, visible,* and *history.*

Repetitious Wording

As we've seen, several short sentences are usually better than one long one. But it's sometimes better to *combine* two or three short sentences to avoid unnecessary repetition. If done correctly, the resulting sentence is significantly shorter than the total length of the several sentences that went into it, as in this example:

ORIGINAL

The electric drill is easier to use than the hand drill. The electric drill is faster than the hand drill. The electric drill is a very useful tool. (twenty-eight words)

REVISION

Easier and faster to use than the hand drill, the electric drill is a very useful tool. (seventeen words)

In the original, *the electric drill* appears three times and *the hand drill* twice. By using each of these phrases only once, the revision conveys the same information much more efficiently. Always strive for this level of economy.

EXERCISE A.6

Revise these sentences to express the ideas more concisely.

1. The company cannot maintain full employment during the summer months.
2. In the event that the conductor becomes hot, shut down the unit.
3. I sent a check in the amount of $379 on April 3.
4. This airbrush has a tendency to leak.
5. The security office should take into consideration the feelings of the other employees.
6. Fire drills are important because fire drills provide students with practice in emergency evacuation procedures that they will have to know in the event of an actual fire.
7. On all our computers, the Delete key is red in color.
8. The Desert Storm war was relatively brief in duration.
9. In view of the fact that Christmas falls on a Monday this year, we will have a long weekend.
10. Prior to entering the factory, please sign the visitors' log book.

7. Choose Simple Language

Most readers don't respond well to fancy or unnecessarily complex wording. Therefore, you should use ordinary terms your reader will immediately recognize and understand.

Of course, there's no reason to avoid *technical* terms—specialized words for which there are no satisfactory substitutes—if your reader can be expected to know them. An electrode is an electrode, a condenser is a condenser, and an isometric drawing is an isometric drawing. If you're writing in a technical context, most of your readers will share your knowledge of the subject area. If you're not sure whether your readers will be familiar with the vocabulary of the field, provide a glossary (a list of words with their definitions), as discussed in Chapter 11. If there are only two or three questionable terms, you can insert parentheses—as in the previous sentence, in which *glossary* is defined.

Generally, however, the best policy is to always use the simplest word available: *pay* rather than *remunerate, transparent* rather than *pellucid, steal* rather than *pilfer.* Another advantage of using everyday vocabulary is that your spelling will improve. You're far more likely to misspell words you're unaccustomed to seeing in print because you won't know whether they "look right" on the page or screen.

EXERCISE A.7

Revise these sentences by replacing the underlined words with simpler ones. You may have to consult a dictionary to determine what some of the underlined words mean. (Of course, that's why they are poor choices.)

1. These guidelines cover everything germane to the procedure.
2. In February, we will commence to use the new equipment.
3. The worst scenario would be if the company had to relocate.
4. Supervisors should transmit accident reports to the personnel office.
5. The summer schedule will terminate on September 10.
6. Please utilize safety glasses when working with the grinding machines.
7. All workers should eschew procedures that are obviously dangerous.
8. You must complete the requisite forms before we can consider your request for personal leave.
9. The union will endeavor to avoid a strike, but the company must meet certain conditions.
10. Let me explain what transpired at last Thursday's meeting.

8. Avoid Clichés

Sometimes a catchy or cleverly worded phrase quickly gains widespread popularity and becomes a permanent part of the language. Ironically, however, the phrase then loses much of its original energy, becoming stale and lifeless through overuse. In short, it becomes a cliché. Countless clichés exist in English (as in most languages), and their number has increased greatly during the past couple of decades because of the growing influence of advertising and the mass media.

Indeed, clichés have become so much a part of the culture that many people rely heavily on them when speaking. This is hardly surprising because such phrases require no real thought and are readily understood. However, clichés should be avoided in writing. Because they are by nature "prefabricated," they create an aura of trite predictability that robs language of vitality. In addition, clichés are often wordy. For example, why write *at this point in time* or *easier said than done* when *now* or *difficult* would suffice?

Here are ten more common examples:

Cliché	Alternative
Between a rock and a hard place	In a difficult situation
Beyond the shadow of a doubt	Undoubtedly
Few and far between	Scarce
First and foremost	First
In the final analysis	Finally
Let bygones be bygones	Forgive
Needless to say	Obviously
A rude awakening	A shock
See eye to eye	Agree
Tried and true	Proven

EXERCISE A.8

Revise these sentences by replacing the underlined clichés with more original wording.

1. When the company switched insurance carriers, we went from the frying pan into the fire.
2. For all intents and purposes, the agency is now performing the duties of two or three agencies.
3. The heart of the matter is that the employee parking lot is too small.
4. If we could expand our product line, this would be a whole new ball game.
5. Certainly it would be a step in the right direction to expand the company's marketing base.
6. The outdated machinery sticks out like a sore thumb.
7. It is time for the company to throw caution to the wind and make a major financial commitment to expansion.
8. If profits continue to decline, somebody will have to face the music.
9. If we play our cards right we will be able to survive this crisis still smelling like a rose.
10. Last but not least, we must consider the possibility of relocating the downtown office.

9. Use Numbers Correctly

Because much workplace communication involves quantitative information, writers often must decide whether to spell out a number or use a numeral (e.g., *three hundred* or *300*). This issue is somewhat complicated because several different systems exist. In general, workplace writers prefer numerals to words. Often, however, words are used from zero to nine and sometimes for other amounts that can be expressed in one or two words, such as *thirty-one* or *fifty*. (Note that two-word numbers under 100 require a hyphen.)

Here are a few guidelines that may help.

- Never begin a sentence with a numeral. Either spell it out or, if the number is large, reorder the sentence so that the numeral appears elsewhere.

  ORIGINAL   781 people have registered for the convention so far.
  REVISION   So far, 781 people have registered for the convention.

- For very large numbers, combine numerals and words, as in "100 million."

- Combine numerals and words whenever such an approach will prevent misreading, as in this example:

  ORIGINAL   You will need 3 6 inch screws and 10 4 inch nails.
  REVISION   You will need three 6-inch screws and ten 4-inch nails.

  Note that a hyphen is required when a number is used with a word to modify another word.

- Be consistent about how you deal with numbers in a given piece of writing. Pick one approach and stick with it, as in this example:

  ORIGINAL   We will hire 5 masons and two plumbers.
  REVISION   We will hire five masons and two plumbers.

- Use numerals for all *statistical* data, such as the following:

  Ages and addresses
  Dates
  Exact amounts of money
  Fractions and decimals
  Identification numbers
  Measurements (including height and weight)
  Page numbers
  Percentages, ratios, proportions
  Scores

  When dealing with statistics, it often makes sense to combine numerals with other symbols rather than with words (e.g., 6'1" rather than 6 feet, 1 inch and $375 rather than 375 dollars).

  Always review your completed draft to ensure that you have handled numbers correctly and consistently.

EXERCISE A.9

Revise these sentences to correct all errors involving numbers.

1. A test of thirty one control valves at a major factory revealed more than seventy significant operating deficiencies, and in another series of tests conducted on a random sample of 60 control valves, 88 percent exhibited substandard performance.
2. $15,140 in "play money" is included in every Monopoly game.
3. This machine offers a calculated mean time between failures (MTBFs) above one hundred thousand hours, or more than eleven years if used twenty-four hours per day, three hundred sixty-five days per year.
4. The job involves undersealing, lifting, and stabilizing a fifteen thousand square foot concrete slab.
5. In nineteen ninety three, a one hundred eighty foot long, three hundred twenty eight ton replacement span for the historic Grosse Island Bridge in Michigan was set in place in one piece, using the "sinking bridge" method.
6. In the nineteen seventies, baseball's Major Leagues comprised 4 divisions—the American League East, the American League West, the National League East, and the National League West—each with 6 teams.
7. The population of the United States is now more than three hundred million.
8. It is unusual for a high school basketball team to have more than 1 or 2 20 point scorers.
9. The temperature in Death Valley often exceeds one hundred degrees.
10. When it is six o'clock in New York, it is 3:00 o'clock in California.

10. Use Bias-Free Language

English (like most other languages) tends to be male-oriented, as is the traditional view of society itself. Since men's and women's social roles have changed, language should reflect that.

Here are three examples of sexist (i.e., gender-biased) writing:

> Every welder must sign his name on the login sheet before beginning his shift.
>
> Lollipop Nursery School requests that each child's mother help out at the school at least one lunch hour per month.
>
> It will take twelve workmen to complete this job on time.

Although all these sentences are grammatically correct, each is sexist. The first sentence, by twice using the word *his*, implies that all welders are male—certainly not true today! But the sexism can easily be removed by cutting or changing a few words:

> Every welder must sign the login sheet before beginning work.

The writer of the second sentence implies that child care is solely the responsibility of mothers—hardly the case! A far better phrasing would be to replace *mother* with *parent(s):*

> Lollipop Nursery School requests that each child's parent(s) help out at the school at least one lunch hour per month.

The last example implies that only males (work*men*) could do this job. Avoid gender-biased terms such as *workman, fireman, mailman,* and *policeman.* Instead, use gender-neutral ones such as *worker, firefighter, mail carrier,* and *police officer.*

Here is one possible revision of the example:

> It will take twelve workers to complete this job on time.

In the interest of simple fairness, we must all develop the habit of nonsexist expression.

EXERCISE A.10

Revise these sentences to eliminate sexist language.

1. To keep his knowledge up-to-date, a doctor should read the leading medical journals in his field.
2. Every man needs the satisfaction provided by meaningful work.
3. The average employee is dissatisfied with his wages.
4. As we move through the 21st century, every U.S. president will have to work very closely with his advisors to avoid international conflict.
5. There will be a policeman posted at each of the entrances, and nobody will be allowed into the plant without his ID card.
6. I now pronounce you man and wife.
7. In the early days of public education, a schoolboy's parents had to purchase his textbooks.
8. Increasingly, manufacturers are using man-made materials rather than natural ones.
9. If a patient decides to leave the hospital against medical advice, he must first sign a waiver of hospital responsibility.
10. Throughout history, man has created many remarkable inventions.

Appendix B

Review of Mechanics: Spelling, Punctuation, and Grammar

Spelling

Most writers experience at least some difficulty with spelling. However, you can become a better speller simply by observing the following basic guidelines.

1. Do not concern yourself with spelling while you're composing. Concentrate on content instead. But at the rewriting stage, check carefully for obvious errors—words that you know how to spell but got wrong through carelessness. Don't permit obvious blunders to slip past you. When in doubt, consult a dictionary or an electronic spelling checker. Virtually all word processors are equipped with such devices. But these are not foolproof. Consider this little poem that was making the rounds a few years ago. It illustrates quite well (if somewhat jokingly) the shortcomings of spelling checkers.

> I have a spelling checker.
> It came with my PC.
> It plainly marks **four** my review
> mistakes that I **cant sea.**
> I **rote** this poetry **threw** it,
> I'm **shore your** pleased **too no.**
> **Its** letter perfect in **it's weigh.**
> my checker **tolled** me **sew.**

Of the forty-four words in this small poem, fourteen (the ones in bold print) are incorrect—an error rate of nearly 30 percent! Yet no standard spelling checker would identify these mistakes because all are actual words.

Although quite helpful in spotting typographical miscues and other such flaws, spell checkers are no substitute for vigilance by the writer.

2. Certain pairs of homonyms—words that sound alike but are spelled differently—give nearly everyone trouble. Memorize this list of commonly confused words:

accept: to receive willingly
except: with the exception of

affect: to produce an effect upon
effect: that which is produced, a result

alot: [no such word]
a lot: many

a while: a period of time
awhile: *for* a period of time

cite: to quote or mention
sight: something seen
site: the position or location of something

its: possessive form of **it**
it's: contraction meaning **it is**

loose: not tight
lose: to misplace

passed: past tense of **to pass**
past: gone by in time

their: possessive form of **they**
there: in or at that place
they're: contraction meaning **they are**

to: a word used to express movement toward
too: also, more than enough
two: 2

whose: possessive form of **who**
who's: contraction meaning **who is** or **who has**

your: possessive form of **you**
you're: contraction meaning **you are**

3. We all have certain words we nearly always misspell. Identify your own "problem" words, make a list of them, and consult it whenever you must use one of those words. Eventually, you'll no longer need the list, as the correct spellings imprint themselves on your memory.

4. As mentioned in Appendix A.7, you should stay away from fancy terms you are unaccustomed to seeing in print. Use ordinary, everyday words instead. Not only will your reader understand them more easily, but you will also be more likely to notice if they "look wrong" because of misspelling.

5. To spell specialized or technical terms, check manuals and the indexes of textbooks in your field or major. For the spelling of the names of local persons, businesses, addresses, and so forth, consult the telephone directory. (The Area Code section even lists all states and major cities.) Most businesses and organizations provide in-house directories of employees; these are frequently available through an online database.

6. Memorize some basic rules. English spelling is highly inconsistent and filled with exceptions, but there are some generally reliable patterns:

   - *i* before *e,* as in

     achieve, believe, retrieve

     except after *c,* as in

     receive, conceive, deceive

     Notice that in all the above examples, the two letters *i* and *e* combine to sound like a long *e.* If they combine to sound like anything else, the *i* before *e* except after *c* rule no longer applies, as in

     height [long *i* sound] and **weight** [long *a* sound]

   - When adding a suffix (an ending) to a word that ends in *e,* keep the *e* if the suffix begins with a consonant, as in

     complete, completely
     require, requirement
     wire, wireless

     Drop the *e* if the suffix begins with a vowel, as in

     electrocute, electrocution
     wire, wiring

   - When adding a suffix to a word that ends in a consonant followed by *y,* change the *y* to *i* unless the suffix begins with *i,* as in

     photocopy, photocopier
     hurry, hurried
     fry, frying

     When adding a suffix to a word that ends in a vowel preceded by *y,* keep the *y,* as in

     dye, dyes

   - When adding a suffix to a word that ends in a consonant, double the consonant only if

     The consonant is preceded by a vowel
     The word is one syllable or accented on the last syllable
     The suffix begins with a vowel, as in

     begin, beginning

- When choosing between the suffixes -*able* and -*ible,* remember that most of the -*able* words are "able" to stand alone without the suffix, as in **laughable** and **paintable,** while most of the -*ible* words cannot, such as **horrible** and **responsible.**

- To make a word plural, add -*es* if the pluralizing creates an extra syllable; otherwise, just add an -*s.*

  1 switch, 2 switches
  1 hammer, 2 hammers

  If the word ends in a vowel followed by *o,* add -*s.*

  1 radio, 2 radios
  1 video, 2 videos

- If the word ends in a consonant followed by *o,* add -*es,* as in

  1 tomato, 2 tomatoes
  1 potato, 2 potatoes

  Remember never to pluralize a word by using an apostrophe. The apostrophe is used only in contractions and to indicate possession (see pages 246–247).

EXERCISE B.1

Each of the following sentences contains at least one misspelled word. Rewrite the sentences to correct all spelling errors.

1. Specialized method's must be used for recycling hazardous waist products such as batterys, paint, and used oil.
2. Although bridges often go unoticed, there function is esential to modern America.
3. The principle component's of natural dry gas are methane, ethane, and propayne.
4. The viscosity of oil varys, but oil is allways lighter then water.
5. Biologists have mounted tiny bar codes on bees to moniter the insects' mateing habbits.
6. In the snowbelt states, highway agencys have been experamenting with new kind's of salt products during the passed severel years.
7. Obviousley, not all technological problems are easily solveable.
8. Its extremely dangerous to allow an open flame anywhere near a combustable gas.
9. American moterists have been slow to except the idea of anything but a gasaline-powered car.
10. When shifting to a lower geer, a vehikle gains power but looses speed.

Punctuation

Punctuation exists not to make writers' lives more difficult but to make readers' lives easier. A punctuation mark is simply a symbol, like a road sign on a highway. It tells readers when to slow down, when to stop, and how to anticipate and respond to what appears before them on the page. This brings us to a basic principle: *Trust your ear; listen to the sentence and insert punctuation marks wherever you can hear them.*

However, be careful not to overpunctuate. As on a highway, an incorrect sign is even more misleading than a missing one. For example, consider this sentence:

> The Carrier Corporation manufactures a wide variety of air conditioning units, ranging from small household models to huge industrial installations.

If the comma were removed, no real harm would result because the reader would probably still pause after *units* instinctively, just to draw breath. Although the removal of the comma would in no way change or hide the meaning, look at this version:

> The Carrier, Corporation manufactures, a wide, variety of air conditioning units, ranging from, small, household models, to huge, industrial installations.

See how much harder it is to read the sentence? All those unnecessary commas cause the reader to hesitate repeatedly, thereby derailing the train of thought. The reader will keep pausing because people automatically respond to symbols, whether they want to or not. This leads to a second basic principle: *Do not punctuate at all unless you are absolutely sure you must; when in doubt, leave it out.*

Of course, there's more to punctuation than these two principles. As you know, there are literally hundreds of punctuation rules. But the good news is that, unless you plan to become a professional writer or editor, you need to know only a small percentage of them. This section of Appendix B covers the basics of punctuation—the fundamental rules everyone must know to write clearly.

End Punctuation: Period, Question Mark, and Exclamation Mark

Practically everyone knows how to use periods, question marks, and exclamation marks at the ends of sentences. Sometimes, however, we simply forget to use end punctuation because our minds are faster than our hands. As we write, we tend to think ahead a sentence or two, and it's easy to overlook the punctuation in our rush to express the next thought. This is something to watch for at the rewriting stage. Make sure that every sentence ends with punctuation. Be especially vigilant about question marks. A common error is to hastily insert a period even though the sentence is actually a question. As for exclamation marks, use them rarely. If they become commonplace, they lose their impact. Use exclamation marks only when necessary to signal great emphasis.

Comma

The comma is probably the most difficult of all punctuation marks to use correctly because it's required in such a wide range of situations. However, if you study the following comma rules, you'll notice that it's also the easiest punctuation mark to "hear." As mentioned earlier, trust your ear for determining where to insert the comma. And when in doubt, leave it out. The following rules will help guide you.

1. Use a comma to separate words or phrases in a sequence, as in these examples:

   The most common crimes are murder, rape, robbery, assault, burglary, and theft.

   There are five main types of metering devices used in refrigeration: the automatic expansion valve, the thermostatic expansion valve, the capillary tube, the low-side float, and the high-side float.

   Notice that there's a comma before the *and* in both of these sequences. Some writers choose to skip that last comma, but using it ensures that the reader will not misread the sentence.

2. Use a comma after an introductory word or phrase, as in these examples:

   Obviously, safety is an important consideration in the workplace.

   Because of its flexibility, a drive belt can be used to connect nonparallel shafts.

   In a typical transistor, the collector-base circuit is reverse-biased.

3. Use a comma before "linking" words such as *and, but,* or *so* if the word is linking two complete sentences, as in these examples:

   The upper number in a fraction is called the *numerator,* and the lower number is called the *denominator.*

   The risks involved in underwater welding are great, but the pay is excellent.

   Pressure within a fluid is proportional to the density of the fluid, so gasoline exerts less pressure than water.

4. Use commas between two or more adjectives in a row, but only if those adjectives would make sense in any order, as in this example:

   This task requires a large, heavy sledge.

   In the following example, there is no comma between the adjectives (*three, more,* and *full*) because they make sense only in the order given:

   Give the valve handle three more full turns.

5. Use commas to surround words or phrases that are not essential to the sense of the sentence—words or phrases that could just as easily appear in parentheses, as in these examples:

> The catapult, a device for hurling large objects, was an early war machine.
>
> Pavlov, a Russian physiologist, demonstrated the existence of conditioned reflexes by conditioning dogs to salivate at the sound of a bell.
>
> The Louvre, a museum located in Paris, is a major tourist attraction.

6. Use a comma before an afterthought—a word or phrase "tacked on" to the end of a sentence—as in these examples:

> Lead is highly toxic and extremely dangerous, even more so than previously believed.
>
> The first really good synthetic abrasive was carborundum, introduced in 1891.
>
> Drunk drivers cause many accidents, often after falling asleep at the wheel.

Colon and Semicolon

The colon and the semicolon are obviously related, but they serve different purposes and should not be used interchangeably.

The four main uses of the colon are after the salutation of a business letter and after the headings of a memo (see Chapter 2), to introduce a complicated list, and to introduce a long quote, as in these examples:

> At an 1874 meeting in Switzerland, delegates from twenty-two countries decided on four main principles that still govern postal service today: The postal service of the world should be regulated by a common treaty; the right of transit by sea or land should be guaranteed by every country to every other country; the country of origin should be responsible for the transmission of mail, and all the intermediate services should be paid for by fixed rates and according to periodic statistics; and each country should keep all its postage collections on both paid and unpaid letters.
>
> All U.S. school children are required to learn the Pledge of Allegiance: "I pledge allegiance to the flag of the United States of America and to the Republic for which it stands, one Nation under God, indivisible, with liberty and justice for all."

Other uses of the colon are in denoting time of day (3:05 a.m.) and "stopwatch" time (1:07:31), in Biblical citations (Corinthians 3:22), in two-part book and article titles (*Workplace Communications: The Basics*), and in various locations within bibliography entries (see Chapter 11). It can also be used to serve a "stop/go" function, as in *Some people are motivated by only one thing: money.*

There are really only two uses for the semicolon: to link two complete sentences that are closely related and to separate the items in a complicated list, as in the *postal service* example.

However, the semicolon should be avoided because there is usually a better alternative. For example, when linking closely related sentences, a comma along with a linking word like *and, but,* or *so* not only establishes the connection but also clarifies the relationship between the ideas. Compare these examples:

> He ate too much; he became ill.
> He ate too much, so he became ill.

Clearly, the second version is better. It not only connects the two sentences but also plainly shows that the second idea is a result of the first.

As for separating the items in a complicated list, simply arrange the items vertically, like this:

> At an 1874 meeting in Switzerland, delegates from twenty-two countries decided on four main principles that still govern postal service today:
>
> - The postal service of the world should be regulated by a common treaty.
> - The right of transit by sea or land should be guaranteed by every country to every other country.
> - The country of origin should be responsible for the transmission of mail, and all the intermediate services should be paid for by fixed rates and according to periodic statistics.
> - Each country should keep all its postage collections on both paid and unpaid letters.

Again, the second version is obviously preferable. It enables the reader to differentiate better among the separate items.

Quotation Marks

Quotation marks are used to surround a direct quotation (someone else's exact words) or to show that a word is being used sarcastically, ironically, or in some other nonliteral way. Here are examples:

DIRECT QUOTE   As Thomas Edison said, "There is no substitute for hard work."

NONLITERAL USE   An athlete must not "choke" under pressure.

Quotation marks must be positioned correctly in relation to other punctuation, especially end punctuation. Follow these guidelines:

1. A period at the end of a sentence always goes inside the quotation marks.

   Caesar said, "I came, I saw, I conquered."

2. A question mark at the end of a sentence goes inside the quotation marks if the quote itself is a question.

   Juliet cries, "Wherefore art thou Romeo?"

3. A question mark at the end of a sentence goes outside the quotation marks if the whole sentence (rather than the quote) is a question. Notice that in such a situation, there is no period within the final quotation mark.

> Did Caesar say, "I came, I saw, I conquered"?

4. A question mark at the end of a sentence goes inside the quotation marks if the quote and the whole sentence are both questions.

> Does Juliet cry, "Wherefore art thou Romeo?"

5. If an attributing phrase follows the quote, the comma goes inside the quotation marks.

> "I came, I saw, I conquered," said Caesar.

6. If an attributing phrase follows a quote that is a question, omit the comma but leave the question mark inside the quotation marks.

> "Wherefore art thou Romeo?" cries Juliet.

Apostrophe

The apostrophe is often misused, but the rules governing this punctuation mark are actually quite simple.

1. *Never* use the apostrophe to make a word plural.

   INCORRECT   Carpenter's use a variety of tool's.

   CORRECT   Carpenters use a variety of tools.

2. Use the apostrophe to make a word possessive, as follows:

   - If the word is singular, add *'s:*

     > one man's hat
     > one woman's hat
     > John Jones's hat
     > Jane Smith's hat

   - If the word is plural and does not already end in -*s,* add *'s:*

     > the children's hats
     > the men's hats
     > the women's hats

   - If the word is plural and already ends in -*s,* add an apostrophe:

     > the boys' hats
     > the girls' hats
     > the Joneses' house
     > the Smiths' house

3. Use an apostrophe to replace the missing letter(s) in a contraction.

I am, I'm	I will, I'll
should have, should've	could have, could've
would have, would've	it is, it's
she is, she's	she will, she'll

EXERCISE B.2

Punctuation has been omitted in each of these paragraphs. Rewrite the sentences, dividing them into new sentences if appropriate, and inserting end punctuation and other punctuation wherever necessary.

1. Refrigerants are used in the process of refrigeration whereby heat is removed from a substance or a space a refrigerant is a substance that picks up latent heat when the substance evaporates from a liquid to a gas this is done at a low temperature and pressure a refrigerant expels latent heat when it condenses from a gas to a liquid at a high pressure and temperature the refrigerant cools by absorbing heat in one place and discharging it in another

2. Full-mold casting is a process in which a green sand or cold-setting resin bonded sand is packed around a foamed plastic pattern (for example polystyrene) the plastic pattern is vaporized when the molten metal is poured into the mold an improved casting surface can be obtained by putting a refractory type of coating on the pattern surface before sand packing the pattern can be one piece or several pieces depending on the complexity of the part to be cast

3. The first step in bias circuit design is to determine the characteristics of both the circuit and the transistor to be used will the circuit be used as an amplifier oscillator or switch what class of operation (A, AB, B, or C) is required how much gain (if any) is required what power supply voltages are available what transistor is to be used must input or output impedances be set at an arbitrary value.

EXERCISE B.3

Punctuation has been omitted in each of these paragraphs. Rewrite the sentences, inserting commas and other punctuation wherever necessary.

1. If the Bonneville Salt Flats have meant one thing to nature lovers to enthusiasts for speed their meaning has been something else again. There has been no finer natural speedway on earth or at least none so readily accessible. The water table generally about a foot down rises to the surface during the rainy season and water collects to a depth of a foot or more. This water is gently swirled around by the wind and by the time it evaporates the surface is left smooth level and almost as hard as concrete.

2. Emotional players have no place on a Japanese baseball team. Those who get into fights in the clubhouse or enjoy practical jokes may be relieving tension on a U.S. team but are only contributing to it on a Japanese team. The good Japanese team is composed of players who never argue never complain and never criticize each other. The good team is like a beautiful Japanese garden. Every tree every rock every blade of grass has its place. When each players ego detaches itself and joins twenty-five others to become one giant ego something magical happens. All the efforts and sacrifices the players have made at last become worthwhile for they are now a perfectly functioning unit.

3. Several avenues are open to baseball card collectors. Cards can be purchased in the traditional way at the local candy grocery or drug stores with the bubble gum or other products included. For many years it has been possible to purchase complete sets of cards through mail order advertisers found in traditional sports media publications such as magazines newspapers yearbooks and others. Sets are also advertised in the card collecting periodicals. Many collectors begin by subscribing to at least one of the hobby periodicals all with good up-to-date information. In addition a great variety of cards can be obtained at the growing number of hobby retail stores around the country.

EXERCISE B.4
Consult newspapers and magazines to find ten examples of sentences in which the colon introduces a list and ten examples in which the colon introduces a quote.

EXERCISE B.5
Using the examples you found for Exercise B.4, copy the sentences in which the colons introduce lists. Then rewrite each sentence, removing the semicolons and arranging the entries as a vertical list.

EXERCISE B.6
Consult newspapers and magazines to find ten examples of semicolons linking complete sentences. Rewrite those sentences, replacing each semicolon with a comma and a linking word.

EXERCISE B.7
Consult newspapers and magazines to find ten sentences in which quotation marks appear. Have the quotation marks and surrounding punctuation been correctly positioned in relation to each other? Copy the sentences, rewriting any that are incorrect.

EXERCISE B.8
Consult newspapers and magazines to find ten sentences in which an apostrophe appears. Try to find examples of both possessives and contractions. Have the apostrophes been used correctly? Copy the sentences, rewriting any that are incorrect.

Grammar

As with spelling and punctuation, there are a great many grammar rules. For practical purposes, however, you really need to know relatively few. This section focuses only on the basics—the rules governing sentence fragments, run-on sentences, and agreement.

Sentence Fragments

As the term itself denotes, a sentence fragment is an incomplete sentence. Most fragments are actually the result of faulty punctuation—when a writer inserts end punctuation too soon, thereby "stranding" part of the sentence. Consider these examples:

Rabies has been a problem since the 1950s throughout New York

(Fragment)

State. <u>Including Long Island and New York City</u>.

[The first period should have been a comma.]

(Fragment)

<u>If you cut yourself while skinning an animal</u>. Have your local health agency check the animal for rabies.

[Again, the first period should have been a comma.]

You can usually avoid sentence fragments if you remember three basic principles:

1. To be complete, a sentence must include a subject (actor) and a verb (action).

   (Subject)   (Verb)
   <u>Snowmobilers</u> sometimes <u>take</u> unnecessary risks.

2. If a sentence begins with a word or phrase that seems to point toward a two-part idea (for example, "**if** this, then that"), the second part must be included within the sentence because the first part is a fragment and therefore cannot stand alone.

   Here are some examples of words that signal a two-part idea:

after	if
although	since
because	unless
before	until
for	when

3. Certain verb forms (some *-ed* forms, *-ing* forms, and *to* forms) can't serve as the main verb in a sentence.

(Fragment)
Opened in 1939. The Merritt Parkway in Connecticut was one of America's first freeways.

(Correct Sentence)
Opened in 1939, the Merritt Parkway in Connecticut was one of America's first freeways.

(Fragment)
Winding from Chicago to Los Angeles. Route 66 covers 42,000 miles.

(Correct Sentence)
Winding from Chicago to Los Angeles, Route 66 covers 42,000 miles.

(Fragment)
To succeed in your own business. You need both energy and luck.

(Correct Sentence)
To succeed in your own business, you need both energy and luck.

Notice that the *-ed, -ing,* and *to* forms frequently appear in introductory phrases. Learn to recognize these phrases for what they are—not sentences in themselves but beginnings of sentences—and punctuate each with a comma, not a period (see Rule 2 in the section on commas).

Run-On Sentences

While the sentence fragment is something to avoid, even worse is a sentence that goes on and on after it should have stopped. A run-on sentence spills over into the following sentence with no break in between. When that happens, the writing takes on a rushed, headlong quality, and ideas become jumbled together.

There are two ways that a sentence can overflow into the next: either with a comma weakly separating the two sentences or with nothing at all in between. Here's an example of each:

A surveyor's measurements must be precise, there is no room for error.

A surveyor's measurements must be precise there is no room for error.

Technically, only the second example is a true run-on. The first is really an instance of what grammarians refer to as a *comma splice.* Nevertheless, the problem is essentially the same. In both cases, the first sentence has collided with the second. Obviously, the two sentences must be separated with a period (or a semicolon).

A surveyor's measurements must be precise. There is no room for error.

Another option would be to use a linking word to join the two sentences. Sometimes a comma is needed before the linking word.

A surveyor's measurements must be precise, and there is no room for error.

Or you may prefer to turn one of the sentences into a fragment and use it as an introductory construction.

Because there is no room for error, a surveyor's measurements must be precise.

It should be clear by now that fragments and run-ons alike are usually the result of faulty punctuation. Certain patterns are correct, whereas others are not, as the following list indicates:

Correct Patterns	**Incorrect Patterns**
sentence.	fragment.
sentence. sentence.	fragment. fragment.
sentence, link sentence.	sentence, sentence.
fragment, sentence.	fragment. sentence.
sentence, fragment.	sentence. fragment.
fragment, sentence, fragment.	fragment. sentence. fragment.

Subject–Verb Agreement

Another common grammar error is to use a plural verb with a singular subject or vice versa. Remember that a singular subject requires a singular verb, whereas a plural subject requires a plural verb.

(Singular (Singular
Subject)   Verb)

A <u>welder</u> <u>welds.</u>

(Plural   (Plural
Subject) Verb)

<u>Welders</u> <u>weld.</u>

Note that singular subjects rarely end in -s, but singular verbs usually do. Conversely, plural subjects usually do end in -s, but plural verbs never do.

Although the subject–verb agreement rules may seem obvious, many writers commit agreement errors simply because they fail to distinguish between singular and plural subjects. This sometimes occurs when the subject is an indefinite pronoun, most of which are singular. Here is a chart of the most common indefinite pronouns, indicating which ones are singular, which plural, and which can function as either.

Singular			**Plural**	**Either**
anybody	everybody	no one	few	all
anyone	everyone	nothing	many	any
anything	everything	somebody	several	more
each	neither	someone		most
either	nobody	something		none
				some

Agreement errors can also result when there's a cluster of words between the subject and its verb, thereby creating a misleading sound pattern.

INCORRECT   A pile of tools are on the workbench.

CORRECT   A pile of tools is on the workbench.

Even though *tools are* sounds correct, the first sentence is incorrect because *pile*—not *tools*—is the (singular) subject and therefore requires the singular verb *is*.

Pronoun–Antecedent Agreement

Just as subjects and verbs must agree, so too must pronouns and their antecedents (the words that the pronouns refer back to).

(Singular
Antecedent)   (Plural
                                 Pronoun)
For <u>a woman</u> to succeed as an umpire, <u>they</u> must overcome much prejudice.

(Singular
Antecedent)   (Singular
                                 Pronoun)
For <u>a woman</u> to succeed as an umpire, <u>she</u> must overcome much prejudice.

The first sentence is incorrect because *a woman,* which is singular, disagrees with *they,* which is plural. (Although *they* is often used as a singular in speech, it must always be treated as a plural in writing.) The second sentence is correct because both *a woman* and *she* are singular and therefore agree.

Once again, indefinite pronouns can create agreement problems.

(Singular
Antecedent)
<u>Everyone</u> on the men's basketball team should be proud of

(Plural
Pronoun)
<u>themselves.</u>

(Singular
Antecedent)
<u>Everyone</u> on the men's basketball team should be proud of

(Singular
Pronoun)
<u>himself.</u>

The first sentence is incorrect because *everyone,* which is singular, disagrees with *themselves,* which is plural. The second sentence is correct because both *everyone* and *himself* are singular and therefore agree.

Let us consider one more aspect of agreement, using this sentence as a starting point:

(Singular   (Plural

Antecedent)   Pronoun)

<u>Everybody</u> should mind <u>their</u> own business.

Clearly, there is disagreement between *Everybody,* which is singular, and *their,* which is plural, even though this is how the sentence would probably be worded in speech. However, because writing is more formal than speech, the problem must be corrected. There are two ways to do so: The pronoun and its antecedent can both be either plural or singular.

Here are three different singular versions:

(Singular   (Singular

Antecedent)   Pronoun)

<u>Everybody</u> should mind <u>his</u> own business.

(Singular   (Singular

Antecedent)   Pronoun)

<u>Everybody</u> should mind <u>her</u> own business.

(Singular   (Singular

Antecedent)   Pronoun)

<u>Everybody</u> should mind <u>his or her</u> own business.

Here are two plural versions:

(Plural   (Plural

Antecedent)   Pronoun)

<u>People</u> should mind <u>their</u> own business.

(Plural   (Plural

Antecedent)   Pronoun)

<u>We</u> should all mind <u>our</u> own business.

The plural approach is almost always better because it avoids gender-biased language without resorting to the wordy *his or her* construction. For a more in-depth treatment of this topic, see Appendix A.10.

EXERCISE B.9

In both of the following passages, nearly all punctuation and capital letters are missing. Copy the passages, inserting punctuation and capitals to prevent fragments and run-ons.

1. In many parts of the United States building codes had long ignored the severity of earthquakes and the damage they can cause nevertheless research has revealed that earthquakes and earth tremors are a threat in a far greater percentage of the country than most people commonly believe while documentation shows that earthquakes have not resulted in loss of life or costly damage along the east coast cataloging of this kind of information has been sporadic and inconsistent it was not until 1900 that instruments were used to record and locate this activity ever since then information has been gathered and more uniformly recorded by several organizations designers of building codes nationwide have used this information to define requirements for withstanding the lateral forces of earthquakes these forces are generated from the movement of the ground due to seismic activity and converted into horizontal and vertical loads building frames architectural components and mechanical and other equipment must be designed to withstand these forces in areas where quakes have occurred more recently and cause extensive damage and loss of life these design parameters have long been incorporated into structural design elsewhere however the building codes are just beginning to reflect the potential damage of seismic activity.

2. One of the fears associated with electric cars is that the batteries will run down and leave you stranded this is not the same as running out of gasoline because you cannot bring electricity back in a can or make a quick stop at a service station when you're empty even an on-board battery charger won't do any good by the side of the road because such recharging requires time and a source of electricity within reach of an extension cord one way to eliminate this fear is to avoid electric cars the general public has taken this course ever since electric self-starters were added to gas buggies in 1912 however the oil embargoes in the mid-1970s created such hysteria over the thought of gas rationing that electric vehicles became plausible once again even crude electric cars that were little more than golf carts with headlights and turn signals were finding buyers that fear of being stranded still existed though and one answer to the problem was a hybrid gasoline/electric car it was in this atmosphere that Briggs & Stratton commissioned a hybrid electric car using conventional batteries in conjunction with one of its larger gas engines.

EXERCISE B.10

All of the following sentences contain agreement errors. Rewrite the sentences to correct the errors.

1. Regularly scheduled sessions of hypnotherapy creates a state of complete mental and physical relaxation.
2. Each of the players on the women's basketball team will receive their trophy next week.
3. Although secretaries are often underpaid, their role are essential to any workplace.
4. Neither of the security guards were in the plant at the time of the break-in.

5. Sophisticated harvesting machines like the one shown in Figure 3 is in use on many farms today.
6. A student must study hard if he or she expect to succeed in college.
7. Classes in soil science provides future engineers with experience in testing various types of soil to determine its characteristics.
8. There is more than 2 million miles of paved roads in the United States.
9. Everyone in the apartment building will have their rent raised next month.
10. Either Smith or Jones are guilty.

Index